Crossing the Green Line

The Ethnography of Political Violence

Cynthia Keppley Mahmood, Series Editor

A complete list of books in the series is available from the publisher.

Crossing the Green Line Between the West Bank and Israel

AVRAM S. BORNSTEIN

PENN

University of Pennsylvania Press

Philadelphia

10 9 8 7 6 5 4 3 2 1

Published by
University of Pennsylvania Press
Philadelphia, Pennsylvania 19104-4011

Library of Congress Cataloging-in-Publication Data
Bornstein, Avram S.
    Crossing the green line between the West Bank and Israel / Avram S. Bornstein.
        p.   cm. — (Ethnography of political violence)
    Includes bibliographical references (p.) and index.
    ISBN 0-8122-3635-1 (cloth : alk. paper); ISBN 0-8122-1793-4 (pbk. : alk. paper)
    1. West Bank—Social conditions. 2. West Bank—Economic conditions. 3. Palestinian
Arabs—West Bank—Social conditions—20th century. 4. Palestinian Arabs—West Bank—
Economic conditions—20th century. 5. Palestinian Arabs—West Bank—Ethnic identity.
6. Arab-Israeli conflict. 7. Palestine—Historical Geography. 8. Bornstein, Avram S.
I. Title
DS110.W47 B67   2001
305.892'74056953—dc21   2001043108

Contents

Preface

That which is hateful to you, do not do to your neighbor. This is the
entire Torah. The rest is commentary. Go and study it.

—Rabbi Hillel (c. first century B.C.)
   Babylonian Talmud, Shabbat 31a

The recognition of mutual personhood is a profoundly widespread (although
not exclusive) principle of human morality. It is often called the Golden Rule,
and Rabbi Hillel's quote above is not unusual. Similar statements are attributed to Jesus and Confucius and can be found in the ancient Hindu epic poem
the *Mahabharata*. Most humans have significant abilities to empathize and act
morally when face to face with other humans, despite the opportunity to neglect or harm. Carolyn Nordstrom, who has been at the forefront of anthropological studies of violence, while amid devastating bloodshed in Sri Lanka and
Mozambique said that even in warzones most people work to create a healthy
society (1997: 212).

   Despite the popularity of this moral wisdom, great violence has been
committed in the name of righteous traditions by individuals and by organized
groups. Severe violence and oppression come not necessarily from those *without* an understanding of morality, but from the systematic exclusion of particular people from empathy. We detach ourselves from the pain of others by
placing them outside "our" community, which is often understood and identified by reference to overlapping distinctions of gender, class, race, ethnicity,
or ideology. "We do not acknowledge the destruction of beings outside our
moral community as suffering" (Morris 1997: 40).

   Stopping suffering often requires broadening a moral appeal and disrupt-
ing power holders enough to scare them into concessions or collapse (Heyman 1998a: 11). Although it has not posed a threat to power as of yet, ethnography has made effective humanist appeals because it "is well equipped for
moral witness of the documentary style" (Heyman 1998a: 12). At its best, "I-
Thou relationships, impossibly intimate, are at the heart of the anthropological
enterprise" (Mahmood 1996: 25). Cynthia Mahmood argues that the work of
recognition is what "humanistically inclined ethnographers do in the research
setting, in the writing of monographs, and in the courtroom. Not to praise or
condemn our interlocutors, but to discover with them the challenges they face"
(Mahmood 1996: 267). Such ethnography can help expand the boundaries of

a moral community and widen the circle of those called neighbors. Lila Abu Lughod (1993) advocates using a technique called tactical humanism. Humanism as a style of representation should be deployed tactically within particular struggles to broaden political support for a particular group, but it should not be a general strategy for every group an anthropologist might study. Josiah Heyman urges that anthropologists "diagnose contexts and ideologies that weaken, restrict, or distort mutual personhood" (Heyman 1998a: 7; see also Scheper-Hughes 1992, 1995). By learning about human interchange, anthropologists can better advocate ways to increase moral recognition of mutual personhood (see Heyman 1998a: 3).

An anthropology based on the human-to-human, ethnographer-to-host relations formed in fieldwork is naturally open to healthy skepticism from those familiar with the presumption of objective scientific inquiry. Some readers will be more comfortable and convinced by writing (representational) techniques, like statistical norms, ideal types, chains of linguistic analogies, or symbolic grammars, that produce an aura of objectivity and factuality achieved partly by extracting the researcher from the view of the reader. However, it is naive to think that disinterested styles of anthropology do "not reflect the predominant worldviews and preoccupation of an era" (Heyman 1998a: 10). Ethnographers cannot extricate themselves from unequal relationships and should be careful about writing texts that attempt to stand outside the world of struggle, contest, and competition. In fact, the obfuscation of the researcher's position is itself a technique of authority, a political technique. The objective language of the scientific report, dislocated from any social position, has become an important tool for the production of the modern state as a rational bureaucracy. While fascism requires objectivity, the strength of the scientific tradition is the transparency of method and epistemology which require political and personal reflexivity, not the obfuscation and denial of subjectivity. "Partisanship does not change the answers social science finds-though most people who have not tried it assert that it does. It changes the questions one asks" (Sider 1993: xxii).

This ethnography is about the conflict in Israel-Palestine. I argue that the conflict is hardly about an ancient Jewish-Muslim religious dispute, but is mainly a consequence of a drastic political and economic inequality. This national apartheid in the Middle East developed mainly during the nineteenth and early twentieth centuries, in the era of high colonialism, and was shaped by the converging struggles of the British, Zionists, and Palestinians. It has been sustained and reinvigorated with the rise and collapse of the Oslo process. In Palestine, the border, as opposed to parliamentary quotas as in Lebanon, was always the officially preferred mechanism for governing separation. State powers have drawn and redrawn the shape and practice of borders in Palestine, carving it into increasingly smaller pieces, but this form of administrative violence has remained a central factor in the conflict.

In order to learn about the importance of the border in the daily life and struggle of Palestinians, I visited Palestine-Israel eight times between 1988 and 2000 for a total of about three years (September 1988 to June 1989, the summers of 1992 and 1993, June 1994 to September 1995, the summer of 1996, the winter of 1998–99, and the summers of 1999 and 2000). Between 1988 and 1993, I spent a significant amount of time at Hebrew University in Jerusalem and Birzeit University in the Ramallah District of the West Bank, traveled widely, and defined a research focus on state violence in general and borders in particular. Since 1994, I have spent most of my visits living with a Palestinian family in a village in the Tulkarm District in the northern West Bank. In addition to complete immersion in social life during these visits, I worked alongside Palestinians in construction, agriculture, and other jobs in the West Bank in 1994 and 1995.

For those in the West Bank, the Green Line (the former Jordanian-Israeli armistice line that separates the West Bank from Israel proper) shaped everyday life, more than ever, in the opportunities to make a living. Border policies restricted Palestinian agriculture and industry, pushing many to serve Israeli producers and consumers. Tens of thousands of West Bank workers crossed the border to work in Israel almost every day. Tens of thousands of others, like car mechanics and textile workers, worked for Israelis in the West Bank. The border limited the claims most of these workers could make on those who made the profits. Subcontracting agents, who made business across the border possible, also suffered from restrictions at the border, but the border brought them new sources of wealth, creating new internal tensions. Labor and production processes in the borderland were an important part of the national conflict often missed in descriptions of the Israel-Palestinian struggle.

Palestinians often spoke to me about these problems in relation to the border, but they also reflected on the border in more indirect ways. The border became a location separating cultural worlds. The customs of gender, age, and marriage of most West Bankers were demonstrably different from those of their relatives only a few kilometers away across the border. Palestinians were marking inter-ethnic and intra-ethnic cultural borders. Customs indicated inequalities and solidarities, and reinscribed relations made by the border as well as the personal identities they imply. The making of borders established a distinction and connection between West Bank and Israeli Palestinians and also distinguished those who remained inside historic Palestine and those in diaspora communities in Jordan, the Gulf, and beyond.

The focus of this study is not the essence of Palestinian culture, but the geopolitical border that enforces difference and shapes cultural affiliations. This ethnography of the Green Line uses very particular Palestinian experiences as the framework for an analytical and moral critique of how borders work in the modern world. When the role of the border in creating inequality is made evident, the practical and moral legitimacy of its maintenance becomes open to question. From the borderland, the debates of politicians and nationalists about where and how to redraw the border seem inadequate as a solution. The agreements between Israel and the Palestine Liberation Organization (PLO), although politically expedient, were beneficial to a limited few, reorganized an apartheid for most, and have proven to be temporary. The militarization of borders for workers and their selective opening for trade, appearing unique in Israel-Palestine, are also persistent features organizing inequality in the old/new world order.

1. Locations

The quintessential Palestinian experience, which illustrates some of the most basic issues raised by Palestinian identity, takes place at the border, an airport, a checkpoint: in short, at any one of those many modern barriers where identities are checked and verified. What happens to Palestinians at these crossing points brings home to them how much they share in common as a people. (Khalidi 1997: 1)

Near the Palestinian town of Tulkarm, in the northwestern West Bank, in the middle of a two-lane road that ran past olive groves, small wheat fields, and plastic hothouses that grew vegetables and flowers, sat an Israeli military checkpoint marking the Green Line, the border between the occupied West Bank and Israel. At the checkpoint a half a dozen concrete blocks, each about a cubic meter in size, fortified the Israeli soldiers manning the crossing. On each side of the formidable obstruction ran parallel lines of red plastic barricades that guided drivers and pedestrians around the blocks, past the soldiers and across the border. An Israeli sniper with a machine gun stood watch in a three-meter tower protected by concrete slabs and sandbags. On one side of the checkpoint, smooth, soft, black asphalt paved the way to the coastal plains of Israel along the Mediterranean. On the other side, the surface of the same route was old, hard, and broken from years of neglect. This ragged road twisted into the hilly lands of the West Bank that border the Jordan River. Permanent army checkpoints like this were created on the Green Line between Israel and the West Bank in March 1993.

The Green Line was the armistice line between Israel and Jordan established in 1949 that ended Israel's war of independence. From 1949 to 1967, the border was closed and the West Bank was occupied and annexed by Jordan. In the June 1967 War, the West Bank was taken from Jordan and became an occupied territory under the Israeli military. The border was opened soon thereafter. Palestinians began crossing for work and Israelis began to confiscate land to build settlements. There were no permanent checkpoints from the 1970s until 1993, when they were established to enforce work permits. This occurred as Israel and the PLO were secretly negotiating in Oslo. (More descriptions of these changes are provided in Chapter 2.)

Crossing a checkpoint from the West Bank into Israel, after 1993, required all men between adolescence and old age to show their identity card, known to Palestinians as a *huwiya*, and, if they were West Bank or Gazan Palestinians, to have a *tasrih*, a permit to be in Israel between 5:00 A.M. and 7:00 P.M. The identity card, issued by the Israeli army's Civil Administration, had a sword and branch inside a six-pointed star (a Jewish star) printed on its face. It showed the name, place of residence, and file number of its carrier. Israeli ID cards had blue plastic holders. Jewish-Israelis and Palestinians who became citizens of Israel around the time of independence in 1948 (henceforth called Arab-Israelis) had the same blue ID and could pass Israeli checkpoints with relative ease. But after the Israeli army took the West Bank in 1967, West Bank Palestinians did not become citizens of Israel. They became "residents" of Judea and Samaria, which is what Zionists call the West Bank. Identity cards for Palestinians who were just "residents" came in orange plastic holders (red for Gazans) that stood out like neon signs when they came out from the pockets of their owners. Israeli soldiers and policemen asked Palestinian men for their *huwiya* any time or any place. Taking a person's ID was the first act of taking the person into custody.

While everyone was required to have an ID at all times, most West Bank Palestinians could not get a permit to enter Israel. Tens of thousands of workers who built, picked, cleaned, and manufactured every day in Israel had to sneak across the Green Line without military permission in order to get to work. From 1993 to 1997 this was a formidable task. Plenty got caught and could be seen sitting in groups on the ground next to the checkpoint with their IDs in an Israeli soldier's pocket. When the morning traffic subsided, the police would write them a ticket, sometimes for 450 New Israeli shekels (NIS) (about $150 in 1994), about a week's wage for most people, and send them home. Nevertheless, tens of thousands of men crossed clandestinely in the hours around dawn. Few women crossed among the men. If they did, neighbors might gossip about how they were vulnerable to an immoral world. Those women who did cross, mostly to work in cleaning and agriculture, were usually in the most difficult financial circumstances. They were often allowed to pass through the checkpoint without showing any identification or permission. This was also the case for small boys or very old men. When workers got across the border, there were usually many vans and trucks waiting to transport them to locations all around Israel.

1. A clandestine path in a valley, cutting through the Green Line, 1995.

During the midmorning hours, after the workers' traffic ended, Israeli vans and trucks came across into the West Bank. Just over the border they waited for transport vehicles to deliver or pick up their goods. Largely, Israelis sent cut fabric and labels into the territories where Palestinian women assembled and packaged the clothes. Some Israeli merchants delivered supplies to the checkpoint, business to business, especially for light industry, automobile garages, and construction. Most heavy construction deliveries were made all the way to the site in an Israeli truck. Some deliveries, like petroleum or tanked gases, usually had Israeli army escorts. On Thursdays, there was an animal market on the West Bank side of the checkpoint where Israelis sold horses, cows, sheep, and chickens to Palestinian farmers and butchers. Most imports came from Israel, and the West Bank was open to the dumping of Israeli goods, but Israel's market was protected from goods coming in.

About a hundred meters from the checkpoint inside the West Bank there was an unplanned industrial zone where Palestinians fixed Israeli cars. There were some semi-permanent fruit and vegetable stands, but the main industry in these zones was auto service. There were paint and body shops, engine mechanics, electricians, carburetor, air-conditioning and muffler specialists, oil and tire changers, and even simple car washes. There were Mercedes specialists and American car specialists, and everyone could fix a Subaru. These industrial zones grew on the outskirts of all major towns to service the villages, but they were especially numerous near the border where they could service Israeli customers. Most of the customers were from nearby Arab-Israeli towns, but a number of Jewish-Israelis were also regulars, even wearing sidearms and military fatigues or carrying an M-16 rifle.

2. Men going around the checkpoint in view of the soldiers' tower, 2000.

Like the merchants who stopped at the checkpoints, many Israeli labor contractors, Jews more than Arab-Israelis, were often scared to enter the Occupied Territories because Israeli cars were regularly stoned by children during the uprising (1987–93), and a handful of attacks occurred against Israeli drivers and passengers in the middle and late 1990s, although most were in Hebron and Ramallah. Around 4:00 P.M., most Israeli contractors would simply drop off their workers at the checkpoint, and the workers would pile into shared taxis that carried them from the crossing to the garage in town where other taxis traveled to more distant towns and villages.

In the evening there was little movement across the checkpoint. West Bank Palestinians, even with permissions to cross, were not allowed in Israel between 7:00 P.M. and 5:00 A.M. Some Arab-Israelis came into the Occupied Territories to visit friends and family or to contract workers. The infrequency of movement during these hours made soldiers suspicious enough to closely scrutinize any car coming into the crossing, even from Israel. The only visible activity at the checkpoint was one Arab-Israeli, parked on the side of the road

3. Men going around the checkpoint, passing vending carts, 2000.

inside the territories, who sold ice-cold beer from his van from sundown until about 9:00 P.M. This was the only place to buy beer in the entire Tulkarm District.

Saturday was the one day of the week when the flow at the border was reversed. The Jewish Sabbath was everyone's day off, and many Arab-Israeli families from areas of Israel like the Triangle and the Galilee crossed the border to shop in the West Bank for clothes and food. The largest segment of Palestinian business, retail sales (Palestinian Bureau of Statistics 1995), was visibly dependent on Arab-Israeli money. Before the uprising, many Jewish-Israelis went to the crowded vegetable markets on Saturday for the great bargains; after the uprising, only Jewish soldiers on patrol could be found in the market. Even Jewish-Israeli drivers who employed Palestinian mechanics were scarce in town. The Oslo negotiations and the arrival of the Palestinian Authority led to the gradual return of Arab-Israelis to the Tulkarm market, though Jews were still rare. This normalization collapsed with a renewed uprising and intensified closure in Fall 2000.

4. Netanya checkpoint with crowd of workers being stopped by a soldier, 2000.

Violence and the Border

Acute forms of violence that inflict or threaten to inflict physical pain in a punctuated way to the body (by abrasion, rupture, temperature, pressure, electric shock, etc.), are often woven closely together with economic and "structural" violence in which pain is inflicted slowly and in a chronic fashion, by keeping people in poverty, depriving them of the ability to reproduce themselves, forcing them into hunger, or systematically preventing them from pursuing their chosen life on an equal playing field. Structural violence is built into everyday life, into the economy, a political system, and into the landscape. In the Palestinian refugee camps, for example, poor living conditions, overpopulation, and poverty were ongoing forms of structural violence caused partly by the war more than half a century ago.

Obviously, both acute and structural violence can destroy natural resources, community infrastructures, and the ability to make a living, and they can kill and maim people. But the power of violence goes beyond the act of destruction or deprivation. Long after physical suffering, violence can work

5. Israeli junk collected by Palestinian workers for sale on the West Bank side of the checkpoint, 2000.

through the fear or trauma it produces (see Robben and Suárez-Orozco 2000). The fear of violence is largely produced by experiences of violence and stories of violence or "talking terror" (Taussig 1992). Understanding the role of the border as a particular form of violence in daily life requires situating it within the larger repertoires and discussions of violence "on the ground" in the West Bank.

At about 11:00 P.M. one spring night in 1995, after a leisurely evening of socializing in the village of al-Qarya, I drove a few friends back to their homes in the town of Tulkarm, about a ten-minute journey by car. It was a common and routine event for me. Listening to music and enjoying the weather's pleasant change, I turned a corner on a small street in a relatively new residential area, and we found ourselves squinting into the spotlights and headlights of two Israeli army jeeps. I turned off the music, and our conversation stopped. My companion in the front seat said "slowly, slowly." We came closer into the bright lights and I began to see in silhouette a group of about ten or fifteen soldiers, spread out, moving down the street, some with their M-16 rifles raised to their eyes, aimed at us, with clips in their guns and fingers on their triggers. In a loud, screaming voice, one soldier ordered us in Hebrew to stop and get out of the car. We got out slowly with our hands up and stood looking down the barrels of several rifles held by nervous and aggressive young men. They ordered us to put our hands against the wall on the side of the street. They frisked everyone and collected our identification cards. Because it was my car, they ordered me to open the trunk. Two soldiers searched the vehicle, while my friends were ordered to remain against the wall. We had no weapons and the soldiers moved on down the street. My four friends remained standing there, with their hands against the wall, not turning around. I realized I did not have my ID, my American passport, even though my friends' ID cards had been returned to them. I ran after the soldiers to get it back and caught up with them about two blocks away. I called out from about thirty meters distance. They turned, raised their rifles, and ordered me to stop. I told them that they had my passport. One of them had put it in his pocket, and he gave it back. I walked back to my friends, who were still standing facing the wall as they had been ordered to do, although they had put their arms down. I assured them the soldiers were not coming back, and we left. One companion remarked, "You ran after the soldiers," sounding somewhat surprised. Running toward or away from soldiers, another said, was stupid, but, he said I did not know any better.

Violence in the occupied territories was imminent, possibly around the next corner, and it shaped lives in obvious and subtle ways. I could not drive around at night without some cautious hesitation. When I was walking through the village at night, the sight of oncoming headlights or the sound of a car motor from just over the hill inspired a physical desire for flight that I had to resist. When people approached a checkpoint on the road, experiences of violence, either from personal memory or from the stories of friends and family, could flood forward, and these thoughts could compel potential victims to be compliant, at least for the moment. The lingering effects of violence continued to work even when it was not actually happening because it created permanent scars, both physical and psychological. It weighed in the air with imminence.

In the West Bank and Gaza, the effects of violence were intense because the use of violence by the state was continuous under the Israeli occupation, especially to crush the uprising called the Intifada, which began in December 1987. During the Intifada, villages, town councils, labor unions, student groups, women's organizations, and Islamic centers all became politicized to the point of confrontation (Nasser and Heacock 1990; Hiltermann 1990, 1991, 1992). Harassment by the Israeli military government in the name of tax collection pushed shopkeepers and small businessmen to become willing activists in the uprising (Tamari 1990b: 163). Palestinians shut their stores every day at noon and observed strike days when called by the secret leadership. All Palestinians were encouraged to boycott Israeli goods, refuse to pay taxes, and resign from jobs as tax collectors and customs officials. Women were encouraged to create an "alternative economy" based on cottage industries (Tamari 1990b: 160). These activities were directed, in part, by dozens of statements signed primarily by the pro-PLO Unified National Leadership of the Uprising or the Islamic Resistance Movement (HAMAS), and also by Islamic Jihad and leftist parties, like the Popular Front for the Liberation of Palestine (PFLP) and the Democratic Front for the Liberation of Palestine (DFLP).[1]

Statements from the leadership, photocopied in the thousands, were distributed and enforced by decentralized and often anonymous groups of youth, referred to as the *shabab* (the youth). They often wore Palestinian scarves (*hattat*) or homemade cloth masks to protect their identity. The *shabab* ruled the streets. They also threatened, attacked, and sometimes killed "collaborators." Collaborators, mostly Palestinians who gave information to Israeli intelligence, but also drug dealers, women accused of loose morals, and merchants or moneylenders taking economic advantage of the people, were chased from their villages, often fearing for their lives.

The *shabab* also confronted IDF patrols in the refugee camps, towns, and villages with stones, Molotov cocktails, and burning tires. Children and teenagers enthusiastically played the game of hit-and-run, seemingly fearless of the possible consequences of their adventure. Street battles, often called demonstrations, were the most dramatic kind of violence in the Occupied Territories since the late 1980s. Crowds of stone-throwing Palestinian youths and Israeli soldiers would square off. Young Palestinians would often pick strategic locations and set up barricades of stones and burning tires. Stockpiles of rocks were gathered to throw at IDF patrols or yellow-plated Israeli cars.

IDF soldiers would usually respond with tear gas, rubber or regular bullets, sound bombs, beatings, and arrests. During the Intifada, these street battles claimed the lives of over a thousand, mostly Palestinians; thousands more were maimed or wounded, activists had their homes destroyed, and entire villages suffered days or weeks of curfew. Economic punishments to suppress protest and civil disobedience were regularly enforced by the Israeli military government in particular villages, municipalities, or districts. The Israeli Defense Force (IDF) Civil Administration would refuse applications for permits (drivers' licenses, permits for travel, building, retail, etc.), uproot "illegal" fruit trees, destroy merchandise in stores, factories, or street carts, cut the supply of fuel, water, or electricity, prevent harvesting or marketing of produce, and force payment of taxes and confiscation of property to that end (Al-Haq 1990: 241–58). Ironically, these forms of economic violence, these deprivations and assaults on property and livelihood, intended to suppress the uprising, were largely the cause of the uprising and the reason Palestinians demanded an independent Palestinian state.

In the fall of 1988, street battles were regular in Gaza and the West Bank. I wanted to witness it myself. At first, like the media, I considered these events exciting and worth seeing. One afternoon in Ramallah in 1988, still brand new to the area, I decided to wait around to see what would happen as the ever present IDF patrols closed a downtown street for no reason apparent to me. They parked their jeep blocking the middle of the street, and two soldiers screamed and raised their guns at anyone who attempted to pass. Crowds began to gather a short distance, twenty-five meters or so, from the soldiers to watch what some said was an investigation or arrest.

I stood there less than ten minutes before a bottle came from over a roof-top and smashed about twenty meters from the soldiers, closer to the nearby Palestinians. The person who threw it was not visible. A soldier calmly walked to where the bottle landed and lobbed a tear gas grenade in the direction from which the projectile came. A few moments later rocks and bottles came from over the rooftops: not many, but there were several participants acting simul-taneously in at least two locations, on opposite sides of the street. The IDF threw tear gas in both directions. The crowd panicked and began to run away.

The first waft that hit my face compelled me to run, too. I coughed pro-fusely, my throat and face burned, and, almost blind with tears, I began running with hundreds of Palestinians: men, women, old people, children, rich, and poor, past the jewelry stores and clothing boutiques of downtown Ramallah. About a block away I stopped, still coughing and tearing, and turned to look back. A man handed me a piece of an onion he had snatched from a nearby cart and told me to smell it to lighten the pain in my throat and face. I learned that I never wanted to wait around again, that noncombatant people, neither IDF soldiers nor Palestinian freedom fighters, were the people most likely to get hurt. The more time I spent in the West Bank, the more likely I was to en-counter street battles from a distance, and the more eager I was to turn around and get home safely.

A few months later, I rode an Israeli municipal bus near the Ottoman-built Damascus Gate of the Old City in East (Palestinian) Jerusalem, on my way to my apartment after shopping. A single stone suddenly struck the bus and shattered a window about a meter in front of me. No one was injured. The bus immediately stopped. I and all the passengers rushed off the bus to see two television cameramen, each accompanied by a soundman toting a microphone, stepping out of their parked cars, where they had obviously been sitting in wait for this to happen. Israelis from the bus yelled and insulted the television crews. Some of the police were busy trying to keep the irate Israelis from attacking the journalists. A passenger screamed in Hebrew at the cameramen, "You're garbage! Do you want to get us killed?" Another passenger began a scuffle with a cameraman and attempted to pull a wire out of his camera. Israeli soldiers, who had been sitting at the back of the bus, dispersed into the Palestinian crowd and returned moments later each holding a teenage Palestinian boy in an arm hold. Seven boys were pulled from the crowd and put in the now empty and stationary bus. Peasant women who had been selling fruits and vegetables started to scream. I thought they were being beaten as they pushed their bodies into the police and pleaded for the boys to be released. Two of the seven Palestinian boys were let down from the bus and released. The other five were not; they were put into a police van and driven away.

This incident stuck out in my mind, not only because I was riding on the target, but because several of the different actors of the uprising struggled together in those few moments. There was the anonymous (probably Palestinian) rock-thrower who wanted to smash the window of an Israeli bus and scare or injure Israelis. There were the media, a preexisting, lying-in-wait audience for violence. There were civilian Israelis who immediately transformed their fear into anger at the cameramen. There were Israeli soldiers who jumped into the crowd determined to avenge the attack. There were Palestinian boys, randomly snatched from the crowd. There were Palestinian women who claimed the boys as their children. There were police, plenty of police, trying to deal with scared and angry Jews and Arabs. And there were many people like me, confused and startled participant-observers who would think about it for years and maybe retell the story. For most of those present, the event ended in a few minutes and we were on our respective ways. But for the five boys taken by the police the experiences of violence were probably just beginning.

The number of arrests and arbitrary detentions had been escalating since March 1988, when the Israeli parliament empowered military commanders to issue orders of administrative detention. "Administrative detention, as defined by law, is meant to prevent the actions of an individual whom the authorities believe is liable to endanger security and public order in the future. Administrative detention was not meant to replace the judicial process" (B'Tselem 1992: 81). Anyone could be detained by a policeman or soldier for ninety-six hours, after which time the detention had to be authorized by an officer, who could continue it for up to eighteen days, after which time a military commander or judge could issue a renewable six-month period of administrative detention. Over 100,000 Palestinians were detained between December 1987, the beginning of the Intifada, and July 1993, according to the Israeli army (Human Rights Watch 1994: 3).[2]

Arrest could come at any time. The IDF entered Palestinian homes between midnight and dawn in search of wanted persons. More than a dozen
heavily armed men in bulletproof vests would pull young men from their beds,
still in their pajamas. The IDF raided late at night to avoid crowds and resistance, but this timing also had a meaningful consequence for Palestinians. It
drew the entire family into the experience. Mothers and sisters would sometimes try to force themselves between their male relatives and the soldiers.
Their homes were violated and their ability to sleep soundly permanently
threatened.

Arrest was not limited to this midnight raid procedure. Israeli security
routinely put up checkpoints on auto and pedestrian thoroughfares with or
without obvious provocation. Palestinians traveling along the way would be
stopped. Police or soldiers demanded IDs from Palestinians anywhere and
any time: on a bus, in a market, or just walking along the street. Sometimes
their cars or bags would be searched, too. Their ID numbers would usually
be checked against a list of wanted persons. People did not always know they
were wanted until they were taken into custody. Some people were ordered to
go see a particular officer at the IDF administration facility. This could merely
be a polite interview or the beginning of incarceration.

Israeli forces were given government permission to use violence on political detainees and prisoners during interrogation. The 1987 Landau Report on
the General Security Services (GSS) decided that it was permissible to use
"moderate physical pressure" in security matters (B'Tselem 1991a). Consequently, thousands of detainees were hooded, bound, confined, threatened, and
beaten during their first days or weeks of custody (Al-Haq 1984, 1989, 1990;
B'Tselem 1991a, 1992; Ginbar 1993, 1998; Human Rights Watch 1991, 1994;
Palestinian Human Rights Information Center 1991). The Palestinian Human
Rights Information Center documented patterns of torture involving

sexual harassment, hooding, beating (especially on the head and genitals), forced standing for long periods, kneeling on stones, exposure to sun or cold, electric shocks,
cramped confinement, deprivation of water, food, sleep, toilet facilities and medical
care, cold water dousing, chilling, isolation for long periods of time, threats of death,
rape or expulsion against detainees or their family members, forced exercise, humiliation, cigarette burns and choking. (Palestinian Human Rights Information Center 1991:
24)[3]

In 1994, Prime Minister Yitzhak Rabin declared that, because of the increase
in bombings and terrorist activity, the gloves would be taken off and even the
Landau restrictions would be suspended because of the gravity of the moment,

because of the "ticking time bomb" scenario.[4] The Israeli High Court reversed this decision in September 1999, although reports of torture continued.

The reason for torture during interrogations was getting the victim to confess the names of those active in the uprising. But Cynthia Mahmood argues: "Even when people do have information to give, they typically lose track of it utterly in the torture situation. The goal of torture therefore must be understood in terms other than mere acquisition of knowledge, despite the common claim of torturers the world over that this is why they torture" (Mahmood 1996: 9). The "reason" was important from the standpoint of the Israeli courts, some of the Israeli public, and an international audience, but also for the Israeli interrogators to maintain their own belief that they were right and rational, and fighting against irrational terrorist enemies.[5] Another sign of Israel's enlightened use of force were the "rubber" bullets (never mind their metal core) given to soldiers to shoot at the rock-throwing youth (see Ezrahi 1997).

However, this rationality of torture—the ticking time bomb—seems remote from the experiences of interrogation. Israelis tortured many youths detained for throwing stones and painting slogans who were unlikely to have any information about ticking time bombs. Former detainees

reported constant verbal humiliation—abuse, insults, slander, cursing,—by the interrogators. Almost all reported that their mothers, sisters or wives were cursed by their interrogators: "we will bring your sister and your mother here and we will fuck them while you watch," is one of the sayings reported. "Your mother is pregnant by a GSS man," or, "Your wife is already pregnant? Good thing for you," are also phrases often attributed to the interrogator. (B'Tselem 1991a: 56)

The poetics that structure this violence are too complicated to fully unravel here.[6] However, the attention given by interrogators to beating the testicles and threatening to rape female relatives strikes at the masculinity of the victim and also at the collective representations of national identity (Seifert 1996). They seem intended to humiliate in particular and local ways. Torturing Palestinian boys and young men was partly meant to teach them fear, to destroy their will to resist or participate further in the uprising. But perhaps, as Israeli journalist Yaron Ezrahi suggests, it was also a tragic aspect of a new Jewish identity, "a sign of a recovered masculinity, a repudiation of anti-Semitic stereotypes of the Jew as weak and impotent, a means of restoring Jewish pride, a symbolic revenge for past crimes against the Jews or as the instrument of a redemptive messianic Jewish mission" (Ezrahi 1997: 226–27).

The IDF operated nine detention facilities of their own. These were separate from the twenty-one prisons operated by the Israeli Prison Service, six of which were in the territories, to hold criminal prisoners (Palestinian Human Rights Information Center 1991: 23). IDF prisons and detention facilities were for political or "security" prisoners. Most detainees in these facilities lived in crowded tents with poor sanitary conditions. During the uprising there were five main detention centers: Far'ah, north of Nablus; Dhahriyyah, south of Hebron; Beach Camp (Ansar II) in Gaza; Megiddo, inside Israel; and Ketziot, called Ansar III by Palestinians, also inside Israel, in the Negev desert. Ansar III, created in the mid-1980s to cope with the increasing number of arrests, was the largest detention facility, holding close to 6,000 detainees (B'Tselem 1992: 103). Prisoners at Ansar III, as at Beach Camp and Far'ah, were kept in tents, approximately twenty-five to thirty prisoners per tent (B'Tselem 1992; Isaac 1989). Ansar III was divided into six blocks, including "Prison 7," a section set apart from the other blocks. Each block was an asphalt floor surrounded by high fences, and divided into sections by fences and barbed wire between which prison guards and soldiers patrolled. Only one designated representative from among the prisoners could pass through gates to bring in food, take out garbage, and speak with prison authorities.

The IDF targeted community leaders for arrests and closed community centers to retard organization. However, as the bus stoning incident described above illustrates, detentions, as well as beatings and shootings, could come from enraged soldiers, many only eighteen to twenty-one years old themselves, who were unable to identify or just unable to catch the person who threw the projectile. Nevertheless, they had to bring in a victim for their anger. Israeli soldiers could easily use Palestinians as an outlet for their frustrations or fears with much impunity. They harassed Palestinians, sometimes violently, but more often by making them wait at checkpoints and submit to searches and questioning. Even more humiliating than the checkpoint was the practice of waking people up in the middle of the night and forcing them to come out to the street to paint over walls that had political graffiti written upon them. Soldiers could not catch those who wrote the graffiti, but they could punish adults who lived near it and thereby try to humiliate everyone.

Despite being intimately bound to struggles over material resources and shared human mentalities, violence and the creation of fear are rarely reducible to class struggle or psychology. While economic and individual developmental variables are critical elements, there are socially meaningful motivations for violence and meaningful impacts. These are often the factors shaping who gets terrorized and how. For example, Taussig (1987) describes how the terror-ridden encounters between rubber traders and native Amazonian Indians were structured by elaborate mythologies that often led to the destruction of production, not the increasing exploitation of producers. Cynthia Mahmood's (1996, 2000) description of the Sikh-Indian conflict in the Punjab also indicates that violence is often expressive of a struggle for complicated notions of dignity, rather than a tactic of a larger political strategy. Aretxaga (2000) describes how in Spain the state is imagined in fictional genres, especially about terrorism, that are manifest in the everyday lives of people and, more important here, state officials. There is a "surplus" of violence produced by fantasy and imagination (Aretxaga 2000: 47). Violence cannot be seen merely as functional. Palestinian youth threw stones at passing Israeli civilians or soldiers to express that they would not be silent and complacent, that they were defiant, not powerless and submissive to domination and the confiscation of land. Such resistance should be understood as an attempt to maintain or regain dignity rather than as a clear tactic of a larger political strategy. This expressive or symbolic aspect is critical to patterns and cycles of violence.[7]

Violence, both acute and structural, can destroy natural resources, community infrastructures, and the ability to make a living, or it can kill and maim people, but an anthropology of violence must go beyond the physical act of destruction or deprivation. The power of violence is sometimes in the kind of fear it produces. Fear can destroy communities and the orderliness of daily life (Taussig 1992). Elie Wiesel's (1982) memoir of Nazi concentration camps portrays the gradual breakdown of relations between ethnic groups, fellow prisoners, even father and son. Merely surviving is sometimes the best resistance possible.

After hearing dozens of stories from Palestinians of interrogation, I realized that the issue of confession was rarely mentioned, nor do the human rights publications write of it. Most people like to think that no one made any confessions. But the use of secret evidence in Israeli military courts, sudden arrest at a checkpoint, or being plucked from home in the middle of the night, all flamed suspicions of betrayal. Giving names might have contributed to the process of arrests—only IDF intelligence knows for sure—but it could create doubt and mistrust between neighbors and even self-doubt. Every kind of violence, including at the border, can work in this insidious way against hope, dignity, and normalcy. Grief becomes a weapon that imposes unlivable contradictions (Nordstrom 1997: 125–30). As acute physical violence ruptures flesh, trauma can rupture the social fabric in which people make their lives (Robben and Suárez-Orozco 2000).

With the arrival of the Palestinian Authority in the 1990s and the redeployment of Israeli troops away from Palestinian populations, the number of arrests went down, but the use of checkpoints became more widespread. Passing through them meant being checked, delayed, detained, or maybe worse. Just before the renewed uprising began in Fall 2000, the *Washington Post* reported the following:

JERUSALEM, Sept. 18—After they had finished pummeling their three Palestinian detainees, finished smashing them with their fists, elbows and boots, slamming their heads against a stone wall, forcing them to swallow their own blood and cursing their mothers and sisters, the young Israeli policemen did an unusual thing: Using a disposable camera, they took photographs of themselves with their victims, holding their heads by the hair like hunting trophies. . . .

In fact, this month's incident, which took place within sight of Jerusalem's Old City walls, may never have come to light but for two things, human rights groups say. One is that the policemen photographed themselves with their victims and failed to destroy the negatives. The other is that the Palestinians' boss, an Israeli rabbi, was so furious that after his employees were released from the hospital he took them to the authorities to complain. (Hockstader 2000: A16)

According to the *Post* article, the three Palestinians were heading home after working until 2:30 A.M. delivering groceries, when police stopped them at a checkpoint near the entrance to Abu Dis, a Palestinian autonomous zone near Jerusalem. The police ordered them out of their car, ordered the men to stand against a wall, and, according to the indictment, proceeded to beat the three men for about 40 minutes, despite the fact that they had work permissions.

As this book will describe, the power of the geopolitical border has been especially difficult for Palestinians. During periods of border closures, getting to work meant that West Bank Palestinians had to play cat-and-mouse with the Israeli army. They had to run through dry river beds, hide behind olive trees, or hike far away from the main roads. Even when the checkpoint was open, it was a place where heavily armed soldiers were looking for reasons to open fire or take people into custody. This alone made crossings dangerous. Passing through it could be the first step into detention, which could unfold into an experience of incarceration and torture while under interrogation. This potential threat of physical violence also made symbolic violence all too common. Palestinians often faced the simple but painful humiliation of a soldier's disrespectful questioning or search. Even if none of these things happened, crossing the Green Line peacefully was a form of economic violence that limited the rights of workers and the potential of Palestinian businesses.

The geopolitical border is an important form of acute violence that often underlies structural forms of violence.[8] Borders shape the relations of production and consumption, that is, the macroeconomic situation, by regulating the flow of capital, commodities, and workers and separating employers from their social welfare responsibilities like unemployment and disability insurance. The border also shapes relations at work. Outlawing undocumented workers puts an entire population in jeopardy of arrest or police violence, and this danger is something employers use to exploit employees by paying them less or sometimes not at all (Heyman 1998b).

Examining the impact of the border from the perspective of West Bank Palestinians is somewhat different from an older anthropology based on the idea that cultures were bounded, holistic ways of life. At one time, most anthropologists tried to describe and explain the core elements of different cultures, like the Navaho, the Samoans, the Japanese, or the Nuer.[9] Barth's edited volume *Ethnic Groups and Boundaries* (1969) challenged this essentialist approach and taught anthropologists that identities are dialectically constructed as a kind of boundary maintenance against other identities.[10] Studies in the borderlands since then have provided "a basis upon which to redraw our conceptual frameworks of community and culture area" (Alvarez 1995: 447).[11] It is often not homogeneity at the center but border maintenance at the periphery that makes a group. Sometimes that boundary maintenance is carried out through custom; sometimes it is enforced by the soldiers at a geopolitical border.

Fieldwork

My investigation into this place, the border, was stirred by studies and fieldwork in Israel-Palestine for about thirty-six months between 1988 and 2000, mainly in the Tulkarm District in the northwestern West Bank, but also around Ramallah and Jerusalem. In July 1994, I met Umm Samud and Abu Samud in the village of al-Qarya in the Tulkarm District.[12] I visited them as the guest of their sons, who were students at Birzeit University, in the Ramallah District of the West Bank just north of Jerusalem, where I also studied. They invited me back several times and eventually agreed to take me into their home for an indefinite period. I stayed for thirteen months (September 1994–September 1995), and on subsequent visits to the West Bank (July–August 1996, January, July, and August 1999, June and July 2000). Their home was the center point from which I was allowed to see and experience the border in daily life.

Umm Samud and Abu Samud agreed to take care of me, and they took that very seriously. They had no daughters, only four sons, making the issue of private space in the home much less difficult to negotiate. Abu Samud said he thought my work, writing about Palestinian daily life for an American audience, was a worthy idea. Umm Samud said it was because her second eldest son Sabri was a student in America. He had been unable to return home during the four years of his study. She called his name often, missed him greatly, and wanted me to look out for him when I returned. I think she also felt that, if she looked after me, God would make sure that someone looked out for her son. They took a risk bringing me into their home. Not only might I have been a spy (which had to be considered), but I might have turned out to be an embarrassment.

The front porch of the home looked over a field toward the center of the village, which rose up onto a hill. In the noon village sun, one could watch children with backpacks coming from school, running, screaming, and playing. The little girls wore smock-like gowns with green vertical stripes over their clothes. Later the boys and young girls would raise the dust playing soccer. Women could be seen putting up laundry on the rooftops or shaking out rugs. Most men from the village labored in agriculture, construction, or a skilled trade, but there were also a number of merchants, professionals (such as doctors, teachers, and engineers), and civil servants. Women worked as school-teachers and in sewing factories, but most worked at home. In the evening the men came home and with their wives, daughters, and small children could typically be found watching television. Most were probably watching one of the two Jordanian channels, keeping up with their soap operas. Some might have watched one of two Israeli channels that broadcast American serials with Hebrew and sometimes Arabic subtitles. By the late 1990s, satellite dishes were delivering twenty-one Arab channels. Young men were more likely to be hanging out somewhere else, often in the street, where they could smoke cigarettes away from the view of their parents. Other than people's homes, there was no place to go in the village, no coffee shops, no restaurants, not even a falafel stand.

After three previous summers of visits to Birzeit University, where I met the people who would help me do my research, moving into a village like this was my ideal situation. I had been anxious to move to the northern West Bank, a place the thousands of international journalists in Israel ignore. Most research in the West Bank, except for that of a few anthropologists (Peteet 1994; Swedenburg 1995; Moors 1995), has been done in the Ramallah, Jerusalem, and Bethlehem areas, which are distinctly more metropolitan than the northern towns of Tulkarm, Jenin, Qalqilya, Nablus, and their surrounding villages. I wanted to go to these areas because they were more working class than the Ramallah-Jerusalem area, and it seemed these people, in the villages and refugee camps, were most often ignored by foreign and Palestinian scholars. These northern areas were borderlands between Israel and Palestine. They were proximal to Israel's populated northern areas where there was work, and they were marginal from the economic, political, and intellectual Palestinian centers around Jerusalem.

On my first visit, about two months before I moved in, the mother of the house, Umm Samud, took me upstairs to the roof to see the rabbits, pigeons, and chickens; downstairs to the kitchen to see her jars of homemade olives and pickles, barrels of flour, rice, and sugar, crates of onions and garlic; and to the backyard, where she baked bread in a wood-burning oven and grew sage, *za'tar* (wild thyme), saffron, mint, red chili peppers, almonds, apricots, olives, pomegranates, lemons, three kinds of oranges, and a variety of flowers.

I sat with the father, Abu Samud, on the porch of his home as he explained how he built his concrete-block house with his own hands on this plot that his wife inherited from her father. He took me into the bathroom to show me the tile work and explained how he dug the hole for the septic tank with a shovel. He took me back up to the roof and showed me the solar panels for hot water. He pointed to the iron reinforcement bars sticking up from the roof and explained (in detail beyond my comprehension at the time) how he was going to build a second and maybe third story on this approximately 170-square-meter house for his four sons and their future families.

Fifty years before I arrived in Umm Samud's home in the village of al-Qarya, the area was surrounded by fields, mostly filled with olive trees and wheat. The village stood as a tightly packed cluster of stone homes on a hilltop. Buildings and stone walls were layered in the old village to form small alleys, giving a fortified position to those inside. These arch-windowed houses, some many generations old, belonged mostly to the families of seven clans, with some hangers-on. These old houses made up the center of the village when I lived there in the mid-1990s. They were mostly one-room apartments, often lacking plumbing, and rented to people of little means.

The village expanded beyond the hill during 1970s, into the surrounding fields and onto adjacent hills. These newer houses, like Umm and Abu Samud's, were mostly built of concrete blocks and were more spread out, often standing alone or as a clump of two or three together in a small field. The variety of new housing in the village reflected the differing fortunes of the inhabitants. A few houses were built of stone, three stories high, with conspicuous air-conditioning units, satellite dishes, and built-in kitchen appliances. Others were dormitory-like structures for large families who moved all at once into the village from a refugee camp. The wealthy homes were few, but so were the impoverished. In 1995, the village of al-Qarya had about 2,000 people living in fewer than 300 homes on more than 30 hectares of land.

Adjacent to the village, only a ten-minute walk away, was a refugee camp that housed people (and their descendants) who had fled from what became

Israel in 1948. Here some 12,000 people lived on about 16.3 hectares. The land was owned by a wealthy family and had been leased since 1951 by the United Nations Relief and Works Agency for Palestine Refugees in the Near East (UNRWA). UNRWA distributed food staples like oil, flour, and rice to many in the camp, and everyone with an UNRWA refugee registration card had free access to the camp clinic. By the 1990s, the camp was crowded and had bad sewage and garbage disposal problems. The main roads were filled with potholes. Two- and three-story concrete-block homes were packed unsystematically together, forming irregular alleyways like the old village. But unlike the homes in the village, there were few verandas or courtyards in the camp, so women and children gathered with friends and neighbors inside their homes, in doorways and alleyways, or on rooftops. There was constant movement in the camp. On the center street, men were in garage-style coffee shops, pool halls, and storefronts until late at night. Televisions, radios, and children could always be heard coming from somewhere.

Boys from the camp were watched with suspicion when in the village. They generally were not greeted, as other villagers were, with polite calls of welcome. There were some friendships, but they seemed rare. When I first arrived, village residents expressed concern about parking my car outside at night, fearing that boys from the camp would steal it. Some of my friends from the village seemed very uncomfortable in the camp. Some explicitly refused and others just avoided visits in the camp. Both villagers and camp dwellers recalled days before the Intifada, when there was open and explicit hostility between the children of the camp and the village. The high school students from the village had to walk an extra kilometer to get to school in the main town because they walked around the camp rather than through it. In retrospect I wonder whether this story was retold to express reconciliation or as an ongoing threat.

The tension between the village and the camp was a complicated result of the inequality between villagers, who had property even if it was only their house, and those in the camp, who arrived with nothing and had no land. Villagers' houses, land, and families were a means of upward mobility out of the camp. But villagers were afraid of the poverty, of the desperation poverty brings, and of the intimate burden placed upon them by their more destitute neighbors.

In conversation with friends from the camp one night, they told me a story about a man named Ahmad who asked permission to marry Khadija, a young woman from the village who happened to be my neighbor and the cousin of my adopted family. Khadija's family had lived in the Gulf for many years and were forced to return to the village during the Gulf War of 1990–91. Her father had to work as a day laborer in Israel. Their forced return was a change in their standard of living and their father's occupational status, and also a bitter setback that threatened their desired path to professional and educated children. My friends were disturbed at the manner in which the girl's parents rejected his request. I asked why he was refused. Immediately someone said it was because Ahmad was a "son of the camp." Khadija's cousin, who had come with me from the village and sat with us, did not disagree, but tried to explain that her parents had a misconstrued notion about Ahmad's moral character. Later, no longer with our friends from the camp, Khadija's cousin said that, although Ahmad was a hardworking young man who managed in difficult circumstances to establish himself as a relatively successful petty entrepreneur, Khadija's parents had many expectations of the man she would marry, and, despite Ahmad's honesty, diligence, and good nature, he would not make much money and his family had no land. She would only end up living in the camp.

Many people have assumed that doing fieldwork in the refugee camps and villages of the West Bank presented problems of personal danger. I am often asked, "Did the Palestinians with whom you lived know you were Jewish?" Most people in the Occupied Territories immediately recognized "Avram" as a Hebrew name, and I would use it freely. The question that often follows is, "How did the Palestinians treat you?" The answer, that I acquired a second life, complete with friends and an adopted family, usually comes as a surprise. "But didn't you feel scared?" I am asked. I say that I had little reason to be scared because the Israeli army had no intention of hurting a foreign, Jewish American; they were only after Palestinians. My questioners usually think I have misunderstood their question. "Not scared from the army, but from the Palestinians?" they inquire. The question indicates a misapprehension of the relations of power that actually existed on the ground in the Occupied Territories. It was I who presented the greater potential danger and my hosts who were taking a chance. Umm Samud was always keeping track of my whereabouts and warning me to be careful, but sometimes she would joke, "If something happens to you, the Israelis will put all of us in prison." In my experience, violence from Palestinians was a freak occurrence, but violence against Palestinians was systematic. I was often mistaken by Israelis as a Palestinian if among Palestinians, especially in winter when I wore a Palestinian scarf, a *hatta*. I was regularly stopped, made to get out of cars, had my own car searched numerous times, sometimes at gunpoint with my hands up. Most of the time the soldiers or police looked at my name and asked, "Are you Jewish? You're not afraid?" meaning to be with Palestinians, and they soon backed off.

Despite the restrictions on Palestinians (and me by mistake), as a Jewish American the occupying Israeli authorities gave me complete freedom of movement within their jurisdiction. I received tourist visas at the airport and the bridge to Jordan, like almost any American. More importantly, I could renew my visa without much question. These conditions made my stay and subsequent visits easier, but were based upon the real life inequality between Palestinians and foreigners. I could come and go, to the beach in Tel Aviv, to Jordan, Europe, almost anywhere, while they could not even get to their Arab-Israeli cousins ten kilometers away for a wedding on the weekend without fear.

As for the reception given to me by Palestinians, during the Intifada, when I first began to visit the territories, I was made to feel welcomed as part of the sympathetic foreign community familiar in the Ramallah, Jerusalem, and Bethlehem areas. Palestinians were trying to push out Israelis and most Israelis were scared to enter the West Bank, but Palestinians invited foreigners, especially journalists, human rights workers, and representatives of nongovernmental organizations, to bear witness to the occupation and the uprising. My Jewish name made some Palestinian men curious to see my passport when we first met to confirm that my birthplace was Florida, that I was visiting on a tourist visa and not concealing Israeli citizenship. Many people, in fact most people, asked why a Jew decided to live among Palestinians. I would explain that, after visiting Israel as a child and teenager, I went to study at the Hebrew University of Jerusalem for a year abroad. Arriving in September 1988, after a summer in West Africa, I found the city being torn apart by an uprising going into its tenth month. The overseas school catered to foreign students who wanted to strengthen their ties to Israel by building their nationalist ideology. The contradiction between the histories taught in this branch of the university and the events of the occupation I was witnessing with my own eyes was too great to ignore. While visiting with Palestinians in the West Bank and Gaza, or even in East (Arab) Jerusalem, during those first and second years of the uprising, I chronically encountered beatings, tear gas, checkpoints, and harassments in the markets, neighborhoods, and roads. These experiences broke my heart and shattered my vision of redemption in the reclamation of the Holy Land as claimed by Jewish nationalism. Over my ten-month visit in 1988–89, while I was living in Jerusalem and moving back and forth between Israelis and Palestinians, the clashes of soldiers and civilians in the streets and the callous denials by many Zionists increasingly inspired my sympathy for the spirit of the uprising. It was this emotional and intellectual challenge that, in 1990, became the focus of my graduate research. I have told this story so many times that my close friends in the West Bank could recite it themselves.

Crossing the border without caging myself behind steel and weapons inside a car or settlement, being forthright with my Jewish name and identity, and stating a clear political position on the colonial nature of the Israeli occupation usually seemed appreciated. Many were well aware of how they were portrayed in America, how they were feared by Jews. Many joked or asked if I were not afraid that I might be stoned or stabbed. It was not unusual for Palestinians to deal with a Jew; it happened every day for many, especially at work. But my intention to write an ethnography of the border while living full time in a Palestinian village was unusual. Sometimes being Jewish produced interesting theological and historical discussions. I was always being asked about Jewish texts, traditions, philosophers, and history and, in turn, told about the Muslim parallels. Being Jewish was always a topic, merely because it was so odd and had to be explained to every new person I met, but I felt judged by my character and behavior, not by the conditions of my birth. I always believed my actions might be under close scrutiny, but everyone seemed to feel watched by their family and neighbors in the village.

These dialogues and dialectics of my fieldwork in the context of the larger political struggles had a tremendous impact on the methodology I chose to use and the subjects I chose to investigate. Several summers of pilot research taught me that the most comfortable and extensive dialogues came in the least formal circumstances. Therefore, my primary method was participant observation: working in construction, agriculture, light industry, and the government sector, living with a family, and spending all my social time with my Palestinian peers. I carried index cards or a small pocket notebook with me and made quick notes immediately after a conversation or event. As soon as I got a chance, which usually meant when I got home, using my quick notes and memory I wrote a detailed description in a larger notebook or on my laptop computer. I would only take notes in a formal manner when I was doing a "formal" interview, which only happened if I went to visit the office of a public official I did not know and who expected me to take notes. I did formal interviews with friends, but they became more reserved than usual and the sessions were unproductive and awkward.

Finding connections between daily life and the violence of the border was not difficult. My Palestinian hosts offered many first- and second-hand examples, and I could offer my collection of ethnographic observations and readings to them. Such dialogue with my Palestinian hosts and their personal histories were critical, but the data I sought to document the border in daily life were also experiential: participating in work and household reproduction, joining public celebrations and ceremonies, and, most important, participating in the conversations and decisions that come only from living with people for months and years.[13] When you live with people for an extended period, their stories, concerns, fears, and silences become part of everyday life. While working as a laborer I developed calluses on my hands that gave me a knowledge of daily life that dialogue alone could never produce. This kind of record, more than any other form of social history, the bread and butter of ethnography,[14] shows how society and culture are shaped "from the ground up—a process invisible to Hobbes and his proponents who write far from civilians' experiences of war on the front lines" (Nordstrom 1997: 13). Although I have made use of available statistical research, rather than attempt a broad survey of the border, I have chosen to examine individual cases in detail.[15] "The dread with which Palestinians regard such boundaries, and the potent—albeit negative—reinforcement of their identity this fear engenders, can be understood only in light of the many anecdotal examples of incidents at crossing points" (Khalidi 1997: 2).

I lost data not only by forgetting and misunderstanding a language that is not my own, but also by paraphrasing and writing in English conversations that occurred in Arabic. That is why there are fewer quotations in the words of individuals in this text than can be found in many ethnographies. Even though using a tape recorder would have provided a more precise transcript of conversations, it created uncomfortable situations and would never have been appropriate at the really critical moments. Electronic recordings jeopardize confidentiality, anonymity, and deniability, all crucial when studying people's activities in the borderlands. I was fearful that our house would be raided by the Israeli army because of my unusual presence, and that my notes would be confiscated. That never happened, but I was very careful about writing anything I thought might be potentially compromising to my friends or adopted kin. It was necessary to give up these tools of documentation in order to open communication, maintain access, and protect my hosts. I also omitted identifying details, and changed the names of all the people, even of the village in which I lived, to protect the privacy of those about whom I wrote. Admittedly, anyone who lives in al-Qarya, who knows me and these people, will be able to identify them, but at least the outsider will remain outside.

Most of my observations were recorded as entries in a daily journal, and I have turned them into stories, peppered with complementing research from archives and secondary sources. Stories are more readable than arguments that extract details and arrange them according to theory. With stories readers are more likely to imagine themselves in the place of those being written about. Storytelling also maintains the "positionality" or role of the author in the events reported, and reduces the tendency of anthropologists to overgeneralize, or even stereotype, the behavior of their hosts (Abu-Lughod 1991, 1993).

I wanted to investigate something that people wanted investigated. The borders and the closures were widely accepted objects for my investigation. It was Umm Samud, the mother of the home in which I lived, who told me over and over again to write about the border closures so Americans would know what is really happening. Bearing witness to some of Umm Samud's pains and frustrations makes clear how state violence is still part of the "new world order" and still productive of the inequalities of daily life. When her husband, Abu Samud, was unable to go to work because the border was closed, Umm Samud would say, "Write about that in your book. Tell them in America." Umm Samud intuitively knew that representations of suffering can expand the boundaries of sympathy and "help to mobilize the will, passion and intelligence needed to change the world" (Morris 1997: 42).

Despite the difficulty of facing this daily violence, representations of suffering can "become the currency, the symbolic capital," to negotiate political and personal problems (Kleinman and Kleinman 1997: 10).[16] For example, one of the most popular posters, sold in bookstores and hung on the walls of many Palestinian homes and offices, was of a portrait of a fair complexioned boy, about four or five years old, wearing a black and white Palestinian scarf. The little boy had chains draped upon him, he was crying, and tears flowed down his red cheeks. In some ways, this poster gave "voice to the unspeakable" and in so doing could

render it at least somewhat more controllable. Words serve to mourn the dead and create meaning in a new and brittle world. Words serve to construct a tomorrow in the face of chaos. People also feel the need to convey their stories to challenge the "factx" of war spun by the politico-military institutions and by outsiders with vested interests- and thereby to break the "reality" these people have constructed upon their victims. (Nordstrom 1997: 79)

"Hanging paintings of martyrs and bloodshed in one's home, in an atmosphere of deceit and denial, is an insistence on an alternative truth" (C. Mahmood 1996: 189). Although violence against Palestinians was meant to secure their passivity, compliance, or flight, this poster used a representation of violence to speak a different truth, and to create solidarity in a community of resistance.[17]

This ethnography is partly meant to fulfill my responsibility as a witness for my Palestinian hosts, for the people that trusted me and allowed me into their homes, of the border checkpoints in their lives. However, it is intended to do more intellectually (if not politically) than the poster. I do not neglect my obligation as analyst by just telling sympathetic stories. The last section of each chapter makes broader generalizations from these particular cases aimed at analyzing the power dynamics of geopolitical borders. The final chapter explains how the problem Palestinians face at the border resembles problems faced by other oppressed people, suggesting that shared learning about this tactic of power might help bring smarter resistance and more equitable solutions.

2. Making Maps Real

Looking at the Green Line that partitions Israel-Palestine at the beginning of the twenty-first century, it is important to remember that it has not always been there. It emerged and changed in the struggle of people who live in the borderland and of global players in powerful governments and businesses. This geopolitical border,[1] meaning a geographic boundary enforced by a state or states, is of relatively recent origin, like most borders of the world. The Israeli-Palestinian conflict is also of recent origin, despite the fact that many have used clichés like "ancient tribal conflicts" or "thousands of years of bloodshed." The names Palestine and Israel are ancient, at least as old as the Hebrew Bible,[2] but these names have not continually referred to the same groups of people or territories.[3] The idea that Palestine and Israel refer to a bounded territory with a homogeneous people emerged in the nineteenth century and continues to shape the conflict into the twenty-first century.

For purposes of clarity, the complicated history of partitioning Palestine, the multiple causes and effects of borders, have been reduced below to four phases of development with bounded dates: European imagining (1840–1917), the Partition (1917–67), the Occupation (1967–87), and the Closures (1987–2000). While no history is ever so simple, most of these dates mark major shifts in the presence and functioning of borders. The era of European imagining was the period when colonial powers, Britain and Zionist Jews in particular, designed a state in the region of Palestine that would be separate from surrounding Arab communities. This period began in 1840, when Muhammad 'Ali withdrew to Egypt from Greater Syria, and ended when British and French armies took control of the region in World War I, that is, when the European powers established borders that resembled what they had already designed. The second phase, the Partition, began with the physical creation of the borders of the British Mandate in Palestine in 1917. A plan for further partition caused fighting and eventually broke into a war that ended with an armistice line in 1949, called the

Green Line. This remained the border until the June War of 1967 when Israel crossed the Green Line and captured the remaining areas of former Mandate Palestine, the West Bank and Gaza Strip. The Occupation, the third phase, erased the Green Line for business and settlement, but did not extend political rights to those living in the West Bank and Gaza. The fourth phase, the Closures, began in 1987 with the Palestinian Uprising, called the Intifada. Although permanent closures of the Green Line by the Israeli army actually began in 1993, it was during the Intifada when Palestinians began to redraw the map.

Histories are political because they create legitimacy and justice out of time-space narratives. The failure of Israelis and Palestinians to *understand* each other can usefully be conceived as a clash of histories.[4] Jewish nationalist ideology situates the struggle within histories that include European anti-Semitism, Roman persecution, and even exile to Babylon. The Palestinian nationalist perspective does not usually conceive of history using these same markers. The settlement of Palestine by Jews is seen largely within the history of European colonialism and, sometimes, the Crusades. All histories are necessarily selective in what and how they tell a story, how they order events and point to particular causes. This history is not a comprehensive history of Palestinians[5] and will probably be unsatisfactory to those who sympathize with either Jewish or Palestinian nationalism. The four phases described here emphasize how space was reorganized over the last two centuries in a particularly "modern" way that delineated nations and forced them into territorialized forms.

European Imagining and Interventions: 1840–1917

For centuries, neither Palestine nor Israel was a name that had geopolitical significance, although Muslims, Christians, and Jews had extensive literature describing the Holy Land that focused on Jerusalem (Khalidi 1997: 29). For three and a half centuries Palestine was the common term for an undemarcated region of the Ottoman Empire and was divided by tax districts called *sanjaqs*, distinct from what became Palestine (see Map 1).[6] Most of the people were peasant farmers, *fallahin*, living in villages in the central highlands, paying taxes to elites who collected in the name of the Ottoman sultan (Baer 1966). Most farmers lived in the rocky central highlands, instead of the more fertile coastal plains, because the hills made them less vulnerable to Bedouin raids (Reilly 1981: 83).[7] Unlike most of Ottoman Syria, where the elite were urban (Khoury 1983), in Palestine (as in Lebanon) sheiks often lived on their rural

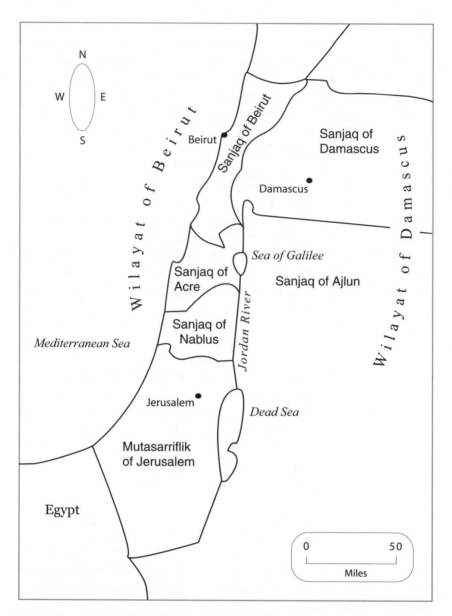

Map 1. Ottoman period, nineteenth century. During Ottoman times southern Palestine was in the *Mutasarriflik* (semi-autonomous province) of Jerusalem; northern Palestine was in the *Wilayat* (province) of Beirut and divided into the *Sanjaq* of Acre and the *Sanjaq* of Nablus.

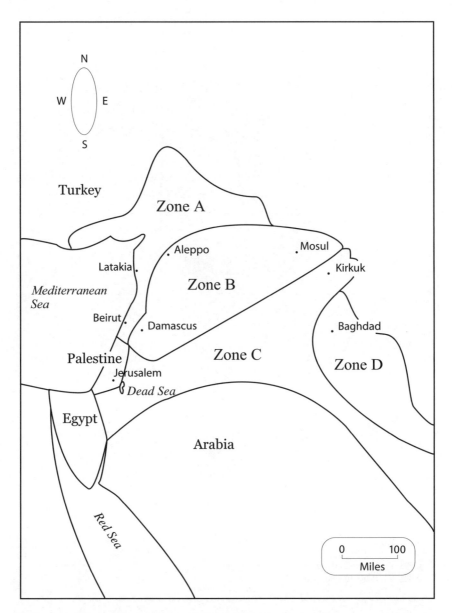

Map 2. The Sykes-Picot Agreement of 1916 divided the Fertile Crescent into four zones. Zone A was to be under direct French control, zone B was to be under French influence, Zone C was to be under British influence, and zone D was to be under direct British control. Under this agreement the future of Palestine would be decided by an international body composed of French, British, and Russian representatives in consultation with Sharif Hussein of Mecca.

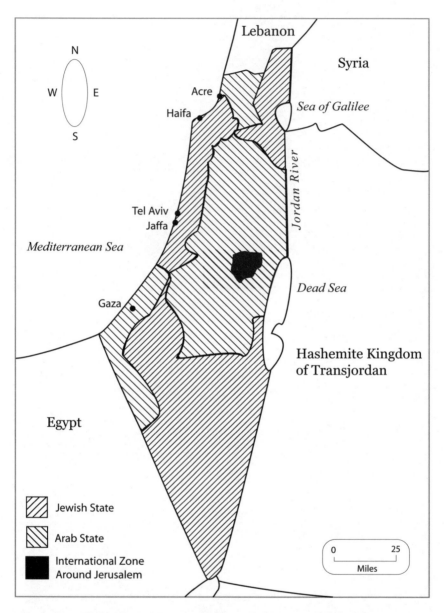

Map 3. The UN Partition Plan of 1947 divided Palestine into six checkerboard sections, three Jewish and three Arab, with neither group getting a single contiguous area. Jerusalem was to remain an international zone.

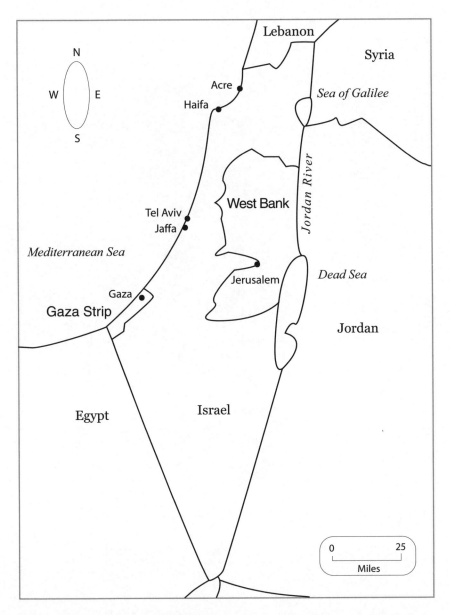

Map 4. The armistice line of 1949 left the new state of Israel in control of approximately 77 percent of Palestine, including much of Jerusalem. The Gaza Strip fell under the control of Egypt, and the West Bank was soon annexed by Jordan. The Gaza Strip and the West Bank became territories occupied by Israel after the 1967 War.

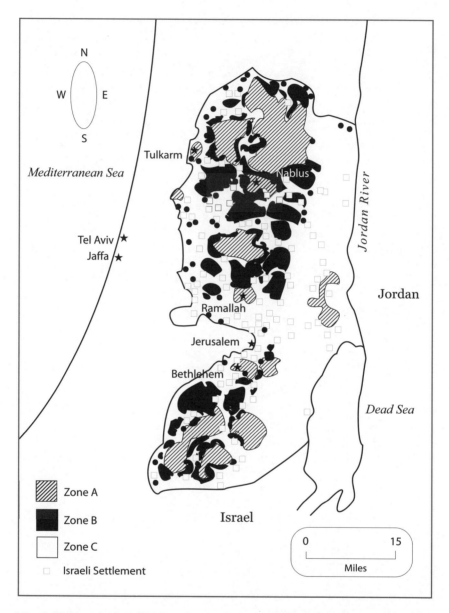

Map 5. The interim Israeli-Palestinian agreement of 1994, amended by the Wye River agreement of 1998, designated three zones in the West Bank. In Zone A, Israeli forces withdrew and ceded control to the Palestinian Authority. In Zone B, Israeli and Palestinian authorities were to collaborate on security and administration. In the remainder of the West Bank, Zone C, the Israeli government had sole authority.

estates.[8] Although tax-farming elites were officially subordinate to the sultan in Istanbul, several ruled the land with relative autonomy for long periods.[9] Despite this relative autonomy, experiences of Palestinian identity were rooted in long-standing forms of affiliation like family, village, region, and attachment to Jerusalem (see Khalidi 1997). Until the twentieth century, most of "the people of Palestine considered themselves Syrian Arabs" (Abboushi 1990: xiii).[10]

Napoleon's forces landed in Palestine at the close of the eighteenth century, and although they were not there for very long, the region soon emerged as an important concern of colonial politics. Early in the nineteenth century, Muhammad ʿAli, a vassal of the Ottoman sultan, built new cities, schools, agricultural estates, bureaucracies, and armies in Egypt. His power became so strong that he challenged the sultan by invading Syria (which included Palestine and Lebanon) in the early 1830s. Muhammad ʿAli's troops "pacified" the Bedouin in the coastal plain of Palestine, making it safe for settlement and commercial agriculture (Issawi 1982). But his occupation of Greater Syria lasted less than a decade because of the intervention of the British navy in 1838. British, Prussian, and Austro-Hungarian officials did not want Muhammad ʿAli to control Syria because they feared it would give an advantage to the French who were on good terms with the Egyptian ruler, so they supported the weakened sultan in Istanbul (Macfie 1996).

The increasing inability of the Ottoman government to defend the empire encouraged the sultan to make capitulations to the foreign powers. These capitulations included granting special privileges to local "protected minorities," mainly Christians (Armenians, Orthodox, and Catholics) and Jews who acted as the commercial agents of European capitalists. The struggle between European colonial powers to exploit Ottoman resources and markets emerged as a campaign over who would ensure the well-being of these protected minorities. The tsar claimed to defend the Orthodox Christians, the French claimed to protect Catholics, and the British were to protect the Jews. It was these struggles among local Arabic-speaking minorities, the Ottoman authorities in Istanbul, and foreign involvement that gave birth to the institutions (like scholarly and popular presses and schools) and ideologies shaping Palestinian Arab nationalism (Abu-Ghazaleh 1991).

The early imperial designs were evident in newspaper reports from the period. On August 17, 1840, for example, the *Times* of London ran three front-page articles on the Eastern Question. One article sympathetically described the celebration of Passover by Jews in Jerusalem. A second described an ongoing saga in which Syrian Jews were being accused of ritual murder based on confessions made under torture. A third article discussed the value of settling

Jews in Palestine to establish a colony against Muhammad ʿAli and the French. The "Eastern Question" became an important subject of foreign policy and public opinion. The topic tied imperial interests, religious convictions, and racist orientalism into one overlapping project.

In the 1850s the British and the French stood together with the Ottoman sultan against the armies of the Russian tsar in Crimea. Victories in the Crimea left the sultan with a financial debt to England and France, which created the impetus for a second wave of modernization. This opened a wider door for colonial "free trade," or concessions, and led to the privatization of peasant lands and the arrival of thousands of European tourists.

By the mid-nineteenth century, Palestine had become more sharply defined by colonial strategic interests, as well as central to British popular imagination (see Ben-Arieh 1979). British fascination with the "Holy Land" generated over 5,000 publications by more than 2,000 writers between 1800 and 1878. Thousands of pilgrim-explorers attempted to confirm biblical scripture by finding evidence of sayings or prophecies. By the 1850s, steamships regularly docked in Jaffa, travel facilities had sprung up, and increased security on the main roads made pilgrimage tours possible for a growing European middle class. In May 1865, an organization called the Palestine Exploration Fund was established in the Jerusalem Room of Westminster Cathedral, to pursue "systematic and scientific research" to better illustrate the Bible (Palestine Exploration Fund 1895: 11). The fund financed expeditions to map Palestine, do archaeological surveys, and report on flora, fauna, and the habits and customs of modern inhabitants, and published the results in a quarterly journal. In 1867, the journey of the *Quaker City*, which brought 150 Americans from Henry Ward Beecher's Plymouth Church to the Holy Land, was made famous by the serial publication of Mark Twain's correspondences, later collected and published as the book *Innocents Abroad*. In 1869, newspapers were filled with reports of the many important European visitors who visited Egypt to witness the opening of the Suez Canal, linking the Mediterranean and the Indian Ocean. The event was accompanied by the premier of Verdi's opera *Aïda*. Many of those guests, such as the Austrian Emperor Franz Josef, then toured the Holy Land, which led to construction and road building. From 1868 to 1882, Thomas Cook, printer and Baptist lay preacher (namesake of the British travel agency), brought 4,200 travelers to Palestine, 1,000 on one trip in 1882. This tourism to the Holy Land tangled the Transcendent Kingdom of the Second Coming of Jesus Christ with the very worldly imperial interests of the British Empire.

While the British began exploring and imagining settlement in Palestine early in the 1800s, and had developed an extensive literature about it by the middle 1800s, it was not until the later part of the nineteenth century that

European Jews began to organize around the idea. Moses Hess's book *Rome to Jerusalem*, published in 1862, was the first by a Jewish writer to describe the formation of a Jewish national home in Palestine. But European Jews were scattered from east to west, under very different circumstances, and were slow to get behind the idea of settlement in Palestine.

The first organization among Jews to settle Palestine, called *Hovevei Zion* (Lovers of Zion) was founded in 1882 in Eastern Europe. They were pushed to leave Eastern Europe by instability in the Austro-Hungarian and Russian empires. Extreme nationalisms manifested in anti-Semitic violence called pogroms (organized mobs of Cossacks who attacked Jewish communities). Approximately four million Jews fled from Eastern Europe between 1880 and 1929 (Harris 1990: 229), mainly to the Americas, but some to Palestine.

The leaders of early settlers, like David Ben-Gurion and his teacher Ber Borochov, wanted to settle Jews in Palestine, instead of America or Western Europe, because they believed Jews needed to be *re*-connected to a territory. They were socialists schooled in the struggles of the Jewish left in Eastern Europe. The Jewish Workers Association, the Bund, was the largest socialist organization in Russia before the revolution. The Bund argued that Jewish workers required independent national representation in the international socialist struggle because they were oppressed by the national majority in most countries. Lenin, the leader of the socialist struggle, disagreed with the autonomy of national socialist parties and tried to persuade them into unity (Harris 1990). However, because he distinguished between the chauvinistic nationalism of oppressors and the liberatory, patriotic nationalism of the oppressed (Lowy 1976), he acknowledged the rights to self-determination for oppressed nations (Lenin 1974). Nonetheless, Lenin did not consider the Jews in the same way as the Poles or Czechs because they lacked a common territory.[11] Consequently, some Jewish socialist leaders decided to organize their comrades to settle territory as "pioneers" in Palestine, make the desert bloom, and return a people without a land to a land without a people. The reality that Arabic speaking people already lived there was conveniently ignored.

At about the same time in Western Europe, bourgeois and petit-bourgeois classes of Jews were working for their civil emancipation and social integration. Despite incremental improvements in their rights and general trends toward secularization, discrimination continued and many assimilated professional and petit-bourgeois Jewish families (like Karl Marx's parents) felt compelled to convert to Christianity. The persistence of widespread prejudice in Western Europe became evident in 1890, when the trial of the French Jewish officer Alfred Dreyfus created spectacles of anti-Semitic activity in the streets and cafes of Paris. His conviction for treason made some believe that there could never be Jewish emancipation in Europe, and that they would always be considered foreigners. The Austrian journalist Theodor Herzl, who covered the Dreyfus Affair, began to organize a congress of influential Jews. Knowing they could not establish an independent state in Europe, the World Zionist Organization was founded in Switzerland in 1897 and established the financial and political institutions necessary to colonize Palestine. Herzl's book *Der Judenstaat* (the Jewish State), appeared the previous year to explain the problem and program they would pursue.

Both Eastern European socialists and Western European capitalists came to see a Jewish state with a bounded territory as their central political goal. These movements established institutions on the ground to acquire land and established the financial and administrative bureaucracies to control it. Although quite different in ideology and experience, the interests of the eastern socialist nationalists and western imperialists coincided to lay important foundations for European Jewish settlement in Palestine within the framework provided by the British Empire. Although the exact location of the future Jewish state was not clear (some imagined that all the territories claimed by King Solomon, from the Nile to the Euphrates, would be part of the Jewish State, and this ancient biblical map actually appears in relief on the back of the Israeli 10-agorot coin), the British had already defined the Holy Land and the map of Palestine.

Partition and Catastrophe: 1917–67

In December 1917, toward the end of World War I, Jerusalem surrendered to British troops under General Allenby, and by October 1918 the northern part of the country was also under British administration. The British occupied southern Syria and the French were in the north. After the war, the League of Nations declared all of former Ottoman Syria to be French and British Mandated Territories, in order that they be "developed" by the colonial administration until the indigenous people were civil enough to rule themselves and be independent.[12] Northern Syria came under French control[13] and was divided in two when an independent constitutional republic was created in the Lebanon in 1920.[14] Southern Syria and Mesopotamia came under British rule. This division roughly conformed to the Sykes-Picot Agreement, which the French and British had secretly negotiated in 1916, to divide the entire Fertile Crescent between them (see map 2).[15] "As a result of marks on the map made by an imperial quill, Middle Easterners were forced to share nationality with others from outside their family, village, region, or religion. Nor was the rationale behind such a forced sharing of identity clear" (Brand 1988: 3). Nevertheless, "a universal process was unfolding in the Middle East during this period, involving an increasing identification with the new states created by the post-World War I partitions" (Khalidi 1997: 20).

Farmers were already suffering from land shortages due to natural population growth, increasing numbers of Jewish colonists and land privatization (Tamari 1990a),[16] but these new borders intensified the displacement of Palestinian peasants from their lands. Before the mandate borders were created, the lands around Acre and Nablus were part of the *Wilayat* of Beirut and wealthy Beirutis often owned the best commercial property in the province. When Palestine came under the British and Beirut under the French, these southern properties became more remote and Beiruti owners sold Palestinian lands on an open market. Foreign Jewish companies effectively eliminated potential Arab buyers (Abboushi 1990: 49) and Jewish settlements began springing up along the coast, mostly around the port of Jaffa and in the hills of Galilee.[17]

The British government's Hope-Simpson Report of 1930 described the difficult conditions of farmers in Palestine who were heavily in debt, lacking any capital, and facing rising rents, interest rates, and taxes. Another British report, by the Shaw Commission of 1930, argued that further Jewish immigration would necessarily displace more Arab farmers. Many peasants found it necessary to seek wage work in lime extraction and charcoal burning, mainly for extensive road and urban construction by the British Mandate government, and in plantation agriculture financed by capital from international Zionist organizations.

In these jobs, Palestinians discovered modern discriminatory employment practices (Abboushi 1990: 60). Jewish "pioneers" from Europe were less experienced than indigenous Palestinians at agricultural work, and they were much more expensive. But the leaders of the Jewish socialist movement had to find employment for their settlers. Leaders of Jewish labor agreed to provide settlers for political (capitalist) Zionists, who in turn provided jobs for a workers movement. The Mapai (Israel Workers' Party) leaders "turned to Jewish workers with an appeal—couched in the lexicon of class struggle—to direct their aggression towards Arab labor [instead of capitalists]; and they endowed this aggression with a higher national purpose" (Shalev 1989: 102; see also Shafir 1989; Bernstein 2000).

As the economic basis of life crumbled for the Palestinian peasantry, they were also politically shut out of governance. The British planned to partition Palestine and make two states, one Arab and one Jewish, because of promises they made during World War I. On the one hand, the British government promised to support the rule of Sharif Hussein of Mecca in an Arab state in exchange for his revolt against the Ottoman armies. This alliance was not of great military importance, but it was politically crucial for the British to defuse the risk of mutiny among the many Muslims from India serving in the British forces.[18] On the other hand, Lord Balfour had declared His Majesty's government's intent to create a Jewish homeland in Palestine as a solution to the Jewish problem in Europe. Arabs indigenous to Palestine were not considered in these British plans for the region.

After the war, the British helped establish the creation of the Hashemite Kingdom in the Transjordan in 1928, which became fully independent in 1946, with Sharif Hussein's son 'Abdallah as the king. But west of the Jordan River, the British intention to create a Jewish homeland, stated in the Balfour Declaration of 1917, was met with opposition throughout the Arab world. Arabs protested in writing and by marching in the streets. In 1921, large disturbances, riots, and vengeful retaliation between Arabs and Jews occurred, involving close to a hundred deaths and twice as many injuries. A few years later, in 1929, twice as many deaths and injuries occurred (Abboushi 1990).

In 1936, growing nationalist confrontation over land, labor and political representation exploded in the Great Revolt of the Palestinian peasantry against British soldiers and Jewish colonists (Swedenburg 1995).

Peasants totally abandoned by the system—dispossessed of their lands by Zionist colonies and driven into the towns as a subproletariat—eagerly embraced new ideas and practices that challenged notable dominance. . . . The peasant-led movement represented a congealing of nationalism, religious revivalism, and class consciousness, no element of which can be disentangled from the others. (Swedenburg 1988: 196)

The rebellion was encouraged by a popular preacher in Haifa named 'Izz al-Din al-Qassam who spoke against colonial oppression in 1935. He took to the hills with a small group of fighters but was soon killed by the British in a forest near the village of Ya'bad. This was the first spark of a general strike and armed revolt that lasted from 1936 until 1939. The rebellion was crushed by the British, but the revolt marked the beginning of a full-blown national struggle between Palestinian Arabs and Zionists.[19] The only solution for either side within this struggle became the redemption of national territory.

By 1937, with a major Palestinian uprising continuing into its second year, the British Peel Commission reported that the conflict was unnegotiable, not least of all because the Jews were European and the Arabs were "Asiatic in character" (Abboushi 1990: 127). They recommended that the only option was a surgical partition that could separate the Jewish and Arab communities. They proposed three states: an Arab state, a Jewish state, and a new British Mandate for the Holy Places. The main problem was that there were no all-Jewish areas, making division impossible without transferring thousands of Arabs. Nonetheless, the British sent the Woodhead Commission, a team of experts, to determine where the boundaries of the partition should be. They presented three plans, but each contained significant problems in separating Arab and Jewish populations and establishing equitable property ratios (Abboushi 1990: 130).[20]

The problem became worse as the numbers of Jewish refugees increased due to Nazi persecution in Europe. The Jews had nowhere to go because the doors of other countries had been shut. In July 1938, representatives from thirty-two states, from Western Europe, the Americas, and the British Commonwealth, attended a conference in Evian, France, to discuss a few hundred thousand refugees, many of whom were Jews, that had been displaced by the rise of fascism in Germany and the occupation of Austria. Except for the Dominican Republic, these states, under the leadership of Franklin D. Roosevelt, closed their borders, inviting Kristallnacht later that year and ushering in the Nazi Final Solution. By the end of the war, there would be millions of displaced persons and many Jewish survivors desperate to go to Palestine. As Europe headed into World War II, the British attempted to limit Jewish migration and suppress the revolt of Palestinian peasants (see Swedenburg 1995).

After World War II, the problem of Palestine was handed to the newly formed United Nations, where a partition was designed in 1947 to divide Palestine into six checkerboard sections, three Jewish and three Arab, with neither group getting a single contiguous area (see Map 3). Most Arab leaders, like Mufti of Jerusalem Hajj Amin al-Husseini, found the partition an unacceptable concession to colonization. Jews accounted for only about one third of the population (fewer than 600,000 people), and owned only about 6–9 percent of the land. Despite their minority status and urban concentration, the 1947 UN partition allotted them 54 percent of the land, within which there was a sizable Arab minority.

Zionist leaders accepted the proposal because it put their state on the map. Their concern was only to increase the amount of land they would control. So, as British withdrawal became inevitable, Zionist settlers worked quickly to build "wall and tower" settlements in outlying areas to expand the borders of their future state. As the more organized Zionist forces took control of roads and strategic locations, fighting between Arab villagers and Jewish settlers became more common. "The decisive defeat in 1936–39 had fatally weakened the Palestinians by the time of their desperate final post-World War II struggle with the Zionist movement to retain control of some part of what they passionately believed was their country" (Khalidi 1997: 27). When the British completed their withdrawal in May 1948, the Zionist leadership declared independence.

The United States and the Soviet Union recognized Israel's sovereignty, most UN members fell in line, and it was left to soldiers from the Israeli and Arab armies to determine the borders.

When the fighting ended, a new border called the Green Line, created by the armistice agreement between Israel and Transjordan (later Jordan), partitioned Palestine. Palestine was left divided among three state governments. Israel claimed sovereignty over the coastal plains from Ramla to Acre, the Negev, the Galilee, and a corridor to Jerusalem, 77 percent of the land of Palestine (see Map 4). This was a significantly larger territory than the 54 percent demarcated by the UN partition plan. Transjordan controlled and annexed the West Bank including East Jerusalem. Transjordan gave citizenship to the residents and thus added about 400,000 West Bankers and about 400,000 refugees to its pre-partition population of about 340,000 (Brand 1988: 150). Egypt occupied but did not annex the Gaza Strip, and it did not give its residents citizenship.

Approximately 150,000 Palestinians remained in the land that became Israel. They received citizenship, but lived under military rule until 1966. Even after 1966, these Arab-Israelis suffered as third class citizens.[21] They also became detached from the rest of the Arab world, where they were unable to travel with Israeli travel documents. By the beginning of twenty-first century their descendants numbered over one million.

Some 600,000–760,000 Palestinians became refugees during the fighting between December 1947 and September 1949 and could not return to the land that became Israel (Morris 1987: 298).[22] About 100,000 fled to Lebanon in the north, about 80,000 to Syria, about 300,000 to the hills of the West Bank, about 180,000 to Gaza in the south, and about 100,000 to the East Bank of the Jordan (Kimmerling and Migdal 1993). In 1950, the UN Relief and Works Agency (UNRWA) began to organize those without housing or resources into camps.[23] Those with money or family connections settled in Arab cities like Beirut, Cairo, and Amman, or in Europe.

The partition was not only devastating for those displaced by or living within the new state of Israel, but also for those communities that received refugees. The arrival of about 300,000 refugees in the West Bank intensified the land shortage that had already been present. The new border also separated thousands of Palestinians in the hills from their work in the coastal towns and plantations (Brand 1988: 149). Approximately 160,000 West Bank farmers near the border lost their fields to Israel. Although they were deprived of their means of livelihood, these farmers did not qualify for UN assistance.

This event, called *al-Nakba* ("Disaster" or "Catastrophe") in Arabic, was the most significant historical trauma to shape the formation of Palestinian nationalism. For almost two decades, the border of the Israeli state remained at the armistice line of 1949. There was no peace between Israel and its neighbors and the borders were closed.

The Occupation: 1967–87

In the mid-1960s, Arab leaders, led by the outspoken President of Egypt Gamal 'Abd al-Nasir, threatened to defend themselves and their Palestinian neighbors from Western colonial aggression by attacking Israel. When Egyptian troops were moved near the border and shipping routes in the Red Sea were closed, Israel launched a surprise attack on June 5, 1967. Within six days the war was over and the Israeli army enjoyed an overwhelming victory against Egypt, Syria, and Jordan. Israeli planes destroyed most of the Egyptian and Syrian forces and Israeli infantry more than tripled the land under Israeli rule. From Egypt they took the Gaza Strip and the Sinai Peninsula. From Syria they captured the Golan Heights. The Israelis moved into the West Bank, took East Jerusalem, and were left controlling all of Mandatory Palestine. A second diaspora of 350,000 Palestinians was created, most fleeing to Jordan, leaving about 1.2 million behind.

On June 29, 1967, the Israeli Ministry of the Interior extended the Jerusalem municipality to East Jerusalem, thus annexing the city, and Israeli Defense Minister Moshe Dayan tore down the dividing wall. Some members of the Israeli government aspired to exploit their military victory by annexing all the new territories and extending Israel's borders. But the Labor Party leadership decided that the territories could not be annexed because that would require giving citizenship to more than one million Palestinians. Annexing the territories and not giving them citizenship would outwardly contradict the idea that Israel was a democracy, a crucial point during the Cold War for U.S. foreign policy in the Middle East. The "Allon Plan," which became the policy de jure, masked this contradiction by distinguishing between security borders, which were extended to the Jordan River, and political borders, which remained at the Green Line. Israeli forces and settlements would be built along the mountain ranges of the West Bank and in the Jordan valley to prevent incursions of conventional military forces or guerilla groups from Jordan. However, the official political border would not be extended in order to avoid extending citizenship to the 700,000 Palestinians in the West Bank. By this mechanism Israel could incorporate the land of Palestinians without giving them political rights.

On the ground, Israeli Defense Minister Moshe Dayan pursued a policy he called "Open Bridges. No other term could more aptly express Israeli policy in the territories" (Gazit 1995: 176). By summer 1968 regular movement began between Gaza, Israel, the West Bank, and even, in a more restricted way, Jordan. Dayan proceeded to link the roads, electricity, water, and telephones in the West Bank to Israeli networks (Gazit 1995: 169). The first Israeli commander of the West Bank explained the policy thus:

"Give them something to lose" was one of the basic slogans of Israeli policy in the territories. This roundabout approach may have been preferred for international political reasons, on the basis of legal considerations, or perhaps on purely ethical grounds. In any case, the military government was certainly limited in its options concerning punishment, and pursued as an alternative a system of benefits and privileges that could be revoked. Threatening to close the Jordan River bridges jeopardized the most important privilege enjoyed by the local population and many outside Arab elements as well.

Israel's control over traffic through the open bridges—ranging from total closure to selective measures effecting certain areas, communities, goods, vehicles, or individuals—became a powerful instrument of leverage and a first-rate deterrent, from both a psychological and a practical standpoint . . .

The military government also made effective use of banishment beyond the Jordan River as a punishment. This might not have been possible if the bridges had not been open to traffic.

The policy of unrestricted two-way traffic inadvertently became a central pillar of Israel's international "hasbara" [publicity] efforts. (Gazit 1995: 179)

Bridge policy was a mechanism of control and punishment, but it was also, ironically, a point of public relations illustrating Israel's enlightened and benevolent policy.

Dayan had envisioned an occupation in which residents of the Territories could "live a normal life, having to encounter few if any Israeli administration officials" and he ordered the removal of as many Israeli field-level workers as possible (Gazit 1995: 142).

The Defense Minister concluded that every Arab, so long as he or she broke no law, should be able to go through the routine of life without having recourse to the services of Jewish administrative personnel. (Gazit 1995: 170)

Dayan believed that "mutual acquaintance might induce coexistence and greater understanding [between Israelis and Arabs], and integration would certainly influence the nature of any future political settlement" (Gazit 1995: 137).

But the continuing military occupation was not benign. The Israeli occupation immediately redrew the internal borders of the West Bank, thus dividing the population. Under Jordanian rule (1949–67), there were three administrative centers in the West Bank: Hebron, Jerusalem, and Nablus. Defense Minister Dayan separated East Jerusalem from the West Bank, made the surrounding towns of Bethlehem, Jericho, and Ramallah independent districts, and separated Tulkarm, Qalqilya, and Jenin from their center, Nablus. This policy created a more fragmented polity by decentralizing authority.

Palestinians also suffered from a color coded bureaucracy that distinguished citizens from noncitizen residents of the Occupied Territories. West Bank residents carried their identification cards in orange holders, Gazans red, and Israeli citizens blue. Similarly, cars were easily distinguishable by their color-coded license plates: Israelis had yellow, West Bankers blue. The blue West Bank plates also had a Hebrew letter that identified the district in which the car was registered. Blue-plated Palestinian cars learned to drive slowly behind army jeeps, keeping a safe distance, and approached Israeli army checkpoints cautiously in order to avoid fatal accidents. Meanwhile, yellow-plated cars easily drove past checkpoints and overtook military vehicles without a thought. These color-coded differences made enforcing discrimination easier.

Israeli policies restricted the building of factories and other facilities, only allowing a few industries (textiles, footwear, and chemicals) to develop in the West Bank and Gaza.

The desire to protect Israeli-made products was so great that Israel even attempted to prevent the establishment or reactivation of Arab-owned factories if there was any danger that their products might compete with Israeli products. (Gazit 1995: 221)

In almost all areas of the economy, Israeli policy discouraged investment in the territories by

making the cultivation, harvesting, processing, manufacturing, marketing and exporting of any crop or product contingent on the acquisition of a permit from the military authorities. To protect Israeli growers and manufacturers, permits would be withheld from those who wished to engage in economic activities that might compete with Israeli products. (Al-Haq 1990: 242–43)

In January 1985, Defense Minister Yitzhak Rabin said that "there will be no development [in the territories] initiated by the Israeli government, and no permits will be given for expanding agriculture or industry [there], which may compete with the State of Israel" (Al-Haq 1990: 243; see also Abdulhadi 1990; Tamari 1980).

Agriculture, which remained the West Bank's biggest single economic sector at about 40 percent of the economy through the 1990s (Palestinian Bureau of Statistics 1995: 73),[24] was also significantly transformed by occupation policies. Israelis freely marketed their government-subsidized agricultural produce in the West Bank, which drove the prices of local produce down.

Palestinian farmers either altered their production to the needs of the Israeli market or gave up farming to become wage earners (Samara 1989: 15).[25] Production shifted from subsistence to market (i.e. from home consumption to sales) and employment in agriculture dropped from 42 percent in 1968, to 30 percent in 1980 (Tamari 1981). Agriculture declined as a source of employment and few industries developed in the West Bank to take its place.

In the early 1970s, land confiscation and settlement in the West Bank began and approximately twenty-five settlements were established in the West Bank, totaling about 3,000 people. However, some Israelis were dissatisfied with this hesitant pace. In order to settle the territories more aggressively, religious nationalists established Gush Emunim (Bloc of the Faithful) in February 1974 at Gush Etzion (Lustick 1988).[26] When the Labor Party lost to Likud in the 1977 national elections, this new movement had significant influence on the ruling government coalition,[27] under Prime Minister Menachem Begin, and settlements expanded rapidly.[28] In 1976, there were 3,176 Jewish settlers in the West Bank and Gaza; by 1979, 10,000; in 1982, over 20,000; by 1987, 57,000. By 1995, there were 147,000 Jewish settlers in the Occupied Territories (Settlement Report Spring 1996: 136). By the beginning of the twenty-first century, there were about 400,000 settlers, half of whom were in neighborhoods in and around an expanded Jerusalem.

The settlers were an armed-to-the-teeth encampment that confiscated land with impunity from the surrounding one million Palestinians. By the mid-1980s, settlements surrounded by razor wire and flood lights were conspicuous on hill-tops across the West Bank. Israelis built prefabricated homes on straight streets, at equal distances from each other and, usually, with red ceramic tile roofs. The settlements looked completely different from surrounding Arab villages, which had no such geometric order and where roofs were flat, providing a private, outdoor place to sit on summer evenings.

Uprising and Closures: 1987–2000

Increasing Israeli settlement was accompanied by a more formidable Israeli military presence. This led to increasing hostility between the occupation forces and local Palestinians. Antagonism was also fueled by the Israeli invasion of Lebanon in 1982 to eject the PLO, and by a general recession in the Arab world due to falling oil prices. In 1982, Israeli Defense Minister Ariel Sharon also placed new burdens on economic life in the Occupied Territories, including restrictions on the entry of money from abroad, limitations on the acceptance of loans for public institutions, and the imposition of new taxes.[29]

Conflict brewed on the ground throughout the 1980s, and exploded into the Intifada (Uprising) in Jabalya Refugee Camp in Gaza in December 1987. It soon spread to the rest of Gaza and to the West Bank.

The Intifada began a transformation of the borders around the West Bank. In early 1988, Israeli authorities at the bridge to Jordan limited drivers to 200 Jordanian dinar (JD) per trip and travelers to JD 400 per trip. Israeli Coordinator of Affairs in the Territories Shmuel Goren said the restrictions were made to prevent the transfer of PLO funds (Al-Haq 1990: 248), but the consequence was debilitating to the social welfare and monetary income of the general public. Frequent bridge closures during the Intifada stranded hundreds, sometimes thousands of Palestinians at the bus stations waiting to cross. In Jordan, shared taxis left Amman early in the morning, as early as 4:00 A.M., to arrive at the bridge before 5:00 A.M. On the West Bank side, Palestinians would simultaneously begin arriving at a special bus station east of Jericho. Palestinians described extensive searches and questioning by Israeli secret police about their activities while abroad. Young men, sixteen to forty years of age and unmarried, were the primary targets of interrogation.

In 1988, Jordanian King Hussein ordered his government's administrative and legal disengagement from the West Bank, cutting off funds to pay civil servants and withdrawing full citizenship from West Bankers. They kept their Jordanian passports, but these were easily distinguished from East Bankers by their shorter two-year expiration; East Bankers had five-year passports. This two-year passport was recognizable to most Arab border guards in the Middle East, making Palestinians vulnerable to accusations of either collaborating with Israel or being operatives in the resistance.

The Intifada also began to alter the Green Line and Israel's approach to the territories. Fear recreated a partial border as yellow plated Israeli cars became targets for stone-throwing adolescents. Those settlers and soldiers who continued to cross were forced to cage themselves behind steel grating, razor wire, and floodlights. Despite continued Israeli settlement in the Occupied Territories, a renewed border was made by this fear that kept most Israelis out, the economic war that refused Israeli goods, and an effort to create an internal unity through patriotism and the preservation of Palestinian culture. The popular phrasing of this tripartite resistance was to refer to the occupation as military, economic, and cultural; defense on all fronts was the call to arms.

The Intifada remained at the center of most people's political attention until the Gulf War in 1991, which set the stage for a reorganization of the conflict. General curfews were declared by the Israeli army throughout the war. Weeks went by without anyone going to work. Hundreds of thousands of Palestinians, perhaps three quarters of a million, fled the Gulf after the Iraqi invasion of Kuwait and were not allowed to return. Many lost property in Kuwait. This was a double burden to the Palestinians in the territories and Jordan who lost a significant source of remittances from abroad and had to house their returning families. After embracing Sadaam Hussein, the Palestinian leadership was weak, cut off from Gulf countries, and was ready to cut any deal that would keep them functioning. After having SCUD missiles land on Tel Aviv, the Israeli government realized that strength could not be maintained by military means only. Despite the overwhelming military power of the IDF, the most significant lesson of the Uprising was that "stones can be much more eloquent than bullets" (Ezrahi 1997: 204). When thousands of Palestinian children confronted armed Israeli soldiers, they placed the Israeli citizen-army in the dilemma of either using firearms against civilians or finding other solutions. With Israelis feeling the economic and emotional fatigue of maintaining a belligerent occupation, and with the burden on Palestinians to maintain the Uprising, each respective leadership took the opportunity offered by the Gulf War coalition to rearrange the conflict. The meetings in Madrid in October 1991, and the secret negotiations of Oslo soon thereafter, began a reformulation of border procedures for the West Bank.

In March 1993, while the Oslo negotiations were underway, the Israeli army put up checkpoints on the major roads between the West Bank and Israel, ending almost twenty-five years of open bridges. For the first time, East Jerusalem was physically separated from its surrounding Palestinian villages and its neighboring towns of Ramallah and Bethlehem. The immediate reason for the checkpoints was in response to Palestinian attacks killing fifteen that month, but it soon became clear that this security measure was permanent. The Israeli government said that the closures were a step leading toward the separation of Israelis and Palestinians, and a move toward Palestinian autonomy. However, settlers and soldiers remained free to cross, and only Palestinians were denied freedom of movement. West Bankers and Gazans often spoke of these closures as imprisonment. Workers and businessmen suffered, and even students were prevented from getting to their universities (Perry 1995). Israel had negotiated a more circumscribed form of control by withdrawing from Palestinian population centers and increasing border control.

The Declaration of Principles on Interim Self-Government Arrangements of September 1993, otherwise known as the Oslo Agreement, opened the door for the PLO's [30] entrance into the Occupied Territories of the West Bank and the Gaza Strip. The Palestinian Authority was created in May 1994 with the signing of the Agreement on the Gaza Strip and Jericho, also known as the Cairo Agreement. The Interim Agreement on the West Bank and Gaza Strip, signed in September of 1995, also known as the Oslo II or the Taba

Agreement, facilitated the complete withdrawal of Israeli forces from six major towns of the West Bank (3 percent of the land area), cooperative Israeli-Palestinian patrols in an additional 27 percent of the West Bank, and the election of an eighty-eight-member Legislative Council. Oslo II also established specifications for the Palestinian administration and economic protocols for relations with Israel and Jordan. Additional agreements were signed, most notably the Wye River agreement,[31] but the overall terms of Oslo II did not change by the end of the century.

At the beginning of the twenty-first century, Israel remained in military control of most of the territory in the West Bank and land appropriation and colonization continued with the expansion of settlements. While Israeli troops redeployed out of West Bank towns, there were still Israeli roadblocks and patrols throughout the West Bank. More important, Israel maintained control over the borders around the West Bank. Even if the Israeli military had turned over more territory to the Palestinian Authority, the Israeli administration made it clear that it would maintain control over external trade and the movement of people by controlling "security" at the borders. After Oslo Palestinians faced a double repression from Israel and their own Palestinian Authority, resulting in a deteriorating human rights situation.

Palestinians did not accept this new status quo. In the fall of 2000 street battles began in the Occupied Territories and, for the first time in years, in Arab-Israeli towns. Unlike clashes in the 1980s and early 1990s, Palestinian militiamen with guns joined stone throwing youths in their confrontation with the IDF and the settlers. The IDF responded by escalating their repression with helicopter attacks and tanks in order to maintain their overwhelming military superiority.

3. Work in Israel

Abu Samud in Construction

Abu Samud worked in the Israeli construction industry. Mostly he built the concrete structure of residential houses. The job consisted of several stages. First, he constructed reinforcements by bending and tying together iron bars. Second, he nailed wooden forms around the reinforcement bars. Third, he poured concrete into the forms. Fourth, he laid concrete blocks between the sections of poured cement. Finally, he finished the exterior with plaster. For me this was tiring and difficult work, and I was only in my twenties while Abu Samud was in his fifties. Abu Samud said many times, as he rubbed and rotated his aching right shoulder while watching television in the evening, that all his work was for his sons, so they can study and graduate from the university, so they do not have to work in Israel for their whole lives. Despite all the challenges he had faced, Abu Samud was quick to smile and loved to laugh.

Abu Samud was born in 1944 in the Arab town Ara' in the coastal plain that became part of Israel in 1948. His grandfather had moved down to the plains from al-Qarya around 1910. When fighting began in 1948, Abu Samud's family fled to the Jenin district of the West Bank where they found refuge with in-laws. They were officially refugees; they had UN refugee cards but were saved from the camps by family who took them in. Consequently, Abu Samud grew up in a small village outside Jenin under Jordanian rule.

When he graduated from high school in the mid-1960s, there were few employment opportunities in the West Bank. He went to Kuwait where his older brother was already working. With a nostalgic smile he told me how he just got into a car and rode all the way to Kuwait, via Amman and Baghdad. He worked there for three months in construction and then received a letter from a friend inviting him to Cairo. In 1965, he went to Egypt where he studied radio and television electronics. He spent two years working in Cairo, receiving additional support from his father, who was still in the West Bank, and his brothers in the Gulf. Those were the years when Gamal 'Abd al-Nasir was at his apex, and Abu Samud said, sitting straight up and pointing to his eyes, "I saw him in person."

In early 1967, before the June War, he returned to the West Bank, to the village in Jenin, where his eldest brother, who had been a student in Syria, was starting a well-drilling business with a Swedish company. But the occupation began with the June War of 1967, and easy travel to other Arab countries was no longer possible. The drilling business never opened. There was also no work to be found in his trained profession, television and radio repair.

But there was work in Israel over the Green Line. The IDF had immediately opened the border,[1] even though the Israeli government was divided about letting Palestinian workers into Israeli industry. The Israeli labor minister complained to the police about illegal workers; the police minister denied responsibility, arguing that labor ministry employees should locate illegal workers and then call the police. The defense minister, meanwhile, viewed increasing numbers of workers in Israel as beneficial to security because, he believed, it contributed to Palestinian quiescence (Gazit 1995: 224).

Regardless of these debates in government, Israeli labor contractors and employers in agriculture, construction, food-processing factories, sanitation, cleaning, and service industries welcomed the arrival of Palestinian workers. Israeli industry had slowed down in the second half of the 1960s because it could not compete internationally and was too reliant on foreign support. The Israeli government even fostered recession to strengthen the capitalist sector, thus threatening relations between employers and employees. The entrance of Palestinian labor into the Israeli market kept Israelis from having to take manual jobs and allowed them to move into more desirable occupations (Ben Porat 1989).[2]

Palestinian workers began going to work in Israel slowly and tentatively. Palestinian leaders, both the local landowning elite and the PLO abroad, had reasons to be hesitant about condoning Palestinians working in Israel. For the PLO, work in Israel might compromise resistance to the occupation. For the local elite, comprised mainly of landowning families who also monopolized trade, control of the peasantry (as sharecroppers and consumers) was threatened by peasants earning and spending money in Israel. With their monopoly on production now challenged by Israel, landowners faced the difficult reality that they might have to join the peasants and work in Israel if they were to earn any living at all. The nationalist objections of the elite might be seen as an attempt to maintain their dominance.

In the summer of 1968, Abu Samud's father arranged a marriage with a distant cousin in their grandfather's natal village, al-Qarya. The woman to be his wife, Umm Samud, was the youngest daughter in a family of nine and two years older than he. They lived with her family in al-Qarya, and Abu Samud began to look for a job across the Green Line. First he worked for an Israeli construction company from 1969 through 1973. Going to work in those days was only a matter of walking to the main road, about a kilometer away, and waiting for the Israeli bus. Permission was easy to receive, requiring only bureaucratic procedures of taxes and deductions, and these could easily be avoided.

In October 1973, Egypt and Syria attacked Israel and security intensified in the Occupied Territories. The village was often under curfew, and employers inside Israel were hesitant about employing Palestinian laborers. Abu Samud said that the events of war during the later months of 1973 caused him to leave the Jewish Israeli company and join an Arab-Israeli contractor in the nearby town of Tayiba. He said that he experienced the same problems then, army checkpoints and curfews. The Arab-Israeli contractor specialized in private home construction, mostly in that same Arab-Israeli town. Abu Samud stayed with this employer for two years.

In 1976, his wife's brother, Abu Thaki, who had become a successful entrepreneur in Jordan, invited him to work as a foreman in the construction of research and teaching laboratories. This was a better job. He would oversee teams of workers, but it meant leaving his wife and four sons (born 1969, 1970, 1970, 1974) in the village. He took the job and moved to Amman without his family. Despite the proximity of Amman to the village (by car it is at most a two-hour drive) the road was blocked by the Israeli border. The bridge was open but had become a difficult and threatening crossing. Anyone could be subject to intimidation, unreasonable searches, and confiscation or destruction of property. The family made the journey, visiting for three months each year during the children's summer vacation.

The move to Amman, to the East Bank, was never intended to be permanent. Umm Samud refused to leave her home village or her father, despite having many close relatives in Jordan. Her determination to stay was confirmed in 1978 when, instead of her going to Amman to visit Abu Samud, he returned to the village for three months. With the money he earned in Jordan, he and Umm Samud built a house on a piece of land she was to inherit from her father. They built the house with their own hands, and Umm Samud often told me how she helped twist hundreds of wire ties that hold the iron reinforcements in place.

In 1983, Abu Samud was invited to go to Saudi Arabia to work as a construction foreman. When he told me about taking that job more than a decade ago, his expression suggested that it had been a difficult decision to move farther away. Whatever ambivalence he might have felt was resolved one year later when, while home on vacation in 1984, his second eldest son was badly injured in a bakery in Israel. After this trauma he stayed in the West Bank with his family. His return was not financially unreasonable because during the mid-1980s work in Israel was good. He said the pay was slightly less than in Saudi Arabia, but the expenses of maintaining two households, one in the village and one for himself in Saudi Arabia, eliminated the benefit of extra pay. So, along with about 120,000 others, approximately 80,000 registered and 40,000 unregistered Palestinians (Semyenov and Lewin-Epstein 1987),[3] Abu Samud went to work in Israel every day.

Employment in Israel made up about 30–35 percent of all jobs for West Bankers from the mid-1970s until the closures, when it dropped to 20 percent or less. Many came early in the morning without prearranged employment to locations around Israeli cities and towns where they were hired temporarily by Israeli bosses and paid around $15–30 a day. Most West Bank Palestinians employed in Israel worked in construction (approximately 50–67 percent between 1975–97), with large handfuls in agriculture (7.9–17.7 percent) and industry (9–21 percent) (Israeli Central Bureau of Statistics 1999). Palestinians did not make up a large portion of the Israeli labor market, but they were concentrated in, and vital to, construction.

The Intifada erupted in late 1987, and strikes and curfews began to prevent people from going to work. Between 1988 and 1990, the average number of workdays in Israel declined 33 to 50 percent, while net real income declined 40 to 50 percent (Roy 1991: 61). However, the need for construction workers in Israel boomed when hundreds of thousands of immigrants began arriving from the (former) Soviet Union in 1990.[4] For a country of about five million, large numbers of arrivals created an intense need for new housing starts funded by the government.[5] Employers, as well as the ministries of housing and of agriculture, began demanding the import of foreign workers to replace the Palestinians (Rosenhek 2000: 54–55). Foreigners, mainly from Romania, Thailand, and the Philippines, entered by the tens of thousands, peaking in 1996 at around 100,000 (Rosenhek 2000). Nevertheless, Palestinians continued to enter the Israeli labor market because demand continued and there were few available jobs in the territories. Abu Samud maintained steady employment throughout the Uprising, except on days of strike or curfew. He mainly worked for two contractors, both Arab-Israelis from the neighboring town of Tayiba, who built private homes. However, fear and anger in Israel increased because workers were increasingly suspected and threatened. Some workers were attacked,

6. Construction worker on a ladder installing a heavy metal door, 2000.

burned while they slept, or shot at labor pick-up sites, as on May 20, 1991, when an Israeli posing as a contractor killed eight workers and injured fifteen in the Israeli city Rishon Le Zion.

When permanent closures began in March 1993, only men over fifty were allowed across, and by 1995 all were forbidden unless they had permission. Agricultural and construction contractors continued to hire West Bankers, but the day labor pick-up points in Israel began to disappear. With checkpoints on the main roads and security patrols on the back roads, getting to work became a daily confrontation with the Israeli state. Abu Samud was not immediately hurt by the measure. He had been working for an Arab-Israeli contractor in Tayiba for a year and kept his job even though he did not have permission. At the checkpoint he would show his ID and say in Hebrew that he was over fifty.

I first went to work with Abu Samud in the fall of 1994. Abu Samud normally got up the before first light to wash and pray. He left the house at about 5:30 A.M. and met the contractor at the checkpoint at about 6:15 A.M. The contractor would drive the workers to the worksite in his Mitsubishi truck. In September 1994 we arrived at a worksite in Caesaria by 7:00 A.M.

On my first day the contractor explained to me how Arabs did all the work in Israel. He thought he was mistreated by Jewish Israelis who acted as if they were superior. He could not (or would not) give me an explanatory example, but he subsequently expressed his resentment of the condescending treatment he received from many of the Israelis who were the homeowners or who operated the heavy equipment that occasionally arrived at the site (bulldozers, cement trucks, pumps, and the like).

We worked on a large single family home with a crew of four or five. The contractor occasionally worked, but came and left as he pleased. It was Abu Samud who directed the work. He would examine the plans and assign workers to their tasks. He would measure, design, and build frames for pouring concrete, check levels and depths, and do the finishing work. This work involved several steps: tying iron reinforcements, building the wooden forms around them, pouring cement, building walls of concrete block, and finishing with plaster. A team of four men working five and a half days a week could finish a two-story home in about two months. Roofing, flooring, cabinetry, and painting might be done by the same crew, or other specialists might be brought in, depending on the job. Electrical work and plumbing were usually done by insured Israeli subcontractors.

We usually worked in teams of two, and given the repetitive nature of twisting wire ties or nailing boards, there was an opportunity for a lot of discussion about anything. This could make work more fun or more burdensome, depending on the personality of one's partner. Although workers had different levels of skill and wage, I felt a high level of camaraderie. I did not feel this was extended to the contractor or to his sons who sometimes worked alongside us. Relations with the contractor were not usually tense—they were usually friendly—but sometimes he would drink beer, make disgusting jokes about women, or just behave disrespectfully in ways that were outside the bounds of propriety among West Bankers. Although it annoyed me, most of the workers from the West Bank ignored it, probably because they could not afford to let it bother them.

At the end of September 1994, Abu Samud and the three other workers were talking angrily over lunch about money the contractor owed them. In the middle of the discussion, the contractor drove up and the conversation stopped. When lunch ended, the workers tried to talk to the contractor, and the contractor began screaming that he had no money for himself, not even for his own family, that he was the last to get paid, and that the owners were behind on their payments. He turned red and looked angry enough to hit someone. The three workers congregated around his pickup truck. He shouted while they spoke in passive voices. Their postures were slumped and unthreatening, but they were firm about their decision. Abu Samud told me to start packing up the tools because we were going home early. We packed and the contractor took us to the checkpoint. No one said anything.

There was no transportation at that hour from the checkpoint, so we had to walk a few kilometers into town, where we took cars back to our respective villages. Everyone was so glum and silent that I waited until we had arrived in the village and were walking alone before I asked Abu Samud what had happened. Surprisingly, Abu Samud smiled and said jokingly, "Strike!" as he patted me on the back.

He explained to me that a month earlier, when he tried to cash his paycheck, no funds were available in the account. The contractor assured him that it would be made up in the next paycheck. It was not, and after a second month of work without pay, Abu Samud told the contractor that he was now two months behind in his salary. Until the money came, he was not going to work, nor were the other workers. Abu Samud optimistically explained that the contractor would show up at his house within a day or two with some cash and ask him to come back to work. Days passed and the contractor did not come. Weeks passed and Abu Samud heard that the homeowner had already hired a new contractor.

Abu Samud desperately wanted to return to work. But October 1994 was a violent month inside Israel. HAMAS and Islamic Jihad made several strikes: a shooting in Jerusalem, a kidnaped soldier, and then a tremendous bomb in the heart of Tel Aviv. These events resulted in complete closure of the territories. All military permissions to enter Israel for work were canceled. This made looking for work in Israel impossible. Abu Samud was always asking people where there might be work, and if they could bring him a permit. There was a great deal of ambiguity about the quickly changing rules and the bureaucracy involved. Though he kept himself busy with worthwhile projects (planting and pruning, painting and repairing) he often repeated that he hated being around the house "like a woman."

Umm Samud was constantly talking to me about her husband's unemployment. She would not mention it in front of him. She knew it would make him upset. She expressed her own frustration to me. "You see what they [the Israelis] are doing to us! They close Israel and what are we supposed to do? Where should I get money to buy food? Tell me! You write about this in your book!" These words became so regular that I could anticipate them.

In late November 1994, a cousin named Tawil told Abu Samud that he knew a man who was hiring laborers. Abu Samud told the cousin to call the man and arrange something. I gave the cousin my phone card and we phoned the man in Tayiba from the single, sporadically working public phone in the village. Tawil said that the contractor wanted to meet Abu Samud, so we should meet in an hour on the road to the checkpoint. Abu Samud, his son Taysir, Tawil, and I went to the designated meeting place a few minutes early. We stopped and waited on the side of the road. The cousin and son got out of the car, while Abu Samud and I waited inside. He was nervously smoking a lot of cigarettes. He said to me, "I'm really tired of sitting in the house."

About fifteen minutes after the agreed time, two young men drove up in a new BMW. They were wearing knee-length shorts (inappropriate for West Bankers, who were more modest about naked legs), sunglasses, and gold jewelry, and had a mobile phone (not yet widespread in the West Bank). Their conspicuous style, like their closely cropped haircuts, was noticeably Arab-Israeli, not West Bank. The cousin greeted them and introduced them to Abu Samud. Abu Samud, at least twenty years their senior, asked them from which family they came and then said he knew some of their relatives. He asked about work. Could they bring a permission? "No, not necessary. Just cross into Tayiba and we will pick you up near the crossing and drive you to work." Abu Samud asked about the hours, and they said 7:00 A.M. until 3:30 or 4:00 P.M. Abu Samud said, "Hey what are you talking about? There is a system to this: 7:00 A.M. to 3:00 P.M." They agreed to meet the next day, Saturday, at 7:00 A.M. in front of a particular house in Tayiba.

On Saturday, the Jewish Sabbath, there were not many workers going into Israel, and there were few means of transport. The weather was also rainy and cold. I told Abu Samud that I wanted to take him in the morning and would wait for him if they did not show up. We left at 6:30 A.M. and crossed the border without event. I had my U.S. passport and he held up his West Bank ID, saying in Hebrew "more than fifty" to the soldier who stopped us. We drove to the assigned meeting place and waited. We were about ten minutes early and waited forty minutes, until 7:30. Abu Samud then decided that the employers really would not show up. He was obviously a bit shaken and angry. He smoked a lot of cigarettes and was filled with sighs.

He asked me to take him to the old contractor's house, where he would try to collect some of his money and see if he could return to work. We went to the contractor's house. It was early, overcast, and dark. Abu Samud made it clear to me that he was really angry with this man, but he was also afraid. He needed the money owed him and he needed a job. When we parked in the driveway he did not get right out of the car. He was nervous and making me nervous. He said we should wait a few minutes instead of going to the door and knocking. It was not long before the shutters on a window opened and someone saw us waiting there. Abu Samud got out of the car and spoke with a woman inside. She said that her father had gone hunting and was not there. His truck was gone, so that was believable. Hunting seemed like a strange thing to be doing, but as an Arab-Israeli and not a West Bank Palestinian, he could legally buy a gun, even if he were illegally hunting in the hills near Nablus in the West Bank. We left, and Abu Samud said he felt insulted that they did not invite him in at least for some tea.

Abu Samud did not want to return to the village disappointed as he was. He asked me to take him to another home in the town to see another family for whom he had worked a few years earlier. The father was not home, but the adult son, who had his own contracting business, invited us to come inside. We woke him up, but he was welcoming and greeted Abu Samud warmly. The house was filled with marble surfaces, plush carpeting, and expensive furniture. The man threw a log in his living room fireplace and we sat exchanging greetings. Abu Samud and the man asked each other about their respective relatives. The man served us almond-flavored tea from tea bags, quite unlike the loose orange pekoe used in the territories.

Abu Samud let the young man raise the topic of work. Only then did Abu Samud explain his circumstance in detail. The man said that he had always thought the deadbeat contractor was no good and he said the same about the man's entire family. He regretfully said that he had no work to offer Abu Samud, but that he might have something soon. Abu Samud asked if he could get a worker's permit. The man said it would cost 800 New Israeli shekels (NIS ($270) a month. He wanted to help, so he said he would go to Netanya and see what he could do.

Again we left disappointed. We drove back toward the village, stopping in the camp to get some hot *ful* (fava beans) to bring back for breakfast. When we got home, Umm Samud did not ask Abu Samud what happened. She waited until he was out of the kitchen and then asked me. I explained to her, and she bemoaned the situation. "What should I do now?" she asked me with a challenge. "Where should I get money to eat, or to keep the boys in school? You see what the Jews are doing to us? Am I responsible for the problems in Israel? The whole time that you have been here, have you ever seen Abu Samud do or say anything against the Jews? No. So why should we go hungry? Write about that in your book!" I promised her I would.

Days turned into weeks and there was no work to be found. Abu Samud would spend every day working around the house, planting, weeding, fixing, and doing an occasional light construction job in the village, like building a wall or pouring a foundation for a water tank. Abu Samud was sadder than ever. I left the village every other week or so to go down to Birzeit University where the boys were studying. Their first questions were always "How is my mother's health? Did my father find a job?" It was difficult always to say no and tell them about the many leads that inevitably went dry.

In December, the contractor, who owed Abu Samud more than $1000, came by the house. He explained to Abu Samud that a new job had come. He wanted Abu Samud to come to work for him and would pay him back all the money when he started work. Apparently, he would use the homeowner's first payment to pay off his previous debts. Abu Samud knew this was a bad policy because the contractor needed that money to make the payments for initial supplies—concrete, iron rebar, and the like. But Abu Samud was over a barrel. He had to accept the job because he needed the work and wanted the back pay. We began work again before the new year on another private home.

The contractor paid the money he owed Abu Samud, but it was a frustrating process. The contractor complained that the homeowners were trying to delay making further payments. The owners visited the site almost every day, sometimes twice a day. One was in the commercial laundry business, the other was a career officer in the Border Guard. Once, for a joke, the officer came to visit in a Border Guard jeep, with the lights flashing. The three of us who were illegal began to hide, but we saw his face alone in the car and came out enjoying his little joke.

The Israeli owners were surprised when the contractor told them that I was an American Jew living with Abu Samud's family in the West Bank. They asked the typical questions about fear and danger. They were friendly enough with Abu Samud, perhaps realizing that he was the real craftsman among us. The officer asked me if I thought the work and materials were good and up to standard. I assured him that all was good because I was only concerned that he should make the agreed payments so Abu Samud and everyone else could get their money. The fact that he asked me was curious because he knew I was an anthropologist, not a craftsman like Abu Samud. Nevertheless, he asked my "professional" opinion about the workers and materials. I could only interpret this as an act of trust that he did not give to Abu Samud, who was really knowledgeable about the answers; perhaps it was because I was Jewish, American, or educated.

Border enforcement was getting more difficult with each passing month in 1995. Checkpoints required Palestinians from the Occupied Territories to show the soldiers or police their regular identity card, their magnetic identity card for work, and their work permission. The checkpoints also required West Bank registered cars, distinguished by the color of their license plate, to have a military permit for the car and the driver. Consequently, most workers left their transport vehicles and crossed on foot, then took Israeli transportation or waited for their contractors to pick them up. At the Erez checkpoint in Gaza, a huge complex developed where thousands of Gazans passed through multiple screening and metal detectors, but that was not the case in the West Bank, where there were many small crossings.

Most workers did not have the proper permissions, so they had to go around the checkpoints. A dirt path ran from a paved West Bank road, down through a valley and up to the Arab-Israeli town of Tayiba, whose houses began about 400 meters away on the next hill. Looking from the West Bank side in the fall of 1994, the border appeared merely as a stretch of land filled with thorny bushes. The fence that stood before the war of 1967 was long gone. A foot-worn trail cut through the dry, bristly landscape. Looking at it, the eye, like the pedestrian, was carried along its line, from the West Bank into Israel. In 1995, the Israeli army bulldozed a dirt road bisecting the footpath so jeeps could more easily intercept workers. By 1996, after Israeli redeployment in the northern towns, the valley was traversed by many dirt roads to accommodate army jeeps, carving struggle and conflict into the landscape.

Men would tell their stories about getting caught by soldiers, or about how they made a quick escape. There have been some cases of beatings and shootings at border crossings. Soldiers were always capable of fatal violence, merely because they were so well equipped for it. There were police, Border Guards, and various army divisions that performed reserve duty in the Occupied Territories. The Border Guard, Mishmar Ha-Gavool, were the most feared, and were thought to be the most likely to beat Palestinians. Unlike regular army units who were trained in conventional warfare, the Border Guard was a military police force whose task it is to chase non-citizen Palestinians. The Border Guard was often referred to by Palestinians as the Druze. Israelis, too, frequently mentioned that the Druze like to go into the Border Guard.[6]

If a worker was caught, he was delivered to the checkpoint or police station, or his ID card was confiscated and he had to retrieve it at the checkpoint, while the patrolling soldiers went to look for more workers. At the checkpoint, the commanding officer detained the workers and then turned them over to the police, who wrote violation fines of about $150. Sometimes, after a few hours of sitting on the ground, the officer just let everyone go home. If, on the other hand, one was caught by the police, then he was at least written a summons. On some occasions, illegal workers were taken into custody by the army or police for a few days. This usually happened to young men who were suspected of past or future involvement in nationalist politics. The more than 100,000 former political prisoners felt that they were sure to return to detention if they were caught.

Employers easily exploited undocumented workers when negotiating a wage and conditions of work. A labor intensive job in Israeli construction, depending on the skills required, paid NIS 50–120 ($16–40) to a Palestinian, while Israelis doing the same work received NIS 75–200. Israeli contractors did not pay health insurance or social security taxes for undocumented workers, depriving them of these benefits. They had no leverage even to ensure the payment of their wages. Workers could not go to the contractor's house because it required access to an Israeli car.

To get work permission in the late 1990s, a West Bank Palestinian had to get an Israeli employer to submit a request to the labor office inside Israel and pay taxes based upon the worker's salary the previous month. The labor office then gave a receipt to the employer who passed it on to the worker. The worker gave the receipt, along with a copy of his personal ID, a special magnetic security ID issued by the Israeli military, and an application form to the Palestinian Labor Office in the territories. The Palestinian Labor Office then forwarded the request to the District Coordinating Office (DCO) of the Palestinian Authority, who then forwarded the request to the Israeli military. If the IDF approved the permission, they sent it back to the DCO, where the Palestinian worker could pick it up. Without a patron in Israel to start the process, a work permission was impossible to get. This reinforced dependency on individual employers, increasing the potential for unfair labor practices.

Contractors often underreported the number of days and the wages paid to their Palestinian workers so they could pay fewer taxes. If a worker suffered an injury on the job, he would not receive the compensation due to him by law because his pay and hours were underreported, often by half. Since 1994, the underreporting of taxes has hurt not only the worker, but also the new Palestinian Authority because it became entitled to the largest portion of taxes levied by Israel on Palestinian wages. Years of back taxes owed to the Palestinian people requested by the Palestinian Authority remain unpaid because negotiations failed to bring agreement about how much and for how long.

Workers were not legally allowed to sleep overnight in Israel, but instead of preventing them from staying, this law only meant that workers in odd-hour jobs were pressured to sleep in unacceptable conditions, hidden at construction sites, hotels, restaurants, and other locations. This saved employers the expense of housing and transportation.

Workers abused by their employers could bring legal suit against them, especially with the help of Israeli human rights organizations like Kav LaOved. In 1998, Palestinian unions in the West Bank filed 1,500 complaints in the labor courts over work benefits and false reporting by employers (Lein 1999). However, Palestinian workers must deposit high sums as a guarantee for court costs in case they lose, while Israelis are not required to provide such a guarantee (Lein 1999). Furthermore, because of the restrictions on their freedom of movement, it is difficult for Palestinians even to get to the court or the lawyer.

After only a few weeks of work in 1995, Abu Samud's contractor began to fall behind on payments on his new project and the workers were the first to suffer. The contractor owed too much money, the owner refused to bail him out, and the contractor stopped the work. It was a miserable feeling for Abu Samud to be out of work again. Fortunately, he found new work in less than a month. An old contact, an Arab-Israeli contractor from Tayiba, hired him.

Construction on the previous house had stopped and its owner wanted work to resume. The owner called up Abu Samud's cousins (who had a phone) and arranged a meeting at the checkpoint. He wanted Abu Samud to be the contractor and direct other workers until the job was finished. He had asked Abu Samud once before at his house to do it, but Abu Samud refused. I went along, as I had on the previous meeting, to be driver and translator. We drove down to the checkpoint and waited. The Israeli homeowner showed up late, came no more than twenty meters from the soldiers, stayed in his car, and left it running on the side of the road. Abu Samud sat in the front seat and I knelt beside him at the open car door.

The Israeli asked Abu Samud if he knew what needed to be done. Abu Samud did, but explained that he already had new work. The Israeli asked Abu Samud if his new contractor had gotten him a permission. Abu Samud explained that it was in the process but had not yet come. The owner said, "I'll bring you one right away, don't worry about it." He tried to convince Abu Samud that his pay would be better, although he did not actually name a price. Abu Samud had me explain that he could not be responsible for a project because of the frequent closures. Even if he had a permission, a bomb might go off in Tel Aviv and he would not be able to pour the cement scheduled for delivery. He would not be able to meet deadlines or keep commitments. I also added that Abu Samud needed steady work and could not leave a contractor, who always had several projects, for an owner who had less than one month left on one house. The Israeli argued that it was easy to find work in Israel for a married man over fifty years. Why should Abu Samud be so worried about staying with this contractor? I tried to explain that the closures made it difficult to change jobs and really made it impossible for him to run a project. The Israeli homeowner seemed frustrated that the closure should enter his life so obtrusively.

At that very moment, about thirty meters in front of us inside the West Bank, a large group of people gathered. Most were women and everyone wore very nice clothes. They started to play a handheld Arab drum and sing. There were about eight or nine cars, one decorated with ribbons and balloons. I pointed to the group of people and asked the Israeli man if he knew what was going on over there. I explained that it was a wedding party from the groom's family, who were going to get the bride from her home or village and bring her to the groom's home. The groom's family had stopped here at the checkpoint because they could not go and fetch the bride from Tayiba. They were waiting for someone from inside Israel to bring her across, and then they could bring her home. "Do you understand?" I asked him, hoping he would see how this might be an appropriate metaphor for Abu Samud's situation with work.

Abu Samud's situation was like that of the bridegroom who was all prepared to receive his bride, but was prevented from passing and reliant on someone else to bring her. Abu Samud had his ambitions continually frustrated by the border, by the separation of diaspora and homeland, and by the inequitable passage across the Green Line. He left Kuwait in 1965 because he did not want to work construction, he wanted to study radio and television repair. That job and his work as a foreman abroad were thrown off track by his family's residence in the occupied West Bank. His frustrated aspirations were channeled into a determination to see his sons have a better life.

Abu Bassam in Agriculture

A neighbor of ours, with whom I went to work in February 1995, often commented that it seemed Abu Samud had a very difficult time. He would say things like

Oh poor Abu Samud . . . he is so unfortunate because his sons don't work in Israel . . . they waste his hard-earned money on an education that is useless . . . they could be earning more money and putting it into concrete . . . how will they get married? Who will pay for it all?

Abu Bassam, who lived nearby in the village, had three sons working in Israel, and the four incomes were enough to move out of the refugee camp, buy land in the village, and build a big house. They built on the outskirts of the village. They even hired Abu Samud to direct the concrete part of the construction. The house was two stories high, with six bedrooms upstairs, two more downstairs, a large kitchen, a salon for guests near the front door, and a family television room. Abu Bassam was very proud of the house. He boasted a great deal to me about it being thirty by ten meters. "Oh poor Abu Samud," he remarked, "his house is so small. What is it, ten by ten meters?"

Abu Bassam was born in Wadi Hawarath, near the coast, in 1935. His family was Bedouin and had been in the area for centuries. He began to reminisce about the pastoral aspects of his life as a child and the homemade goods on which his family lived. He told me that his family had sheep and goats and that their surplus income was usually invested in the herd. Children pastured animals, sometimes with the help of adult women or men. They also had rights to the produce of certain lands; he recalled that his mother's family brought them sacks of wheat and barley every year that he referred to as her share. He believed his grandfather was the first to build a home in the village, possibly around 1880 we estimated together. He recalled that in his childhood his uncles worked as laborers in construction.

When Abu Bassam was thirteen years old, fearing attack from the Zionist militia, his family left their house and moved their herds away from the coast. When the Israelis declared independence, the war expanded and Abu Bassam's family became permanent refugees in the West Bank. They pitched their tents for almost two years near Qalqilya, but without jobs or other resources they had to sell most of their herd and the women's gold to survive. Soon they began to feel unwelcome by the local villagers on whose land they were encroaching. In 1950, the UN leased land near Tulkarm and established a camp, one of many, for the refugees. Abu Bassam's family moved there and became residents of the Tulkarm refugee camp.

In 1952, at seventeen years of age, Abu Bassam decided to leave the West Bank for work abroad. He went to the Gulf for two years, where he worked in construction in Kuwait and Saudi Arabia. Then in 1954, preceded by a close friend, he went from the Gulf to Germany to work in an industrial factory in Stuttgart making boilers. He spoke German to me and laughed translating what he was saying into Arabic. I asked if it was difficult to be in Germany for so long. He said it was quite difficult. He worked like a donkey, he lived with other workers in an apartment, and he missed food from home, but he really liked Germany for its advanced industry and modern bureaucratic organization.

In 1965, after eleven years, he returned to the camp to get married. With the Deutsch marks he earned, he married a woman from a large Bedouin family in the refugee camp whose origin was also Wadi Hawarath. Between 1966 and 1979, his wife gave birth to nine children, of whom eight survived, five boys and three girls. There was no work available in the West Bank when he returned in 1965 and he considered using his money to relocate to the East Bank, in Jordan, but his wife resisted the move. She did not want to be separated from her family. Before any decision was made, however, the June War of 1967 began and ended, leaving them in the occupied West Bank. The situation seemed dismal, but leaving was not an option because they believed it would mean never coming back, as had happened in 1948.

Within a few months, Abu Bassam went into Israel to visit relatives and acquaintances whom he had left two decades earlier. He said he was impressed with how well they were doing, with the work they had found in Israel, and the level of technology that had entered their homes, particularly piped water and electricity. With the help of these relatives he found a job working in Israeli agriculture in orange groves near his natal village. He worked the orange harvest for Israelis near Hadera in the winter of 1968–69, and then set out to find more regular work. He worked several jobs, all in agriculture, over the next four years, but they were temporary, seasonal jobs.

In 1973, he met Aaron, a Russian-born Jew a few years older than he, whose family had come to Palestine in the 1930s. Aaron's family had owned land in the Russian countryside, but left in flight from Stalin. They bought fertile land in Palestine and set up a new farm. Aaron gave Abu Bassam work in 1973 and has employed him since. The farm has changed its production over the years, adapting to the market as Aaron saw fit. Throughout most of the 1970s and early 1980s it grew citrus for export and truck vegetables for domestic consumption. By the early 1980s, the profit in truck vegetables began to sink and Aaron began to change his fields over to flowers for export. Abu Bassam worked in whatever field was required and began bringing his teenaged sons to work alongside him.

When the closures began in 1993, Abu Bassam was not significantly affected. He had always had a permit to cross and work for Aaron. Aaron paid the fees and taxes that guaranteed Abu Bassam's documentation, and provided him with insurance and medical care from the Israeli labor federation (Histadrut) and health care (Kupat Holim). Because he was a previously certified worker, and because he was over fifty years of age, he continued working after the checkpoints were set up, except on days of total closure.

His sons, however, were denied renewals of their permits when the closures began, despite Aaron's repeated efforts, because they were under age. Aaron refused to employ workers off the books, so there was no sneaking around the checkpoints to get to this job. Aaron told me that he thought it was not only illegal, but wrong to take advantage of the boys. They would not be insured or protected by the law. Under the circumstances, Aaron said, "we all suffer." The lack of income from the younger sons even forced Abu Bassam's wife back to work in a nearby clothing sweatshop in the refugee camp.

I worked with Abu Bassam for only ten days in the winter of 1995. It was often raining and about 5 to 10° Celsius (40–50° Fahrenheit). We were picked up from his house by a transport van from the village a few minutes before 5:00 A.M. After a few stops in the village and refugee camp, collecting seven passengers in all, we headed to the checkpoint. All the people in this van were men and women over fifty years old because the closures prevented young men from crossing. At the checkpoint, they climbed slowly out of the van to cross on foot. Soldiers checked the IDs and permissions of these gray-haired workers, and they reboarded the bus on the far side of the border. We were at the farm before 6:00 A.M.

This particular farm was part of an old Israeli agricultural settlement called a *moshav*. Unlike the Israeli commune called a *kibbutz*, the *moshav* was a private joint-venture. Aaron's fields were mostly adjacent plots among other privately owned land that shared a common infrastructure. Here and there, older citrus groves remained, but most of the area had been converted to growing stems for the international market in Amsterdam. Each field was covered by a black screen that provided shade in the summer and insulation from cold in the winter.

Aaron mostly grew stems and leaves used in flower arrangements. The stems sprouted directly from the sandy soil, so they needed to be cut from the ground. That meant staying on your knees or bending over. Either way, it was agony for my unaccustomed body. Most agricultural work was like this, but on most farms such work comes at punctuated times of the year, weeding and harvest especially. On this commercial farm, the harvest was a year-round chore. The process was not mechanized because it required cutting only the "ripe" stems, which had to be identified by hand.

Because of the rain, we covered ourselves in yellow slickers while working in the field. It was more tedious work than construction and paid less. Because it paid less, Abu Bassam worked longer hours each day, from before 6:00 A.M. until after 5:00 P.M. After collecting for about two hours, during which time Abu Bassam could cut 700–1000 stems, depending on the field, the stems were divided into 40-, 50-, 60-, and 70-centimeter bunches, bundled into tens, then hundreds, dipped in pesticide and preservative, and packed mechanically into boxes. Aaron was only present once or twice a day to oversee the packing of the boxes. The boxes of sorted, counted, bound stems were picked up every other day and brought to a shipping container at Ben Gurion Airport. The price per stem fluctuated, but Aaron said he could get $0.30 for each 70-cm stem and only $0.05 for a 40-cm stem. If on average he sold stems for $.20 a piece (100 stems = $20), Abu Bassam produced about $400 in stems a day and was paid about $40 for his ten or eleven hours of labor.

Aaron explained that every year, at least once a year, he went to Amsterdam, where buyers and sellers met in the largest flower market in the world. He visited to see what was happening in the market, what was selling, what was new, and to renew the friendly acquaintance he had with his associates. He explained that, although there were several different kinds of flowers growing in the immediate area, he thanked God that several years ago he had chosen to plant decorative leaves. The plant grew particularly well in the sandy soil and ocean climate. It had a thick desert skin that kept it saleable for weeks and simplified packing and transport; because it was a leaf, he believed that it was less prone to go in and out of style, maintaining a steadier market than most flowers.

Because Abu Bassam had been working there many years, he knew the people who owned and operated the surrounding fields. There were Palestinian workers from the West Bank, a handful of men from Thailand who lived on the *moshav* in trailers, a few recent Russian immigrants scattered about (although most of them had moved on to the cities), and the owner families, who were old pre-state European Jewish settlers. I was constantly asking him questions about work on the other farms, so he brought me to see a big conveyor belt cutting, counting, and binding wild flowers. There were a Palestinian from the Nablus area who harvested the ripe flowers in the field, a Thai man who loaded and unloaded stems into the machine, and two Israelis, a man and woman, doing the quality-control work by removing stems with damaged or missing flowers.

Abu Bassam greeted the Israeli man with a big grin saying "Shalom, Shalom Roni. How are you?" in Hebrew. Roni answered, "Okay. Who is this?" referring to me. Abu Bassam told him, "He is from America, he lives with us." Roni asked again, "No, really, who is this? One of your relatives from the territories?" He looked at me very suspiciously. The conversation drew the concerned attention of the Israeli woman. I spoke up, "I'm from the U.S." He was surprised that I spoke Hebrew, "You are from the U.S.? So why do you speak Hebrew?" I told him I was a Jew, and then he could not believe that I lived in the territories with Arabs. The usual questions followed, "You're not afraid? Do they know you are Jewish? What is anthropology?" After answering those questions, Roni explained to me how the Arabs behaved. He insisted it was very dangerous for me. "Ask Bassam. Tell him, Bassam, tell him what you've said about Arabs, about how you know you have to watch out for them." He finished his statement leaving Abu Bassam speechless. Obviously, Abu Bassam was in the habit of swallowing his pride and agreeing with this racist man. Despite the years that they had known each other, Abu Bassam even refrained from correcting Roni's misunderstanding of his name, and allowed him to call him Bassam. Not wanting to fan antagonism between Roni and Abu Bassam, I simply said "Praise God, I've never had any problems." Like many Jewish Israelis, Roni warned me to watch my back because the Arabs will stick a knife in it.

Abu Bassam and I walked out of the building and trying to laugh off the tension he said, "Oh that Roni, he loves to talk about politics." I told Abu Bassam I thought he was racist and I was embarrassed by people like him. Abu Bassam seemed surprised but pleased at my use of the word racist. He often repeated my comment when introducing me to people in the village and camp later that year.

Migrant Labor and the Border

It was impossible to know precisely how many thousand Palestinians were working in Israel after the closures because of the clandestine nature of the crossing. In 1998, the Israeli army loosened security. In Tulkarm, the old clandestine paths were abandoned and a new one emerged passing immediately next to the army checkpoint on the paved road. Undocumented workers no longer had to cross in fear of being discovered by the soldiers or army. The illegal crossing point was out in the open. There were even temporary stalls and carts on both sides where merchants sold food and drinks to workers coming and going to work. The number of illegal workers from the West Bank was estimated to have increased from 35,000 in 1997 to about 52,000 in 1998.[7] The number of legal workers was elusive because of the frequent cancellations and the difficult renewal process. The Palestinian Bureau of Statistics registered an increasing number of permits given to Palestinian workers in the late 1990s, from about 33,000 in 1996 to about 38,000 in 1997 and about 44,000 in 1998.[8] In the Tulkarm District, almost all worker traffic seemed to be going around the border rather than through it. It seemed ironic that they were checking every Palestinian worker who came through the checkpoint and letting so many go around. The only people who had trouble crossing were those who wanted to go to work legally. Anyone who wanted to cross "illegally" could.

During the first half of 1998, as tens of thousands of undocumented workers crossed daily, about 2,500 workers were arrested inside Israel for not having a permit, of whom about 260 were brought before a court. Most of these were fined about $800 (Palestinian General Federation of Trade Unions 1998).[9] This was enough to intimidate. Describing the Mexican-U.S. border, Kearney (1991) says that "the surveillance activities of the Border Patrol are not intended to prevent their entry into the United States to work, but instead are part of a number of ways of disciplining them to work hard and to accept low wages" (Kearney 1991: 61). Economic interests do not fully explain the politics of the border. Exploitability that benefits employers "is not obviously sought by cohesive capitalist elites, but rather is the result of a complex political process" (Heyman 1998b: 173): "the undocumented immigrant is covertly tolerated as a unit of labor, a commodity, while explicitly stigmatized as a person, family and community" (Heyman 1998b: 161). Heyman argues that the

stigmatization of laborers, of varying and complex forms, is a characteristic feature of class societies, because (a) in a class society, varieties of labor are given evaluations, often subtly negative; (b) the narrowing of people to their labor powers, their objectification, eliminates from view their complicated human qualities, and replaces them with simplistic, negative evaluations. (Heyman 1998b: 173–74)

Border policy limits the rights of Palestinians who cross the border to work in Israel by making them illegal, denying them the wages and benefits Israelis receive, making it next to impossible to collect unpaid wages from a deadbeat contractor. And, as Heyman describes, illegality is a factor that stigmatizes Palestinians and makes it morally possible to exploit them.[10]

The maintenance of the border intensified the vulnerability of workers from the West Bank in Israel.[11] The Palestinian press regularly and openly reported the desperation of workers caused by the closures (Musharqa 1996). "Accommodation created both the material basis for dignity and pride . . . and it recreated people's dependence on the interests and needs of more powerful others" (Sider 1993: 29). Enforcement on the Green Line has made Palestinians in the West Bank subordinate to and dependent on Israelis by regulating capital, commodities, and labor. The border provides a way for Israeli builders and farmers to continue using Palestinians as an army of reserve labor, as they have since at least the 1950s (Rosenfeld 1972, 1978; Tamari 1981; Zureik 1976, 1979). The use of coercion at the border in these cases shapes the relations of production by subordinating these workers, but also by separating the point of production from the point of labor's reproduction (Kearney 1986). This creates a boundary on the employer's accountability for the well-being of foreign employees and their families. Neither employers nor their governments are under pressure to subsidize the education, health care, or income of their "foreign" labor. Workers who cross the border are easily disposed of[12] when no longer needed, without paying welfare or unemployment.

Near Tulkarm there were actually two roads into Israel, two different checkpoints. One checkpoint was on the road to Netanya and Israel's main coastal highways. The other was on the road to Tayiba, the Arab-Israeli town a few kilometers away. Jewish Israelis, either settlers or people doing business with Palestinians, came mainly from the highway or from Netanya and therefore passed the Netanya checkpoint. Those coming through the Tayiba checkpoint were more likely to be Arab-Israelis from the Triangle (a region with a significant Arab population). Everyone from Tulkarm and the surrounding villages in the West Bank knew that workers walked around the Tayiba checkpoint. At the Netanya checkpoint, only a few kilometers away, no one was allowed to walk around and every car was scrutinized. Workers without permission went through the Tayiba checkpoint, then boarded vehicles that took them to locations all around Israel.

These two checkpoints were under the administration of the same office. The difference between them indicated that the practice of permission enforcement, whether by design from above or "problem solving" from below, was largely a performance for Jewish Israelis. It was *their* checkpoint that was free from undocumented workers, while Palestinians walked casually around the other checkpoint only a five-minute drive away. Someone, either the IDF or Israeli politicians, wanted to show a response to the panic caused by the ongoing conflict. The closures showed the Israeli voters that something was being done against terrorism. Border maintenance is largely symbolic action, but "symbolic action has quite real effects" (Heyman 1998b: 161). The porous closure of the West Bank did not stop workers, it only succeeded in making them illegal.

4. Work in the West Bank

Abu Hasan's Garage

In border towns like Tulkarm, Qalqilya, and Jenin, industrial zones developed inside the West Bank to service Israeli cars. It was near Tulkarm, about one kilometer from the checkpoint, that Abu Hasan, twenty-eight years old in 1995, had his garage. It was here that I was schooled in the art of changing spark plugs and rebuilding starters and alternators. The sign out front read "car electrician," once in Arabic and three times in Hebrew. Hebrew signs were all over the garages, even around Nablus, where Hebrew-speaking Jewish Israelis no longer traveled.

Abu Hasan's shop employed six people, including his partner. The partner was a paternal cousin who provided capital and labor, but it was Abu Hasan's skills and connections that kept the business in the black. The partners had two teenagers, seventeen and nineteen, who were apprentices, and two younger teens, 13 and 14, who were assistants. Each troubled vehicle that pulled into the driveway was first evaluated by one of the employees. The apprentices would inspect the problem, checking all the easy things first, like loose wires, fuses, and dirty terminals. They would try to identify the problem and then tell Abu Hasan what it was and either let him take a look or just get his permission to begin work on the car. If the starter or alternator had to be fixed, the apprentice would remove the part from the car, take it apart, and get Abu Hasan to fix it. Then the apprentice would reinstall it.

If the apprentice was able to handle the work, the repair, without parts, would cost about NIS 20–50 ($7–17) for an Israeli and about NIS 10–20 for a Palestinian. If the job was more difficult and required Abu Hasan's full attention, the cost per job went to about NIS 40–100 for an Israeli and NIS 20–40 for a Palestinian. Occasionally, someone would want a complicated electrical system installed, and Abu Hasan would charge around NIS 300 ($100). Even though Israelis were charged an inflated price, they were still getting a bargain in comparison to prices inside Israel, which were at least twice as high. The charge for fixing a flat in the West Bank was NIS 5–10, while the same in Israel was NIS 20–30. As Abu Hasan put it, "They pay us half, so we charge them double."

The workers were paid in cash each week and received advances when requested. The younger assistants, who were given easy tasks like fetching tools, cleaning parts, and making tea, made about NIS 15–20 a day depending on the work they did. The apprentices made NIS 40–60 daily. Abu Hasan had to pay them even if the money was not coming, but after splitting the remaining profits with his partner he could normally expect to make NIS 500 to 1000 a week (in 1995), a great income for someone living in the West Bank, even with a family to support.

Abu Hasan could never be sure how much the garage would earn on a particular day; "one day honey, one day onion," the saying goes in Arabic. However, unless there was a closure, the garage was often busy, especially on Saturday, when Israelis poured in from across the coastal plain. He could not take any big projects on a Saturday, only minor repairs—fixing loose wires, replacing the carbon contacts on alternators, installing speakers and stereos. Serious installations and rewiring had to be done during the week. He could not even stop to say hello. Time on Saturday was too expensive. During the week a slow day might only bring in NIS 100, but on Saturday the garage could make up to NIS 150 an hour during the peak at midday. Saturday tended to bring in as much as the rest of the week combined—about NIS 1000. Saturday was the moneymaking day for Abu Hasan's garage, like everyone else's, because Saturday is the day off in Israel.

Israelis brought their cars to West Bank Palestinians not only because they provided cheaper labor, but also because they could purchase cheaper replacement parts and get work done that Israelis would not do. In the West Bank, the mechanic or electrician fixed the part rather than sending it back to the company to be rebuilt. For an electrician this usually meant replacing carbon contacts on starters and alternators. Abu Hasan replaced the carbons in a few minutes at a material cost of about a dollar. In Israel (or in America) electricians replaced the entire part at a much greater cost.

Even the cost of replacement was cheaper in the Territories. For example, a used alternator from an early 1980s Subaru was easily purchased for NIS 40–50 in the Tulkarm District; in Kfar Saba or Netanya in Israel, the used part was more difficult to come by and cost NIS 120–150. A new one would cost only slightly less in the West Bank than Israel because it would be brought in from an Israeli dealer.

The availability of inexpensive used parts also made it possible to make money buying junk cars from Israelis and rebuilding them to sell to Palestini-

7. Car electrician and crew in front of their garage near the border, 1995.

ans. My friend Zahi worked next door to Abu Hasan. He bought cars that had been severely damaged or rusted enough to drop the price significantly. For example, for NIS 7,000 he bought a 1984 Subaru 1600 that had lost the back end, and with less than NIS 2,000 and ten days of his own labor, he completely repaired and painted the car. After driving the car for a month, he then sold it for NIS 10,800. He bought and sold five cars during a one-year period, and this provided an important income.

In 1997 the Palestinian Authority made it illegal to import used cars from Israel. This was an order from the executive of the Palestinian Authority to protect those who held dealerships for new cars, but it devastated the used and rebuilt automobile business. The price of used cars in Israel dropped because the market for cars ten years and older was lost. In the West Bank, the price of used cars increased because of inflation and because the supply stopped. In 1995, the price of a ten-year-old 1.3 liter Subaru was about NIS 12,000–15,000 ($4,000–$5,000). By 2000, the price of a similar ten-year-old Subaru was over NIS 20,000 ($5,000 in 2000) in the West Bank, but about half that in Israel.

Junkyards were filled with stolen property. Thieves from all over Israel and Palestine, including Gaza, would bring stolen cars to Tulkarm. Some of these were not really stolen cars, but cars brought to the territories by Israelis, sold, and then reported stolen. Some thieves were Israelis, Jews, and Arabs

8. Women sewing in workshop in Tulkarm, 2000.

who brought the cars to the territories, but there were a few well-known car thieves who drove around town in new 1994 Subarus and Audis. The Israeli army was still patrolling the town in 1995, and it was common for people to explain the daytime patrols as searches for stolen cars. Helicopters that passed overhead, unless they were military green, were usually assumed to be police looking for stolen vehicles. Police roadblocks between the towns were common and often attempted to recover stolen vehicles.

Late at night in 1995, as I was driving with Palestinian friends through Tulkarm, two jeeps, one army green, one white, shone two intensely bright spotlights at my car from about thirty meters. Three soldiers and two armed men wearing civilian uniforms descended from their vehicles, pointed their guns at my oncoming car and ordered me to stop. One of the civilian men approached my car window. "Where are you from?" he asked in Hebrew. I told him I was from America and my friends from this town. He asked for the papers on the car and our identification cards, and then told us all to get out. The soldiers looked bored, not involving themselves in the matter. The two civilians, men in their forties with older-issue rifles, did the questioning. They had me open my empty trunk. One of them questioned me as the other raised his rifle to his eye, aiming his gun sights at the residential windows of the buildings that lined the road, as if he was imagining terrorists at which he could shoot. "What are you doing here? Do you have family in Israel? Where do you live?" I told him the name of the village just to the east of the town and he questioned me about wanted men he was looking for. Turning toward my friends, he said, "Are you teaching him to fence cars?" My friend Munir was the only one to understand the Hebrew word "fence" and quickly said, "No, he is a professor." They warned me to stay out of trouble and then let us go. Taysir, another passenger in the car, rejoiced saying that he knew they would let us go as soon as they found out I was American. We all concurred that they must be rent-a-cops hired by the insurance companies or detectives working for the police. The point was that they were looking for stolen cars.

Abu Hasan boasted that he had brought the first stolen cars into the district. He said that before the Uprising there were no stolen cars in Tulkarm and few junkyards to sell fenced goods. He claimed that toward the beginning of the Uprising he stole cars from the beach at Tel Aviv and drove them into the district, where he and his friends fenced the parts. In those days, no one from this area stole cars. Our other companion chimed in, "What about Abu Harami and Abu Masruq, they were stealing cars then too, no?" Abu Hasan assured us that each one of them stole his first car more than a year after he brought in his first Subaru. "I'm not going to tell you that it is okay to steal from the Jews," Abu Hasan said. "There are people that say that, that because the Jews are our enemies and stole our land that it is permissible to steal their cars. But that's not true. The guy whose Subaru I took did not do anything to me, right? There is no difference between stealing from the Jews or the Arabs, except that here the Jews are rich and the Arabs are poor and the Jews' insurance pays for it anyway." He felt bad for the "crazy" kids stealing cars from Israel when the Israelis were searching for stolen cars. A car thief could get shot if he tried to avoid capture.

The stolen-car business gave Palestinians the ability to strike back at Israelis, to hit their insurance companies and their pride, by stealing or fencing their cars. It was just about the only way to profit from revenge. Although everyone said they only did it for the money, the only cars that were stolen were Israeli. West Bank cars might have their tape players stolen, but fenced cars were overwhelmingly Israeli.

As an adult, Abu Hasan had no reason to steal cars. He had a successful business, which he attributed to the fact that everyone trusted him. He had loyal customers from Israel whom he preferred to keep as customers by charging fair prices and sometimes not charging customers at all for small jobs. Unlike

most of my friends, Abu Hasan had friendships with Israelis. It was not unusual for him to cross the border (illegally) at night to visit Jewish friends in
nearby towns or even on nearby Jewish settlements. He spoke Hebrew well
and could move easily between the two worlds.

One summer night in 1999, Abu Hasan, Ahed, and I went to the garage,
put some chairs outside, and sat down to enjoy each others' company. We
watched as an approaching yellow-plated Israeli car on the road twenty meters
away began to slow down. We could see two men in the front seat through
the driver's open window. The passenger was gray-haired and bearded, and
the driver was a young clean-shaven man. Both wore *kipot* (skull caps worn
by traditional or religious Jews) and civilian clothes. The driver called out to
Abu Hasan, "Ya Abu Hasan, al-salam ʿalaykum." Abu Hasan responded and
then said to me with a smile, "This is the settler I told you about." The men
parked and got out of the car. The driver explained, in Hebrew with a smat-
tering of Arabic, that the older man had two flat tires and needed someone
to fix them. It was approaching 10:00 P.M. and no one was open. Abu Hasan
scrunched his brow to make his thinking face and said "Yalla. I'll be back in
fifteen minutes."

Abu Hasan fixed the old man's flat tires and returned to the garage about
forty minutes later with the younger of the two settlers. His name was Shmuel,
and he lived on a settlement that was visible from the rooftops of Tulkarm. He
sat with us for about two hours. Ahed and I looked at each other and remarked
how we were very curious about this Israeli settler who came to sit and social-
ize among Palestinians. He was quick to say that he, like most of his friends,
just wanted to live in peace. He explained that he lived on the settlement because he was able to buy a house there for about $30,000, whereas the same
house in Netanya would cost $200,000. He said the commute to work as a taxi
driver was inconsequential compared to the price difference in real estate.

"But how do you feel living there?" I asked. "You mean how do I feel
about myself as a settler?" he asked. I asked about that and about his own sense
of security. Regarding security he said he felt relatively safe. No place is completely safe, he explained. In the towns and cities of Israel there is crime and
sometimes terrorism, whereas on the settlement there is almost no crime and
no substantial fear of terrorism. After Ahed interjected that they stole the land,
Shmuel said in Arabic, "Okay, I stole the land. What do you want from me?"
He explained that taking the land was wrong, but it was not a reason to have an
unending war. There must be some agreement, he said. Either the Palestinians
should be compensated with money, or settlers like him should be given an
opportunity to sell their houses and buy affordable housing somewhere else

inside the Green Line. He said he would leave in a day if it could be worked out financially, and he said 90 percent of his neighbors would do the same. We continued to question him about how many settlers shared his feelings, and I pointed out how unusual it was for me to meet someone like him.

Understanding something about anthropology, Shmuel asked me what conclusions I had made about the underlying basis of Palestinian culture. I explained that my work was about describing the military checkpoints in daily life and I did not seek an underlying cultural structure to explain Palestinian behavior. He then asked what my findings were regarding the checkpoints. I told him I thought it was the basis of a racist system, like South Africa. He protested that the Palestinians have their crazies and the Israelis have theirs. He said that most people just wanted peace and wanted to live together without problems, but there were extremists like Baruch Goldstein, who attacked and killed Palestinians praying at the Ibrahimi Mosque in Hebron, and extremists like HAMAS, who have taken credit for numerous bombings in Israel. He said that, just as Israeli soldiers stopped and harassed Palestinians at the checkpoints, he had been stopped and harassed by special security forces at Palestinian checkpoints as he entered or left Tulkarm. He protested: Why should I call that a racist system like South Africa?

The problem, I tried to argue in broken Hebrew, was the systematic discrimination against Palestinians. Like whites in the United States or South Africa who profited from discrimination against blacks, Israelis profited from the inequality enforced by their government on Palestinians. He asked how Israelis profit from all these problems. "Do you think I want my children to go Lebanon, or to fight with Abu Hasan's children?" he said. I asked him why he came to Abu Hasan to fix his car. He said because Abu Hasan was an excellent car electrician whom he trusted. I said that, although that is true, he also came to him because he was much cheaper than a similar trustworthy worker in Israel. The reason he is cheaper is because he does not have the same rights, freedoms, and protections as workers across the Green Line. I made the same point about the cheaper housing on the settlement. I tried to explain that, just as I profited from being white in America due to the long, historic exploitation of blacks, he was profiting from the continuing exploitation of Palestinians. It was a difficult idea to accept for Shmuel, who drove a taxi, that he was enjoying legal privileges at someone's expense. He considered it and said that there were reasons for these problems of which we were not aware. "It is not as simple as you say," he said.

'Alia's Sewing Job

'Alia, twenty-three when I first met her in 1994, was the eldest daughter of Umm Samud's niece and our neighbor. She lived with her parents, seven siblings, maternal aunt, and maternal grandmother. I spent many evenings with her family sitting in the living room or on their porch underneath an arbor of grapes. There were very few women my age in the village with whom I communicated. 'Alia and her adult sisters 'A'isha, Manal, and Dina were my limited insight into the challenges young women faced coming of age in the village.

'Alia was born in Kuwait and came with her family to the village in the West Bank in 1990 via Jordan (see Chapter 7). For 'Alia, the move meant giving up middle-class suburban living for life in a village in the West Bank. Bored with sitting at home all day with her family and needing more income in the house, 'Alia decided to work. The one opportunity easily available to her was in the clothing industry. Since the age of twenty-one, she had worked in a small clothing workshop. By the early 1990s, businesses operating in the West Bank registered just over 100,000 workers, of whom only about 15,000 were women.[1] Of those 15,000, almost one third (4,294) worked making clothes.[2] Small workshops of five to ten women were ubiquitous in the West Bank town of Tulkarm.[3]

'Alia thought she would enjoy working. Umm Samud encouraged her to work and save money. Umm Samud often spoke nostalgically about her own experience as a seamstress in the 1950s, when she apprenticed with a tailor from Tulkarm and then trained other men and women. She made dresses that were sold in town and she went around visiting women to help them fix bridal gowns. She sent money to her brother who was a student in America. In Umm Samud's memory, like the memories of older women from Nablus as reported by Moors (1995), during the 1940s and 1950s, the most gifted girls from urban middle class families were apprenticed to master tailors who made customized clothing.[4] Umm Samud told 'Alia's mother that she should work for her maternal cousin, Abu Karim, in his clothing workshop in town.

But tremendous changes had occurred in the garment industry since the days when Umm Samud worked. When the Green Line opened, mass-produced clothing from Israel quickly caused a decline in custom-made clothing, which could not compete in price with the ready-to-wear.[5] Israel's clothing manufacturers soon made use of the cheaper and less mobile labor of Palestinian women by locating the work-intensive part of production in the territories. Artisan workshops were transformed into mass-producing sweatshops for Israeli exporters. Designing, cutting, and marketing mostly remained in Israel;

only the cut material was sent to workshops in the territories where the pieces were assembled and returned. By the mid-1990s, clothing manufacturing employed about a quarter of the workers in the manufacturing sector, accounted for about 15 percent of manufacturing establishments, and produced about 10 percent of the gross output (Nasr 1997).[6] By the end of the 1990s, about 80 percent of the garments produced were made for Israeli firms, while 15 percent went into the local market, and the remaining 5 percent were manufactured for the export market (Mansour and Destremau 1997: 41).

'Alia worked for her uncle Abu Karim doing finishing work like clipping the loose threads from the inside of garments, turning them right-side out, and folding them. She clipped thousands of threads each day for month after month from 5:00 A.M. until 1:00 P.M. She often brought bags of clothing home to do piecework at about 5 to 10 agorot per piece. She would sit and have her sisters help as they watched television and talked.

In addition to 'Alia, three other women did the same type of finishing work; they were also relatively new to their jobs. There were usually twelve women employed in this factory, depending on the level of business. Three women made seams, two hemmed, and three made collars. Each used a different technique and each task had a different level of difficulty. Collars were the most difficult; buttons required only a single linear measure. None of the machines were computerized. Cleaning loose threads was the simplest task. Depending on the product, workers were needed to do different tasks, and there were vague distinctions between skilled workers and less-skilled ones. One woman directed everybody's activities when the boss was not there, and she floated from one task to another as necessary to complete the job.[7]

The tense atmosphere in Abu Karim's workshop increased with his presence; he was there about half the day, during which the women did not speak to each other. They listened to the radio, but it could barely be heard when working so close to the noise of the machines. When he left they relaxed, and continued to work at the same pace while having minimal conversation. Because of the noise and the distance between the work stations, except with the person sitting next to you conversation usually had to be loud, which kept it from getting too personal.

Investigating the sewing industry was difficult because I, in my bodily presence, seemed to exacerbate the patriarchal threat of the boss. Women workers seemed embarrassed by my presence and attempts to communicate. Little was discussed in front of me as I tried to visit and do useful tasks. I felt I was a burden upon the workers. Perhaps because I was a foreign man and a friend of the owner, little trust developed. I had worked with women in comfortable circumstances, in business and government offices and in the university, but in this environment the tension was noticeably higher. The town of Tulkarm was not an urban setting where men and women mixed freely in public.

For ʿAlia, the tension of working for her uncle bubbled over into family life. Sitting with Abu Harab's children in Umm Samud's house, we saw Abu Karim coming down the road. ʿAlia jumped up and ran to hide in the kitchen, trying to avoid him because she had told Abu Karim she was sick and had not gone to work that day. ʿAlia did not speak badly of Abu Karim to me, but I caught her glances behind his back. Not going to work was also her way of protesting. She complained that he said he would let her learn to operate more complex machines, but he had not fulfilled his promise. If she stayed on the simple machines, which was repetitive, boring, and required no skill, she would fail to develop her abilities. One day Abu Karim upset her. She went home sick and soon took a new job in another workshop.

The new workshop was very much like Abu Karim's. The owner had been in business only three years, and his sister directly oversaw most of the workers. The hours and pay were the same, but ʿAlia felt more comfortable there because she became friends with one of her coworkers.

In the late 1990s, most women were paid around NIS 25–35 (around $7–$9) per day.[8] Working six days a week, ʿAlia earned about $45 weekly. What she did with the money was up to her, but she said she contributed to the welfare of her family of ten. Besides her, only her father was working full time. Her cousin Ahed encouraged her to put money away for herself, but to what extent she did this I did not know.[9] I asked if she had bought any clothes with her money. She said she had not and that anything nice she owned had been a gift from someone.

I asked if she ever thought of starting her own shop. She laughed and repeated what I had asked as if it made no sense. "How?" she said with a challenge. I stopped myself from saying, "Go to Tel Aviv with clothing samples." I hesitated because I thought it might actually sound rude at the time, suggesting that she would do such a thing, that she would go alone. Crossing the Green Line, especially for work, was understood, at least by ʿAlia, as making a woman vulnerable to disrepute.[10]

I asked if she wanted to work in the future. She did not. She wanted to get married. She was twenty-four years old at the time, and she wanted to leave her home and start her own life. She worked because she earned money and it was a way of leaving the house and doing something. Without a college degree or vocational diploma beyond high school, sewing was her only option. She explained that she felt vulnerable there, going to work in the shop; as she said, "people talk a lot" about women who move about too freely. I asked if that was why she wore a head-covering to work even though she never wore one in front of her male cousins or me. She explained that she wore it when going out formally or going to work, in both cases in order to protect herself from scrutiny and lying gossip. She would have gladly given that up to be married and have her own home. To remain working in this job would mean that she would remain unmarried. (She eventually got married and quit her job.)

Industry on the Green Line

As the Israeli government worked on developing high-tech industries in Israel (*Israel Economist* 1990), underdevelopment in the West Bank made it into a "Third World colony." The territories became "an open market with no competition from outside. As economic integration is accompanied by strong legal, social and residential segregation, labour is very cheap, legal rights are very limited and social security is virtually non-existent" (Moors 1995: 203). In this environment the few cracks allowing livelihoods to take root were in service to Israel: "Of these, two are worth mention. The first was the development of sub-contracting, particularly in the clothing industry . . . [and the second were] garages in the Territories, which offered cheaper repair services for Israeli motorists" (Gazit 1995: 221).

In both industries, as for undocumented migrant workers, the border shapes the relations of production by limiting the opportunity of Palestinians and separating Israelis from labor's reproduction. The border creates a boundary on the capitalists' accountabilities for the well-being of foreign employees and their families. Neither big manufacturers nor their governments were under pressure to subsidize the education, health care, or income of their "foreign" labor. Workers across the border were easily abandoned when no longer needed, without paying welfare or unemployment.

Abu Hasan's garage was largely dependent on Israeli customers, but no single person or job made a big difference for Abu Hasan. His Israeli customers came for his cheaper labor, so he took the work and charged them more than he would his West Bank neighbors. He only suffered when the closures kept Israelis away from his shop. Working with cars gave him an independence that could not be gained from running a clothing workshop or building a greenhouse. His workers also enjoyed a freedom and hope that did not exist in the sweatshop. The young apprentices were paid according to how helpful they were that day, which depended on their eagerness and motivation. If they were ambitious they learned the business, left Abu Hasan, and started their own. It would take them ten or twenty years to build a business like Abu Hasan's, but the opportunity was there.

The textile industry no longer provided improving job opportunities for its workers. Sewing had been the domain of single women from middle-class families, but with the opening of the border it became the job of women from the camps and villages with limited education who did not want to work as cleaners in Israel. Instead of teaching a respected skill, industrial subcontracting only required "guiding material at high speed through the machine, working under great pressure" (Moors 1995: 204).

The emergence of a pool of available jobs for women did not seem to change ideas about women's independence from men, or their desire to enter the labor market on a long-term basis. The West Bank's sewing industry developed a female labor force disciplined by fears of shame under male subcontractors who had connections in Israel (see also Rockwell 1985; Samara 1995). This gendered embodiment of authority made my participant research more difficult than working with men, or even than with women in other circumstances.

Interestingly, "women themselves use gender as a form of resistance":

This "paternalism" is also reflected in the way in which I heard girls addressing their female employer. Rather than using the term "my mother's sister" (khalti; the friendly aunt), a common informal yet respectful way of addressing an older woman, they used "my father's sister" ('ammti; the strict aunt) as a form of address. (Moors 1995: 208–9)

Women intentionally act weak and less capable, and refer to their obligations in the home in "defiance of alienation and resistance to the dictates of the market" (Moors 1995: 209). Sometime they use their paternalist relationship to make claims on their employer, "emphasising their difficult situation rather than their productivity in the hope of getting a raise" (Moors 1995: 210). Women themselves use such relationships to create some autonomy for themselves and as a way of refusing to exploit themselves for wages like men.

Women were disciplined by the border, but in quite a different way from the men who crossed as day-migrants. For women, the border was a place not of physical but of moral danger. In this case, it was the judgment of other Palestinians that kept women from crossing the border and thus, by limiting their mobility, made them more compliant as workers for men who could cross the border. Women's mobility was limited because they are "defined as needing protection and control of male kin" (Moors 1995: 207).[11] "Here the integrity of the Palestinian people is at stake, with women's work in Israel signaling its potential destruction. As younger girls were seen as especially vulnerable, they were particularly condemned" (Moors 1995: 184). This obstacle prevents women from starting their own businesses and makes them more desirable as workers. After getting experience in a West Bank workshop or with a manufacturer in Israel, a man might buy a few used machines and start his own business. Women were unlikely to do this: "even though a female owner is not condemned as strongly as a female labourer if she goes to Tel-Aviv, it is difficult for her to go there by herself and arrange for the delivery of cut material" (Moors 1995: 208). Rather than transform the position of women in society, factory work adapted to existing inequalities.[12]

The border prevented development, intimidated workers, and facilitated the establishment of spontaneous trade zones on Palestinian territory. The Rabin administration, which opened negotiations with the PLO, did not want to eliminate the border, but wanted to transform it. It favored the creation of Israeli-owned industrial zones on the border of the West Bank and Gaza. Accompanied by a large color map, the Israeli paper *Yedioth Aharanoth* described the following in March 1995:

It sounds like a strange dream: ten glass and stone buildings, surrounded by natural green grass, shrubs, and fruit trees.

Between the long buildings, to be built in modern architecture, will be found a large parking lot . . . no chimneys, no smoke. Everything green and flowers. Even the noise of the industrial machinery inside the buildings will barely be heard.

The description is not fiction. This is one of the industrial parks being planned these days, with great discretion, in the top ranks of the ministries of foreign affairs, commerce and industry, and the treasury. The purpose is to establish between eight and eleven of such parks on the seam line between the State of Israel and the Autonomous Territories; and therein empower the soon-to-arrive Palestinian Authority.

. . . the factories could each employ about 10,000 workers on 2,000 dunams (500 acres), with big government and foreign aid and Palestinian labor—close to their homes, so they don't have to enter Israel. The benefits to Israel are clear: 10,000 workers will not be sneaking into Israel. The ministers are already trying to sell the ideas to firms in America, Europe, and the Far East. The Minister of Industry and Commerce [Michah Hanish] and the Minister of Finance [Avraham Shohat] said they really wanted to help Palestinians. "The basis will be Israeli, the set-up plans will be ours, and if it works, it will employ thousands of workers from the Territories." [13]

These plans did not come to fruition in the 1990s, and other projects that were being planned at the time of the report above were also abandoned,[14] but the intention was evident. Despite the description of the factory as modern and pleasing to the eye, the plan indicated how peace could be profitable. Israel could establish in the West Bank a small version of the *maquiladoras* the United States has created in Mexico and Haiti.

5. Entrepreneurs in the West Bank

Abu Karim's New Business

By the 1990s, Abu Karim, Umm Samud's older brother's son, was a successful small businessman doing business with Israeli companies, who could easily get permission to cross the border. He could not drive his own car, because that required an additional permit he did not have, but with an Israeli car he could go. He lived next door to Umm Samud and often came by to visit his aunt. I often asked questions about his business and, noting my interest and the yellow license plates on my car, he invited me to take him to Tel Aviv to arrange work with Israeli manufacturers. First we filled my car with plastic bags of cut pieces of children's jeans and brought them from his shop to a smaller shop. Then we crossed the checkpoint without a problem and drove the 50 minutes to Tel Aviv.

In the early 1970s, Abu Karim went to work as a plasterer in Israeli construction. After a decade, he went to Saudi Arabia for four years where he continued working as a laborer. Having saved about JD 7,000 (about $14,000 at the time), he returned to the village and got married in 1984. He decided to invest his money in sewing machines. He purchased five used machines from an Israeli in Tel Aviv and put them on the ground floor of his house. He hired village women, including his own relatives, to work the machines. At first he took subcontracted lots from larger West Bank workshops, but after two years he moved the workshop from his house to a rented space in town and began doing business directly with Israelis. In the mid-1980s, the number of contracts increased, business expanded, and he purchased more machines for buttons, collars, seams, and pressing.

We talked about how he finds female workers by word of mouth through other female workers. He complained about the "girls" who never work to his satisfaction, who are as undependable as little children. He said they are hard to train and will leave at the slightest problem, or for one shekel more a day. "They are very sensitive. If I give her special work that she doesn't like doing then she might not come the next day," he explained. He must rely on the other workers to bring in replacements, because gender propriety keeps him from searching out women by himself. He complained that it had gotten especially difficult because there were too many workshops, eating up both the profits and the workers. It required JD 7,000–10,000 ($10,000-$15,000) to set up a workshop, and "every woman in the camp now has a machine."

The clothing manufacturers we visited were in southern Tel Aviv's industrial area, near Jaffa Road, among furniture and light industry workshops and stores. The streets were filled with Palestinian workers, and Abu Karim passed men he knew from the territories; one man I even knew. Large trucks loaded and unloaded cloth and clothing. Abu Karim told me most of it came and went to Nablus, the largest town in the northern West Bank, where some clothing factories employ more than a hundred workers. He stopped to talk about transportation prices with some of the drivers and told them to send his regards to their bosses.

Israel's textile industry, which began in the late 1960s, boomed after the government signed a free trade agreement (FTA) with the European Economic Community (EEC) in 1975 that allowed duty free entry for Israeli textiles; 90 percent of Israel's clothing exports in the late 1970s went to Europe (Mansour and Destremau 1997: 6). In 1985, Israel signed a FTA with the United States; by the 1990s 40 percent went to the United States and about 50 percent went to Europe (Mansour and Destremau 1997: 7). As in the construction industry, turnover almost doubled between 1990 and 1995, due largely to the arrival of hundreds of thousands of new immigrants and the growth of a domestic Israeli market (Mansour and Destremau 1997: 17). By 1995, textiles and garments were 6.6 percent of Israel's total industrial turnover, 12 percent of the total labor force, and 9 percent of industrial exports; they ranked fourth among exporting industries (behind machinery and equipment, cut diamonds, and chemicals) and brought a total export value of about $2 billion in 1997 (Israeli Central Bureau of Statistics 1999).

The second half of the 1990s saw significant contraction as FTA negotiations and the implementation of the World Trade Organization (WTO) agreement and associated multilateral trade agreements expanded (Mansour and Destremau 1997: 10). The global market for textile production opened and Israel lost its advantage as Asian goods came into FTAs. This pushed Israeli manufacturers to restructure their production by giving up cheap goods and focusing on knitted wear (hosiery, underwear, and t-shirts), household textiles (towels and bed linens), men's wear, swimwear, and innovative fabrics and design for export markets. They needed a niche different from their massive Asian competition (Mansour and Destremau 1997: 15–16). They have had to move to higher quality clothes.

We dropped off samples in one shop, and then stayed in a second shop for a long time while Abu Karim and the manager (or owner) argued over the price per piece for assembly of a vest. We were there for over forty minutes while the Israeli said NIS 6 per vest and Abu Karim refused to drop below NIS 7.5. The Israeli threatened to give it to some other workshop, and Abu Karim said "give it to them." The manager started to make some phone calls and ignored us. We started to walk out and finally the man agreed. We dropped off samples at another office and then Abu Karim took me to lunch in the neighborhood. He complained about how the manager of the second shop gave him such a hard time. "It is always a fight with these Jews." He said he once made between $3,000 and $4,000 a month, but sometimes doesn't break even.

He said the main problem he faced was that everything had to be done through Israel. He could not market independently. International labels contracted the production of thousands of garments to a select number of Israeli manufacturers; it was highly centralized, with 9 firms accounting for 75 percent of the turnover and half the exports in 1996 (Mansour and Destremau 1997). These firms hired manufacturers who imported, designed, and cut the material. The cut material was sent to workshops in the territories where it was assembled, trimmed, and sometimes washed, ironed, and packaged, before being sent back to Israel for export. Abu Karim received pieces from Tel Aviv, did some of the work in his shop, contracted some work to other smaller shops, and gave some to women at home, all at piece rate.

The assembly and trimming were the most labor intensive aspects of production. Most of this was done in workshops, like Abu Karim's, where women sat at machines on tables arranged in rows, under flourescent lighting in a small warehouse, often on the ground floor of the owner's residence.[1] Cleaning the garments—clipping the loose threads from the inside and turning them right-side out—was usually subcontracted to women working at home at a few cents apiece. Because a large number of shops were in the informal sector, official statistics about this industry probably underestimate the number of workers.[2]

Israeli manufacturers sent fabric to be assembled in the Palestinian territories in order to increase their profits. Israeli workers were too expensive compared to the global market in clothing assembly, especially because in 1994, the Knesset passed a law raising the wages of workers in the textile sector (Mansour and Destremau 1997: 18). Minimum wage in Israel was $695 per month, which equaled about $900 for the employer after taxes. The aver-

9. Plastic greenhouses, field, residential home, and donkey, 2000.

age wage in the territories was $200 to $300 (Mansour and Destremau 1997: 25).[3] The delocalization of the work intensive activities of manufacturing was one of the hallmarks of globalization. Moving operations across borders allowed employers to avoid protective laws, unions, taxes, or codes, pay much cheaper labor costs and take advantage of a substantial military that intimidates all aspects of colonial interaction. In the Israeli-Palestinian case, among many others, no investment was made by global corporations in machines, electricity, buildings, labor recruitment, training, or management. Consequently, they have total flexibility to make short term arrangements and move on at any time. Although Israeli workers might have lost between 20,000 and 30,000 jobs (Mansour and Destremau 1997: 37), delocalizing assembly allowed Israeli firms to maintain their profits.

Some industries are difficult to move across borders because of the distance created between planning and production. Quickly changing demands and trends require communication and geographic proximity. In the case of Israel-Palestine, across the border was not really far away, only an hour from Tel Aviv to Tulkarm (unless it is rush hour), if one has a yellow Israeli license plate. Palestinian entrepreneurs learned to speak Hebrew, and many acquired their skills and experience inside Israel making communication easy. Transaction costs were low. Furthermore, the United States and the European Union considered the Territories and Israel one zone, which meant that production in the Territories was still "in Israel" and met the 35 percent–52 percent rules of origin commonly imposed by international FTAs.

Abu Karim said it was getting more difficult to make a profit in the cloth-ing business, so he decided to invest his money in building plastic greenhouses for vegetables. It did not require the hassle of close management, and he had the land available in his back yard. Abu Karim's and Umm Samud's homes sat on the edge of a ten-dunam (2.5-acre) field. Five houses had been built on the fringes of the land, leaving a field in the center. The land was bought during the British Mandate by Umm Samud's father. By Islamic law daughters get half a son's share, because men are expected to be the providers. These ten dunams would be split into eighths, with the two daughters, Umm Samud and her sis-ter, each getting a sixteenth, and each of the seven brothers getting an eighth.[4] The five houses that had already been built on the perimeter of the land be-longed to Umm Samud and four of her brothers. The two eldest brothers were deceased, but their houses were inhabited by their elderly widows, adult chil-dren, and grandchildren. The eldest living brother, about seventy years old, lived with his wife alone in a third house. The youngest brother, Abu Thaki, in his early sixties, lived with his wife and three sons in Amman, Jordan, but maintained this second house in the village (see Chapter 7). The remaining siblings have lived in Jordan for almost forty years and have not indicated that they will build or even return to the village. The field between the five houses had been given to Abu Samud's father, a cousin of the family, to sharecrop at a generous share-ratio when he came back to the village in 1968. He grew various crops over the years, but by the early 1990s he had grown too old to sharecrop, especially given the difficulty of curfews during the Uprising. The field sat fallow, growing only hay until the fall of 1994.

In the fall of that year, Abu Karim ordered the construction of plastic greenhouses on approximately one third of the family field. He hired men from another village to plow and fertilize the soil, build the greenhouses, install drip irrigation, and sharecrop the first harvest of cucumbers. A team of six built the aluminum structures, and Abu Samud was hired, with his sons and me, to build a steel reinforced concrete 27-cubic-meter water tank. The land, houses, irrigation tank, and water were all provided by Abu Karim. The workers built the structure, planted, picked and sold the crop, deducted the cost of seed and fertilizer, and then split the profits 50–50. Abu Karim was not sure that the workers were really doing all that much, but he did not know enough about agriculture to watch over them effectively. Eventually, Abu Karim became un-happy with both the construction of the greenhouse and the way these farmers cared for the crop. The sloppiness of their work was evident to those with ex-perience, and several neighbors commented on the weeding, ventilation, and irrigation. After the first harvest, Abu Karim did not renew his agreement with them. Instead, he hired a new team, not only to farm the old greenhouse, but to build and farm a second one on another third of the remaining land.

Umm Samud was not happy about building another greenhouse. She said the greenhouse would ruin the breeze that comes across the field to her house and make her house hot. I thought it would be a miserable eyesore, but no one else seemed as concerned with the view. Umm Samud asked me why he needed to make more and more money. Abu Karim said his father had bought the land from his grandfather, so it was within his rights to use it. He also explained that it was good for the Palestinian economy for him to reinvest his money. "Should I just sit on the money, or help put people to work?" he would ask me.

When his first harvest came in, the price of cucumbers had suddenly, although temporarily, plummeted from the high price of NIS 10 down to NIS 0.5 for a quality kilo. Prices in the market usually remained relatively stable at NIS 3 to 6 per kilo, but would occasionally swing one way or the other. Abu Karim did not take it too badly; he said it would eventually pay off.

By the summer of 1995, Abu Karim wanted to start a third greenhouse on the remaining land. He began construction when his paternal uncle (and neighbor) was away in Jordan. The paternal uncle would not care, but Umm Harab, who was ʿAlia's mother, and Umm Samud did not want it built. Abu Karim visited his aunt Umm Samud regularly and he would sit in her living room and explain that he hated to see the field go to hay, that it would be better for everyone, for him and for the workers, to invest his money in a productive enterprise. But when the workers started to dig the holes for the foundation poles, Umm Samud started complaining bitterly to everyone. Umm Samud confronted Abu Karim out in the field in front of his workers and would not talk to him for a few weeks. Abu Karim insisted that he had asked Umm Samud's permission and that she had approved. She said that he began work before he consulted her.

Umm Samud began to organize support among the relatives. Her brother, Abu Karim's father, was no help at all. She called her other brother, in Amman, and told him the details in the hope he would take a stand on her behalf. She also phoned and petitioned her other brother, Abu Thaki, who lived in Amman. Her older sister, Hajji Latifa, who also lived in Amman, said she would come to support her sister. She said she would bring her son from Saudi Arabia and lay the foundation of a new home next to Umm Samud's home. The climax came when the elderly widow, Umm Harab's mother, came limping out of her house screaming at Abu Karim from the street through the doorway of his house, waving her shoe above her head.

He stopped construction and spent the next two months explaining his side of the story every time I saw him, which was just about every day. Abu

Karim bemoaned how instead of congratulating him about his accomplishments, like building the greenhouses or the large stone additions he made to his (father's) home, his cousin-neighbors and aunt complained that it blocked their evening light and breeze. He said that they were just envious and that is why he eventually had a man sacrifice a sheep in order to ward off the evil eye, lest someone's envy cause harm to befall his person, family, or property. He recommended I do the same thing regarding my car, which was always having trouble. He said envy was the reason I was having engine problems; killing a chicken on the hood should take care of it.[5]

Abu Kamash's Vision of the Future

Abu Karim introduced me to Abu Kamash, who owned the biggest clothing factory in the town of Tulkarm. I visited his factory with Umm Samud's youngest son, Taysir. A young secretary, who dressed in Western clothes and wore her hair down—an unusual sight in Tulkarm—greeted us in a front waiting room, and then showed us to Abu Kamash's office.

Without an introduction Abu Kamash began to tell me how American opinion was favorable to Israel and Zionism because Jews were close to Western culture. Arabs, he explained, do not yet have the same ease of persuasion in the West. He complimented me on how smart the Jews have been in their traditions and in their ability to adapt and survive. I interpreted these as diplomatic gestures and responded by mentioning the Palestinian struggle and the injustice of the occupation. We became more comfortable and he took me on a tour of his factory.

He had about sixty operating machines on the floor, where women worked without speaking. He showed me how many of the machines were computerized. The worker only had to run the garment through the machine and the machine made the exact stitch. The second floor was a cutting, packing, and storage room. Here men were working; downstairs there were only women. He showed me the name-brand boxes, plastic wraps, price tags in U.S. dollars, and packaged goods—Jordache, Body Equipment, Casual Corner—ready to ship to U.S. markets. He pointed to the tag reading "Made in Israel," and said "What a joke." He said that his big problem was that he must deal through Israel. There was no recognized export policy for Palestine, so buyers would have to pay 80 percent taxes on his goods if they bought directly from him. But there were tax breaks in the United States and the European Union for Israel.

Indeed, import-export regulations imposed by the occupation forced most Palestinian merchants to market Israeli goods or goods imported through

Israel, thus enforcing their dependence (Samara 1989: 10). Exports of West Bank and Gaza agricultural produce to Europe went through Agrexco, Israel's state-owned marketing agency. Approximately 90 percent of West Bank imports came from Israel, and 50 percent of its exports went there. In 1991, the West Bank balance of trade showed a deficit of $900 million, mainly owed to Israel (Palestinian Bureau of Statistics 1995: 69). To make matters worse, inferior goods were often dumped on Palestinian merchants where no police were enforcing the legal standards. I regularly encountered construction materials not made to specifications (8 mm iron rods were only 7 mm or concrete mix had too much gravel), imperfect clothing, and food seconds.

We went up to the third floor of the building that was his home. He showed me all the public areas. On one wall was a ceramic relief of Jerusalem and the Dome of the Rock. We paused for a moment to look at it, and he said, "That is the problem. Everyone wants a piece of Yerushalayim." Although he was speaking in Arabic, he used the Hebrew name of the city. He listed the desirous parties: the Crusaders, the Muslims, the British, and the Jews.

We sat down on plush couches and I asked about the business. His daughter made us coffee, and he began telling me how the new order was one of economic warfare. Israel's real goal with recent negotiations, he argued, was not so much peace as economic conquest. The main political problems of business that he enumerated were (1) the right to immigration in order to give the diaspora the security to invest; (2) security of life and property against settlers and soldiers; (3) the infrastructure in Palestinian areas of roads, electricity, banking, finance, and education; and (4) the legal and tax structures to work without Israeli exporters.

He told me that recently he had Liz Claiborne sitting with him. He gestured as if she had been sitting in my chair, discussing how they would prefer to do business directly. He claimed that Israel exported about $2 billion worth of clothing, of which he believed 50 percent was produced in the territories. I said it was unlikely that the Israelis would give up their control of the market, but he said that in the end Israel just does not have the workers.

I asked if the closures provided some protection for him and if open borders might create too much competition; other Palestinians could expand their businesses, Palestinian labor costs would increase, and the products of even cheaper labor in Egypt and Turkey would be in the market. He disagreed strongly, saying that he had no competition locally, only internationally. Second, these other labor markets would not disturb his business because productivity really depends on two things: good administration and investment at the point of production. He explained that in Egypt they invest about $1,000 per worker and pay about $2 a day, yielding a production rate (depending on the garment) of about twenty pieces per worker per day. In Jordan, the investment is about $1,500 per worker, with a daily pay of about $6, yielding about thirty pieces per worker, per day. In his West Bank factory, he said the capital investment was about $1,700 per worker, wages were about $15 (higher than average), and production was about seventy pieces per worker per day. In Israel, he said some places invest $30,000 at the point of production, paying $25 per day, and producing over one hundred pieces per worker per day. He stressed the need to "encourage" workers. The computers on the machines could control the quality of the stitch and also count the number of pieces sewn. Counting allowed him to reward those who produced a lot. It also must have been an oppressive device of pressure on the worker.

I asked about workers' rights and how he felt about unionization. He said he did not want a revolution from hunger, and he again emphasized that he thought production increased with increasing wages and better labor conditions—citing Japan as the most obvious example. The key to success, he believed, is keeping a high standard. When I asked if he had a problem with labor he said there were two main problems: (1) the social value of skilled work had gone down so people only want to work at white and pink collar jobs; and (2) nobody trusted the private sector and, instead, wanted a job with the government.

After about two hours Taysir and I left Abu Kamash's house. Taysir, who sat quietly alongside me the whole time, was bouncing with enthusiasm over the experience. "Did you see that house . . . the sculpture . . . the spacious and modern kitchen," he said, amazed at the display of wealth. He fantasized aloud about marrying one of Abu Kamash's daughters. He talked about it in the car all the way back home to the village.

When I walked in the house through the kitchen Umm Samud asked me, "Where have you been all day?" putting her hand on her hip and shaking her head at me with a fixed stare. I told her with whom I had been for the past several hours. "Oh Lord, Oh Greatness, Oh Goodness," she said knocking her fist gently on her chest. Then she laughed and started to sing a little verse about how I will conquer Tel Aviv. She grabbed me tightly by the arm and said, "They [Abu Kamash and his family] came from nothing, nothing!" she emphasized by thumbing her teeth. "It all came from Israel," she said, "since the occupation."

Ahed, who was sitting at the kitchen table eating his lunch, jumped in, saying, "He is a spy." I could hardly believe that. Abu Kamash told me how he spent five years in an Israeli political prison. I asked Ahed exactly what he meant, hoping he would explain something about how comprador-bourgeoisie exploit Palestinians for the benefit of Israelis. But that was not what he said.

Ahed said that Abu Kamash had taped videos of women who worked for him; one of them was supposedly his mistress. Then he used the videos to black-mail the women to entice men to spy on people involved in activity against the Israeli occupation. Taysir jumped in, telling me how Abu Kamash probably had a beautiful mistress for whom he bought a car. Taysir said it as if he was in awe of the man.

There were many problems with Palestinians who worked as Israeli agents during the Uprising, but this accusation against Abu Kamash seemed unusu-ally elaborate. The story of his making videotapes for purposes of blackmail was gossip that I thoroughly doubt, but its repetition by Ahed was meaning-ful. Ahed's accusation was not just about collaboration, it was about exposing women to indignity and blackmail. As the local king of the clothing factories, Abu Kamash worked closely with Israeli industry including, as he explained himself, sometimes using soldiers to protect his delivery trucks. He was also the employer par excellence of women, the gatekeeper between Israeli con-tamination and Palestinian women. Those who facilitated the connection be-tween Israeli capital and West Bank women, like Abu Kamash or Abu Karim, risked being seen as collaborators with Israel. Gossip defined them not as ex-ploiting capitalists, but as men exposing women to indecency on behalf of the enemy.

Entrepreneurial Capitalists and the Border

The first Israeli military commander of the West Bank, Shlomo Gazit, explains that his officers set up demonstration lots teaching Palestinians how to use sprinklers, drippers, chemical fertilizers, tractors, and plastic coverings, and about the "economic advantages of growing flowers and vegetables for ex-port":

The Israeli military government eagerly took on the case of the local Arab agricul-ture. Its staff officers for agricultural affairs energetically applied themselves, first to the rehabilitation and the resumption of routine operations, and later to increasing pro-duction and improving the quality of the produce. The staff officers and agricultural counselors, most of them young but experienced veterans of foreign aid missions to developing countries found wide scope for their initiatives. (Gazit 1995: 218, 219)

Gazit says that "the first years of Israeli rule in the territories were character-ized by phenomenal economic prosperity and a rise in the standard of living" (Gazit 1995: 217).

Without even questioning the sincerity and eagerness of the officers of whom Gazit writes, the interaction between Israeli authorities and Palestinian farmers can hardly be described as a "foreign aid mission." Most Palestinians did not learn about Israeli technology from demonstration lots set up by the army's staff officers. They learned about it working in Israel, from the merchants that marketed such technology in the territories, and in Palestinian agricultural training colleges. It was not Israeli benevolence that extended their technology to Palestinians, it was primarily Israeli merchants who opened new markets for their fertilizers and irrigation technology.[6] According to tax receipts, the Occupied Territories had a deficit that had grown to $1.222 billion with Israel (United Nations Special Coordinator in the Occupied Territories 1999: 6).[7] Ironically, the process of underdevelopment and subordination of the West Bank to Israel was often cloaked as a beneficial process of modernization.

Under the occupation, the "new comprador class has made a quick profit mainly because it alone was granted the right to import to and export from the West Bank by the military government" (Samara 1989: 13). Three main groups have benefited: city merchants who, since Jordanian rule, have intensively exploited local farmers; large landowners; and the new merchant capitalists "created directly and intentionally by the occupation authorities" (Samara 1989: 12).

The entrepreneurial class profited, but remained subordinate to Israel and facilitated ongoing forms of capitalist domination. Entrepreneurs in clothing manufacturing complained mainly about the monopoly the Israelis had over them. The big Palestinian entrepreneurs wanted to work directly with European and American companies, rather than through larger Tel Aviv producers. On the whole, many businessmen spoke about wanting to import and export directly, especially as their children learn to market on the world wide web.

The closures created significant problems for Abu Karim and other medium sized entrepreneurs in garment assembly. Closures limited Palestinian entrepreneurs from meeting on their own initiatives with Israeli manufacturers. Permission was available to individual Palestinian entrepreneurs but not for their Palestinian cars, severely limiting mobility for most. Lack of contact made it difficult to discuss specifications, view product samples, take the forty minutes needed to argue and negotiate a price and payment schedule, identify new opportunities, and find new clients (Mansour and Destremau 1997: 49). The closures also made delivery difficult without an Israeli vehicle. Overall, business became more restricted and hierarchical. "Before 1993, Palestinian subcontractors tended to work for several Israeli manufacturers, but few today have subcontracting arrangements with more than one or two Israeli companies" (Mansour and Destremau 1997: 49). By the summer of 2000, almost all business with Israel in the Tulkarm district was contracted through the largest local Palestinian subcontracting company, Abu Kamash. Dependence of the subcontractor was extreme because there were only a few central clients and a great deal of competitors.

Technically, economic agreements with the Israeli government gave the Palestinian Authority some control over customs, imports, and exports, but most West Bankers continued doing business as subcontractors through Israel or bought from Israeli merchants. Palestinians could not afford to work independently because their companies paid 30 percent higher transaction costs than Israeli companies for identical imports and exports due to Israeli security checks and the necessity of using Israeli shipping agents and ports (Federation of Palestinian Chambers of Commerce 1998). International export was also difficult because it required travel abroad, something that was difficult for Palestinians. The Palestinian Authority did not help with information, research, or supportive policy, unlike many developing countries in Asia (Mansour and Destremau 1997: 44). On the contrary, the Palestinian Authority depended so heavily on foreign aid and so blindly followed World Bank, International Monetary Fund, and World Trade Organization notions of development, that the local bourgeoisie were thoroughly subordinated to foreign capital and monopolies held by the Palestinian Authority (Samara 2000). As the relative value of Palestinian labor fluctuated in the world of deregulating clothing production, the position of West Bank entrepreneurs became precarious.

The owners of manufacturing and service businesses benefited from a border closed to workers. With the border open the price of labor would increase. This would make investments in small commercial agricultural projects like Abu Karim's greenhouses less profitable. Perhaps merchants would benefit from increased spending, but they would also compete with Israeli merchants. It is in the business classes' interests not to completely close or open the border but to monopolize control of what passes across it and profit from that monopoly. It was unclear who could directly benefit from the changing border procedures, but it was clear that not everyone had the same interests.

6. Customs and the Green Line

Umm Samud's Custom

One clear day in November 1994, I sat on the ground on the pavement walk in front of Umm Samud's house. Ahed and Taysir, Umm Samud's sons, sat with me as we shelled a pile of almonds. With a burlap sack spread out on the ground, we smashed the almonds against a rock with hammers and separated the nut from the shell fragments. The almonds went to the kitchen, where Umm Samud sliced and roasted them to sprinkle on dishes of rice, chicken, or soup. The shells went to the outdoor oven where she burned them to cook bread. Nothing was wasted in Umm Samud's kitchen. She often emphasized how most people no longer did things the way she did, like baking bread, making soap, or roasting her own almonds and coffee. Other than worrying about her grown children, these kinds of tasks were her constant concern and labor. Wearing at the joints in her increasingly arthritic knees and hands, her home craft skills were celebrated and praised by the whole the family. She took her housework very seriously.

While we were sitting and cracking almonds on that November day, a shared taxi stopped beyond the gate at the end of the paved walk in the main street. Two women got out carrying big bags of sugar and rice. Not knowing who they were, we stared as they approached the gate. With her arms filled with packages and a cigarette dangling from her mouth, one of the women called out for us to open the gate. Taysir jumped up and opened the gate and Ahed called his mother. She came down from the roof where she had been frying vegetables for lunch, greeted our guests, sat them on the porch, and told Taysir to get cold drinks and make tea. She introduced them to me as the children of in-laws of her father. They lived in the Arab-Israeli town, called Tayiba, just over the Green Line. Despite their geographic proximity, it had been several years since they had been in the village. Umm Samud's sons did not even know who they were when they arrived.

The elder, Umm Dawud, about fifty years old, had a scarf on her head and a dress similar to Umm Samud's. The younger, Sabrin, around forty, wore slacks and a short-sleeved shirt that emphasized her petite figure. Her hair was hennaed red and cut shoulder length. She chain-smoked during the entire visit and spoke with a voice burned rough. While women in the cosmopolitan centers of the West Bank, like Ramallah, Jerusalem, and Bethlehem, or women from the diaspora, smoked in public or in front of men, in the village al-Qarya it was unusual, in fact head-turning, to see women smoking. Sabrin's particular smoking gestures and speaking tones were not from the diaspora, but suggested Israeli to me.

After lunch Sabrin told me she was unmarried, lived at home with her parents, and worked in the cafeteria of an Israeli factory. I asked about her work, and she unenthusiastically told me it wasn't bad, but she looked forward to doing something fun on the weekend. She offered me a cigarette and Umm Samud jumped in and proudly explained that I did not smoke in front of her, which amused our two guests.

I did not smoke in front of Umm Samud and her husband Abu Samud because their sons, who normally smoked, did not do so in front of their parents. Ahed said that it was out of respect. Because I wanted to be an adopted son, as most anthropologists claimed to have become in their fieldwork, I decided not to let them see me smoke. For Umm Samud, this turned out to be something to brag about. She sometimes worried about what other women said about me living in her home, and often felt it necessary to preempt the discussion and justify the situation before it even came up. The potential for gossip was clear to her and she did her best, and let me know it, to quell any negative words that might be circulating. Not smoking in front of her was a repeated point in the narrative of my good behavior, along with not lying and fear of God. Even when I stopped smoking altogether she still said it to other women, like our two visitors from Arab Israel, to vouch for my respectful behavior and, perhaps, to quell suspicions that she had shown poor judgment in allowing me to stay in her home.

In private in the kitchen Umm Samud drew her finger across her upper arm and pretended to hike up her belt to make fun of Sabrin's short sleeves and pants. Then she put her index and middle finger to her puckered lips, took them away, exhaled, and rolled her eyes to parody Sabrin's smoking. She pulled me close and said quietly, as if it was a secret, which it was not, that she wore short skirts and traveled by herself to Nablus to go to the cinema years ago when she was a young woman.

Sabrin's style stood out in al-Qarya because public behavior changed for many women in the 1970s. Many family photo albums showed women across the West Bank wearing short skirts or even sleeveless blouses in the 1960s and 1970s. By the 1980s and 1990s, however, many of these women started wearing head-coverings in public places or when being photographed, as did many of their daughters. Egyptian movies traced the changes quite clearly. In the 1950s, '60s, and '70s, they showed women dressed in gowns with exposed shoulders and arms. Some smoked cigarettes and drank alcohol. There were even belly dancers and passionate embraces between lovers. These sights rarely appeared in Arab movies of the 1980s and 1990s. Even the old movies, when broadcast on local Palestinian stations, were censored. The propriety of women in public settings was one example of the weakened status of secular styles and the recreation of a modern Islamic style, like the wearing of *hijab* (head-scarf). However, among Arab-Israelis, like Sabrin, styles increasingly resembled those of their Jewish-Israeli neighbors who followed European and North American fashion.

Later in the afternoon, I drove our guests back to their town. Once we were in the car and on our way, Sabrin offered me another cigarette. I declined, and she exclaimed, "Umm Samud is not here. Go ahead and smoke." She continued, "You'll like it with us in Tayiba. There is more freedom." Although we were speaking in Arabic, she used the Hebrew word *hofshi* for freedom.

In their town, Tayiba, I met Sabrin's and Umm Dawud's elderly parents and family. Umm Dawud's children were fifteen to thirty years old. The second eldest, a man in his late twenties named Khalid, was unmarried and still living at home. He was eager to become my pal and I made a few subsequent visits to hang out with him. On that first visit I told him what I was doing in the West Bank. It sounded horrible to him. He could not imagine how I lived there. "What do you have there? Stones and *hijab*."

Like his aunt, Khalid smoked continuously. Unlike his aunt, who smoked the Israeli brand Time, he smoked Kent. In the territories, to buy Marlboro, Kent, or Rothman indicated pretensions to wealth or bourgeois elegance at NIS 8–9 a pack. Those who truly aspired to international indicators chose to smoke Marlboro Lights, a very rare sight in the Tulkarm District, or sought out "real American Marlboros" that came tax-free on the black market, which I was often asked to authenticate by taste, which I could not do. Most men in the village and camp smoked Palestinian brand cigarettes because they were cheaper, NIS 4 or 5 a pack. The Israeli Time cigarettes were slightly more expensive, NIS 6–7, but much milder. Hand-rolled cigarettes, called Arabic smoke (*dukhan 'arabi*), were distinctly old-fashioned, most would say peasant (*fallah*), and were smoked by old men. Although it might seem trivial, this habit of smoking was filled with subtle markings of affiliation.[1]

I saw that he smoked in front of his mother and asked if he also smoked in

10. Men dancing at a village wedding, 1994.

front of his father. The question did not even seem to make sense to him, but he made it clear that he did. I asked if he thought it was respectful to refrain from smoking before his parents. He explained that, unlike the "old" ways of people in the West Bank, he had an open and free relationship with his parents. They did not mind if he smoked and he did not need to hide anything from them. "Do you smoke in front of your parents?" he asked me. I explained that my parents would be upset with me if they saw me smoking, merely because it is bad for my health. "But that isn't a question of respect, is it?" he asked. That night he took me out for beer and pizza, which I interpreted as something kindly done for my benefit, to make me comfortable by showing me his modern lifestyle.

A month later, on a December morning in 1994, I sat at the kitchen table with Umm Samud and her older sister Hajji Latifa, who was in from Jordan. We were preparing olives for pickling by poking them with a needle. Commenting on my continuing interest in food preparation, Umm Samud asked me if we made *hilba* in America. No, I told her. "What about *diwali . . . maqluba . . . malfuf . . . ?*" she continued. "No," I repeated, "we don't usually make Arabic food." Umm Samud started to say something, but she laughed, making her joke unintelligible to me. So as not to be impolite, Hajji Latifa repeated

11. Men dancing at the wedding with a tray of henna, 1994.

what Umm Samud had said, saying that if I married their relative Sabrin from over the Green Line she could cook those foods for me. Hajji Latifa explained, while shushing her sister Umm Samud not to laugh, that Umm Samud was only joking because they thought their cousin had been flirting with me and Umm Samud thought it hysterical. Umm Samud considered the woman completely inappropriate for me because she was more than twenty years my senior and uneducated. Commenting on the flirtation, as if to say I should make light of it, Hajji Latifa explained, "She is democratic. She has lived in Israel a long time. She is like you [in the West]. But we are strict (*muta'assibin*)." Hajji Latifa advised me that Islam is difficult, not like democracy. Umm Samud emphasized Hajji Latifa's point, saying how exceptional it was for me to sit with them alone. If Umm Samud had daughters I could not live in her home.

Umm Samud pointed to her adult nieces, 'Alia and 'A'isha, as models of appropriate behavior. 'Alia and 'A'isha, both in their early twenties in the mid-1990s, lived next door with their six younger siblings, their parents, maternal, aunt and maternal grandmother. 'Alia worked in a clothing workshop (discussed in Chapter 4) and 'A'isha was going to college. They came over to

12. Women making rolled grape leaves on the kitchen floor, 2000.

help Umm Samud with housework, especially chores like rolling stuffed cabbage or grape leaves. One or two evenings each week I sat with them and their family in their living room in winter and on their porch in the summer.

On several occasions I went into town with ʿAlia and ʿAʾisha, three of their youngest siblings, and one or two of Umm Samud's sons to "Family Night" at the tea garden. The event had to be scheduled in advance because they had to request permission from their father a few days beforehand. The tea garden was normally filled with young men drinking instant coffee with milk, playing cards, and smoking cigarettes, with only a small section closed off for families. On Thursday night (Friday is the day off in the Muslim world) the tea garden was closed to single men because it was "Family Night" and only families—men, women, and children—were allowed in. This was one of the few times when they could get out to "smell the air" without going to a wedding or funeral. They would get dressed up in a skirt and jacket outfit and elegant lace-edged *hijab*.

In the spring of 1995, after making two trips from the village to town to shuttle the whole group, we sat in the tea garden surrounded by families lounging and children running about. The three kids, ages six, eight, and twelve, bubbled with the excitement of their ice cream and cotton candy. We ordered sundaes and coffees, and I smoked a water pipe filled with sweet tobacco. After gobbling down their sugar, the children went to a playground energized for fun.

'Alia and 'A'isha watched everyone and commented on how particular women looked or what they were wearing. Several times they remarked how a woman had put on or taken off the *hijab*. I asked 'Alia and 'A'isha what made women change their customs that way. The personal choice of the individual was simultaneously their first answer, but engagement and marriage were the conditions they thought of when I pushed the question. I asked what they thought about the imperative for them to dress modestly in public and about the restrictions on their movement. 'A'isha responded by explaining that she did not feel restricted and that modesty of dress was an appropriate thing for everyone. I reminded her of occasions when she or her sisters were disappointed because they were forbidden to do things that were permissible for their brothers, like studying in a college more than an hour away by car, going with male cousins and siblings to the tea garden without permission in advance, or free choice of employment. 'A'isha asked me if my parents ever told me what I can and cannot do, either directly or indirectly. She emphasized that parents should make some decisions for their children, not just say they are adults when they get to be eighteen years old and let them make stupid mistakes. In addition to respecting her parents, 'A'isha explained to me that wearing *hijab* was completely her choice. She pointed out that two of her post-pubescent sisters never wore *hijab* and 'Alia only wore it in public, not in front of familiar visitors (like me) while at home. 'A'isha was the only one of her sisters to always wear it in front of men other than her brothers or father. She was also the only one of her sisters yet to complete a two-year college degree in business and accounting at al-Najah University. She explained that wearing *hijab* allowed her to move about publicly without encountering unsolicited attention from men. "How do you feel about living in a society where you must cover your head from men?" I asked. She said it had nothing to do with Arab or Islamic society; it was human nature with which she was contending. "Love is normal and natural, but we are not animals." Uncontrolled desire and immodesty of dress are against the Holy Qur'an because they have bad consequences in society. When I asked her to explain what kind of consequence, she told me she thought American women were not "free" because there were so many pictures of their naked bodies in films and magazines. She mentioned the epidemic of AIDS and other sexually transmitted diseases in the West implying that it is a consequence of promiscuity. I told her about anorexia and bulimia and the obsession with weight loss. When we seemed to agree that western women were fooled by an ideology of freedom that had nothing to do with happiness, ʿAʾisha smiled and moaned "God knows!" (*Bain Allah*), as if empathetically pondering the shared oppression of women no matter what people or country.

The negative characteristics of morality in the "West" described by ʿAʾisha emerged in many conversations. The use of the word "democracy" often marked the shape of this imagined "West." An old man used the word democracy to describe young people choosing marriage partners for themselves, rather than having them arranged within the *hamula* (clan). Umm Samud and Hajji Latifa used it in the kitchen in reference to their Arab-Israeli cousin Sabrin. Once Umm Samud used the term to describe an outburst of her son. After being nagged about house chores, Umm Samud's youngest son lost his temper and raised his voice to her. She was startled and to rebut without inciting she said to me with angry sarcasm, "You see, we are democratic in this house. We allow our children to speak like this. Democratic." The word was used as if it meant freedom from moral constraint, the opposite of their own customs, which they described as emphasizing generosity, honor, respect, and religion.

The cluster of behaviors and morals that distinguished Palestinians from the democracy of the "West," or even "Westernized" Palestinians, were lumped into a flexible category, sometimes described as customs and traditions (*ʿadat wa taqalid*), or as heritage (*turath*). Standardized material forms of Palestinian custom and tradition were easy to identify. The concepts were not only known, they were celebrated and put on display in schools and museums. At the Society for Family Restoration,[2] Jamʿiyat Inʿash al-Usra, in the West Bank town of al-Birah, a museum and folklore center were created to document and preserve Palestinian customs.[3] They published a journal called *Turath wa al-Mujtamaʿ* (Heritage and Society) focused on popular songs and dance, stories and sayings, medicines, foods and artifacts, and especially the need to identify this material (Kanaana 1986; al-Ghul 1992; Abu-Habda 1981, 1993; ʿAllush 1981, 1982) and teach it to Palestinian children (ʿAnani 1988). Their museum built to serve this purpose (ʿAbd al-Jabbar 1989) had a spectacular collection of embroidered dresses, or *thawbs*, sewn by women from nearby villages. The intricate floral and geometric motifs, hand stitched in bright colors, were testimonies to hours and hours of labor. Some carried a price tag of $1000. The other rooms of the museum displayed dioramas of mannequin men enjoying coffee and a *nargila* (water pipe), mannequin women grinding grain, sewing embroidery, caring for babies, and cooking. It was a picture of the past, of a peasant world. Other display cabinets exhibited costumes, musical instruments, cooking tools, farming tools, and documents from Mandate Palestine.

The museum displays emphasized, especially given the time and energy put into needlework, that the customs of peasant *women* were explicitly valorized by the national movement during the Intifada. Elite women's organizations like the Society for Family Restoration opened public spaces for women who had previously been confined to the private world of home and farm. Women had had an increasing presence in the national movement through much of the twentieth century (Augustin 1993; Giacaman and Johnson 1994; Giacaman and Odeh 1988; Hammami 1990; Hiltermann 1991; Jad 1990; Jawwad 1990; Peteet 1989; Rishmawi 1988; Sayigh 1989, 1983),[4] but during the Intifada women's production became acutely politicized. Because of their status as nurturing mothers, stories of women's participating in demonstrations, putting themselves between their sons (actual or figurative) and Israeli soldiers, and building barricades were repeated to emphasize how committed the Palestinian people were to end the occupation (Augustin 1993; Jad 1990; Jawwad 1990; Peteet 1991).

Relatively early in the Intifada, on March 8, 1988, a leaflet signed by "the Palestinian Women in the Occupied Territories" outlined several important steps to achieve the goal of national independence (see Jad 1990). Central was the development of the home economy, which advocated self-reliance in the production of food and clothing and a general return to the land. The leaflet called for the creation of popular committees to help in this effort by holding lectures on food storage and preservation, caring for plants and animals, and creating women's production cooperatives. The home economy was entrusted by the Unified National Leadership of the Uprising to women and thus incorporated them into the national struggle. The most visible change brought by this campaign was the virtual disappearance of Israeli-made bread. Israeli bread was eliminated partly by the days and weeks of curfews that forced women to buy sacks of flour instead of bread and also by the ideological imperative to boycott Israel and return to home production. The economic aspects of the Uprising began to fail by 1990 and 1991, but their remarkable ability to maintain it for about three years was partly due to their abilities to return to the home economy.

Umm Samud's insistence on continuing her labors, despite the availability of modern conveniences, was partly motivated by her desire to save money to pay for her children's education and marriages. But these activities in the home, which she pursued to the point of physical pain and exhaustion, were intimately wrapped in and echoed by the struggle of many West Bank Palestinians. We all (her sons, husband, neighbors, and I) loved and appreciated her for it. Like the Arabic journal from the Society, which she never read, Umm Samud said people were not doing things the way they used to and she resisted the change.

'Adil's and Amal's *Badal*

In a double wedding, called a *badal* (what anthropologists called a sister exchange) 'Adil and Amal, a brother and sister pair, married Mahir and Muna, also a brother and sister pair. Such a marriage exchange had precedent in Arab history, there was a word for it after all, but old women back in al-Qarya expressed their disapproval of such arrangements. If there are problems in one marriage, it is likely to cause trouble in the second, they told me. Despite such general objections, this particular marriage was openly approved of because of the age of the brides and grooms: the brides were approaching thirty and both grooms were well over thirty.

The unique aspect of this *badal* was that 'Adil and Amal were West Bank Palestinians, while Mahir and Muna were Arab-Israelis. The two families were actually from the same village, but the village suffered the rare (but not singular) phenomenon of being split into two by the armistice partition of 1949. The West Bank side was called Kafr East, the Israeli side Kafr West. After the cease-fire in 1949, the two sides were divided by a barbed-wire fence that ran through a gully and became a no-man's-land about twenty-five meters wide. The fence was removed after the June 1967 war and a road was rebuilt reuniting the two sides. The village was not redivided by a fence or checkpoint when the closures began in 1993, so it was easy to cross in the mid-1990s. There were, however, checkpoints on every road out of Kafr West going into Israel, making it hard to get much further. While the village was no longer geographically partitioned, the villagers were still divided according to those with or without Israeli citizenship. The families in the West became Arab-Israelis in 1949 and remained so, while those in Kafr East remained "resident" Palestinians without the rights of citizenship—without the blue ID.

'Adil's and Muna's wedding celebrations were held near his house in the eastern, West Bank side of the village. The first night in Kafr East was the henna night. It was held at the home of the mother's family, not by tradition but because they had a large house suitable for the event. Inside the house, the bride and the women danced and sang accompanied by two hand drums that women took turns playing. Outside in the street in front of the house, men sat in rented plastic seats and danced accompanied by a hand drum and a *yagh-*

lul (reed flute) playing music called *shibabi*. A man sang *hadaya*, that is, he sang-chanted clever verse praising the groom, his family, and national political leaders. Most of the young and some of the older men arranged themselves in a circle, stepping and clapping to the rhythm of the music and singing a chorus to the *hadaya*'s song. When the flute player and singer took a break, a cassette tape was amplified over the singer's microphone and the young men started free-form dancing characterized by gyrating hips and waving hands. *Hadaya* and dancing continued for hours, punctuated by occasional sessions of young men dancing the *dabka*. Many young men were unable to dance the steps of *dabka*, but this was the centerpiece of the dancing at the henna night. Arm in arm, a group of men stamped out the complex rhythms led by the *luwah*. The different styles of dance and versions of *dabka* were marked by local variation and those idiosyncrasies were explicit markers of local custom, usually in regard to other villages. As a foreigner visiting villages of the West Bank, dancing at these weddings was the best way to become acquainted with my peers.

The culmination of this first night of celebration was when the henna was brought out on a tray decorated with flowers. I had seen henna carried by the brothers or close friends of the groom, but in this case the women of the groom's family joined the celebration, with the mother of the family dancing with the henna tray on her head. 'Adil, the groom, sat surrounded by friends and family, while his friend painted his hand with henna. Taking a small amount of greenish-brown mud-like henna from the tray, thinning it with a bit of water, and using a match or a needle like a quill, the groom's hand was decorated with stars, zigzags, valentines and the first letter of both his and his bride's name, the English letters "A" and "M." When I asked why English letters were used, the response was that it made better decoration. The mound of henna left on the tray became available to anyone who wanted to decorate or dye his or her hand.

The following day I was volunteered to take Amal the bride, her mother, and the younger sister of her soon to be Arab-Israeli husband into Israel to a beauty salon. This was my job because my car had Israeli license plates and because a Jew with an American passport and a carload of women was unlikely to encounter trouble from the military. The sister of the Arab-Israeli groom accompanied us as our guide. At the checkpoint out of the village, the soldier looked puzzled at my name and nationality, but did not bother to ask the women for their identity cards. In minutes we were on the main highway running down the coast of Israel.

Mahir's younger sister led us to the beauty parlor and told me to come back after two hours. More than two hours later, we all went to a park, where the bride from Kafr East and the groom from Kafr West were photographed among the flowers, plants, and tourists visiting Israel. Amal wore a classical white wedding gown, a tiara headdress, and lots of makeup—a white base, bright red blush, heavy black eyeliner, and mascara. Mahir, her groom, wore a black suit and narrow tie. I followed the couple and photographer around the park, watching the bride's mother attend to her daughter's appearance.

As the photographer snapped away, I spoke with our guide, a twenty-one-year-old accounting student wearing *hijab*, who asked how a Jewish American could live among West Bankers. She asked if I found them too strict (*muta'assibin*). I was surprised by the question, and asked her how a woman like herself, who was wearing *hijab*, could think West Bankers were *too* strict. She said that *hijab* was part of her religion, but it had nothing to do with the old customs that oppress women. She thought that most young women in the West Bank would not speak casually with me as she was doing. She said that she was sure the bride's mother would report to all the women in East Kafr that we had been talking and that they would suspect that she wanted to marry me. She pointed out that this was, of course, impossible given our difference in religion. Amusingly, later that afternoon, only a few minutes after I returned with the bride and her mother to East Kafr, a member of the family teased me saying that the woman I spoke to wanted to marry me.

A little after noon, the friends of the groom 'Adil from Kafr East gathered at the home of his close friend. A barber shaved 'Adil's face and cut his hair, while the men played a drum, sang, clapped, and danced. I was once brought into a bathroom where the groom, who was a friend of mine, was standing naked in a tub, being bathed by two of his friends. They were washing him roughly, punctuating the scrubbing by slapping him hard on the back. They invited me to slap him on the back, but I did not understand why. I thought they were just trying to deal with the uncomfortableness of our friend's nakedness by being rough and hitting him. While that might partially be the case, the "real" reason they were slapping him hard on the back was to get the sperm going so he could impregnate his bride. I did not get it at the time, not yet having learned the word for sperm.

When the barber finished, and the groom was dressed in a black suit with a thin red tie, his friends and family escorted him to his home. The procession moved through the dusty streets under the hot sun, led by a truck that carried loudspeakers and amplification. Two men sang *hadaya* as the procession moved along. The men followed the truck through the village, clapping in rhythm and singing with the *hadaya*, "ya halali ya maali." They walked in two rows with a path between them through which the groom slowly advanced. 'Adil was riding a horse and holding an umbrella decorated with ribbons and glitter to protect him from the sun. Women and girls followed the groom, play-ing a drum and singing him praises. They sang a completely different repertoire and style from the men. The groom heard the interweaving of the two songs.

When ʿAdil arrived home from the bathing it was time to make the actual exchange of brides. Some phone calls were made to the other side of the village, and then the two grooms and their respective parties each formed a proces-sion of about ten cars, and crossed the village to the house of their respective brides. The brides and their mothers rode back with the grooms to his house, but the trip was not direct. Each procession circled its side of the village at least three times, honking their horns and singing. The cars carrying the brides and grooms were decorated with ribbons. The lead car of each procession held the video camera men who photographed the whole thing. The drivers following these processions played leap frog, passing each other trying to be the first car after the bride. I witnessed several accidents during my fieldwork, two at one wedding. It was a dangerous and insane game that I sternly refused to play, to the disappointment of my friends.

After the couple were delivered to their new home they were left alone for the afternoon and lunch was served to the visitors. Hummus and pickles were set out on the tables, and individual portions of the customary yogurt beef stew (*labaniya*) with pine nuts on rice were passed around on plastic plates. Men were rushed into the house, quickly served a plate, a piece of pita bread, and a can of soda. There was little formality. Men ate the food, washed their hands, congratulated the parents of the groom (and bride), and left so that the next table of men could come in and eat. As a foreign guest, a second serving of food was urged upon me.

In the evening, the party returned to the street in front of the groom's house. The celebration area was decorated with colored lights strung from houses and electrical poles and a large floodlamp. Over a hundred rented plas-tic chairs were set up around an area cleared for dancing. A "modern" Arabic band with electric bass, organ, full drum set, and Arabic hand drum was hired at a cost of between $1000 and $2000. Other than the cost of food, and gifts of gold to the bride, the band was the single largest expense of a wedding. They performed on an elevated stage decorated with flowers, ribbons, Palestinian flags, and pictures of PLO officials like Yasser Arafat and Abu Jihad. Weddings in the street had stopped during the Intifada because the Palestinians felt pub-lic celebrations were disrespectful to the families of martyrs and prisoners and such weddings were easy targets for military repression. They began again in the summer of 1992, and political decorations and themes were common.

Boys from the groom's family brought around trays of punch and ciga-rettes, young men and teenagers danced in front of the stage, and older men sat around watching. 'Adil sat on a special cushioned armchair on stage most of the night while his friends and relatives lined up to go up onto the stage, one by one, shake his hand, give him some kisses, give him some money, and have their (video) photo taken together. The money was pressed into the hand of the groom, pinned on him, hung around his neck, or made into a crown and put on his head.

As the Israeli military allowed the Palestinian Authority to return, firearms appeared more frequently at weddings. In many Arab countries from Morocco to Iraq and Syria to Yemen, men fired repeatedly into the air to express joy, like Chinese setting off fireworks. Because having a gun was a serious offense in the West Bank under the Israeli military occupation, a gun's appearance in public weddings still caused quite a stir. In Jordan, to discourage the practice the government ran public-service announcements about how women and children, watching from the windows and balconies above, have been accidentally shot.

I do not know whether there was gunplay that night at the wedding celebration in Kafr East, because I went to the other party, to Amal's and Mahir's, held in a banquet hall in a nearby town in Israel. I took female relatives of the bride from Kafr East because men from Kafr East could have been arrested if they were discovered by the police on the way to or from the party in Israel.

The Arab-Israeli wedding celebration was quite different. There were at least two hundred people in the outdoor facility, seated at round cloth covered tables. At one end of the hall was a stage and a dance floor. The band was an electric Arabic ensemble, similar to those hired in the West Bank. There were chairs for the bride and groom, who both sat receiving congratulations and envelopes from their guests. The stage was decorated with streamers, balloons, and plants, but there were no Palestinian (or Israeli) flags, no pictures of any political leaders or signs of political affiliation. We were served several courses by waiters. The food was catered by the hall and resembled the food served in the West Bank, but it was the canned version. The presentation of the food was much more formal, as it would be in an American or European hotel or restaurant.

Umm Samud warned and prepared me for more formal dress. It was the only time I wore a tie all year. In the West Bank only the groom dressed in a suit, but at this celebration many of the men wore suits or sport jackets with ties. The women were dressed in a variety of styles. Some wore sequined evening gowns, high heels, and fancy hairdos. Others wore conservative European styles, and some, mostly older women, wore embroidered Palestinian *thawbs* with their hair covered. A small group of young women wore the modern *hijab* and another group of young women wore the embroidered Palestinian *thawb* with their hair down.

Here women and men not only sat together, they even danced together in public. I believe only married couples and close relatives danced together in mixed gender pairs, but even this was rare in the village across the Green Line. There were times when men took to the dance floor and attempted to dance the *dabka*, but they were very weak and seemed to know only a few basic steps. After the men, a group of young women began dancing the traditional dance; they were more practiced than the men. A number of the young *dabka*-dancing women dressed in embroidered Palestinian *thawbs*.

I sat at a table with guests from other Arab-Israeli towns. They were astonished or amused as I answered questions about my identity and where I lived. The man who was leading the questioning told me I should move to an Arab-Israeli village so I could see how they differed from West Bankers. I asked what the differences were. He said it would be much easier to live among Arab-Israelis: they are much calmer, they do not throw rocks, and they are more modern, he explained, using the Hebrew term *moderni*.

I asked him about the preservation of customs and traditions in Israel and the West Bank. He told me that Arab-Israelis are modern in the world outside and traditional inside the home. "Traditional like the West Bank?" I asked. He explained that women from the West Bank were more traditional and it was good to marry them. My adopted cousins in the village had told me that West Bank women had better reputations for chastity, which made them more desirable for marriage,[5] so I pushed him on how West Bank women were more "traditional" (*taqlidi*). He said they did not want to work outside the home as much as Israeli women and they used the old ways in cooking, especially bread. He also explained that it was really good that young men from the West Bank marry women from Arab Israel so they can get the blue ID card and go to work. He said it was unfortunate that as soon as some of them get their blue ID they leave their wives. He suggested that this family were willing to marry their daughter to the West Bank man because the sister exchange gave them assurance that she would not be mistreated or abandoned.

During the closures, marrying Arab-Israeli women from the other side of the Green Line was a reasonable strategy to escape one's status as a West Bank resident. Marrying to get an Israeli ID allowed men to cross the checkpoints and work in the Israeli economy. In 1990 the idea of a West Bank man seeking out an Israeli ID might have been seen as treasonous. In the first place, Palestinians were seeking to throw off the yoke of Israeli oppression and decidedly wanted their own state with Palestinian identity cards and passports. In the second place, Arab-Israeli women generally had a bad reputation and few men would have subjected themselves to the possible ridicule that would result from such a marriage, unless the woman was from a well-known and respectable family or else very young, sixteen or seventeen years of age. By 1995, however, the desire to marry across the border was common.

My friend Munir sought a marriage across the Green Line in order to get the blue ID. He knew that with his language skills (he spoke English and Hebrew) and wide experience he could make NIS 150 working a ten- to twelve-hour day in Israel, three times what he made in the West Bank. He met a woman he liked. He explained that the marriage made sense because he had known the family for several years, he and his fiancee were the same age, and they were friends. At the age of twenty-nine, she was saved from becoming too old to marry anyone other than an old man. He knew some people would gossip that his fiancee was not a virgin, because she was an Israeli from Tayiba, but he scoffed at such talk. However, the marriage arrangements were problematic because Arab-Israelis living close to the Green Line had become skeptical of the intentions of men from the West Bank. They suspected that the West Bank man would leave his Arab-Israeli wife after he acquired Israeli papers. The bride's family's suspicions of the groom's ulterior motive caused some Arab-Israeli families to set the traditional Islamic prenuptial divorce payment, *mu'achir*, very high at NIS 20–50,000, to discourage the husband from divorcing his wife. Munir agreed to a prenuptial divorce payment of NIS 40,000, got married, and moved to Tayiba. He wanted to raise his family back in his West Bank village, but his wife refused, fearing both the customs that would limit her behavior and the violence of an ongoing Occupation that would threaten her children.

There is always creativity and random chance shaping complex human behaviors like weddings, but anyone living in or visiting the West Bank or Arab-Israeli communities during the 1990s could have observed weddings similar to those of the two couples described above. Some in the West Bank, especially those who had lived abroad and returned with the Palestinian Authority, were more likely to resemble Israeli Arabs in their wedding and gender customs. They often saw themselves as more worldly and modern than the West Bankers they returned to rule. There were Arabs in Israel who rejected Euro-American styles. Arab-Israelis who refused the metropolitan ceremonies modeled on marketing and fashion usually chose the international Islamic alternative, rather than the more provincial Palestinian customs. Of course every celebration, every repertoire of customs was, to some degree, unique. My point is not to create a taxonomy, but to describe one particular axis of difference that is flexibly used: modern or traditional. In the West Bank, wedding customs made claims on the notion of tradition. These claims of affiliation were central to participation in the event. In the Arab-Israeli wedding, emphasis was put on the modern, on affiliation with European and American styles. There were gestures to tradition, the men did a weak *dabka*, some women wore traditional *thawb*s, but these were spices added to a generic catered wedding.

Customs in an Arab "Border Village"

There was a debate, years ago, between two of anthropology's most distinguished theorists, Abner Cohen and Talal Asad, over the politics of custom and the customs of politics in an Arab border village inside Israel before the 1967 War. Cohen argued that traditional family structures were revived despite the "modernizing" influence of Israel because conflict between Israel and the Arab states made life tenuous. In this conflict, the clan or *hamula* "provided a social mechanism for the preservation of Arab traditional values and for the maintenance of political and social autonomy of the village" (Cohen 1969: 173). Asad (1972), however, argued that Cohen overlooked the coercive effects of the Israeli military in manipulating family and village structures. Asad suggested that the military has propped up the *hamula* as a way to counter the emergence of Palestinian nationalism. He indicated that the army attempted to manipulate these kinship structures in order to reinforce paternalism, isolation, and cooptation (see also Ein-Gil and Finkelstein 1978; Lustick 1980; Wood 1993). This debate points to the potential paradox of custom that develops *within and against* multiple inequalities and oppressions (Sider 1993).

The differences in women's custom and self-presentation between West Bank Palestinians and their Arab-Israeli relatives across the Green Line were not simply a result of the Israeli Arabs' "acculturation" or the "diffusion" of Western culture. While that might have been a reasonable hypothesis in 1968, by the 1990s West Bankers had been exposed to Israeli bosses, soldiers, settlers, and the great diversity of Israeli life for over thirty years. Customs drawn from existing material and performative knowledge persist and are transformed by struggles in daily life. As Gerald Sider described them,

customs do things—they are not abstract formulations of, or searches for, meanings, although they may convey meaning. Customs are clearly connected to, and rooted in, the material and social realities of life and work, although they are not simply derivative from, or reexpressions of, these realities. Customs may provide a context in which people can do things that it would be more difficult to do directly; they may provide a context in which to coordinate and coadjust a multiplicity of emotions and interests; and especially, as the loci for international, forward-looking actions, they may keep the need for collective action, collective adjustment of interests, and collective expression of feelings and emotions within the terrain and the domain of the coparticipants in a custom, serving as a boundary to exclude outsiders. (Sider 1986: 94; see also Bourdieu 1984)

The repertoire of customs, or more precisely what are called *'adat wa taqalid* (customs and traditions), tend to differentiate West Bank Palestinians from their Arab-Israeli relatives. Like the geopolitical border, these customs divide and connect. They can be gestures of common affiliation (like the rice and sugar the cousins from Israel brought), they can structure difference and inequality (like Munir's *mu'achir* agreement), or they can define dignity and independence against outside oppressors and exploiters (like Umm Samud's home skills). The choices Palestinians made about how and when to use customs as signifiers of their modernity or their traditionalism were shaped partly by the conditions of living on one side of the border or the other.

Those with Israeli ID cards tended to favor an image of themselves as modern and sought to distinguish themselves from their cousins across the border on that basis. Several said that I, a "modern" American man, would be more comfortable living among them. The Arab-Israeli sponsored wedding celebration was shaped by the styles of Israeli or Euro-American weddings. This signification of modernity reflected their own struggles within the state of Israel to establish their full rights as citizens, which they have never enjoyed. As second class citizens, their claim of modernity was a claim to be treated equally and on parity with Jewish Israelis.

Those in the West Bank, on the other hand, did not have Israeli IDs, and unlike their Arab-Israeli neighbors who were made citizens and given some benefits by the state, most West Bankers experienced severe exploitation in Israel and increasing political violence by the state. For these West Bankers, peasant custom served to confront colonial assaults in several ways.

Customs were part of a practical struggle against the larger system of exploitation. The customs of Palestinian womanhood, both their costume and their home craft practices, protected them from extensive commodification in the market and stood against the super-exploitation suffered by West Bank men. Protecting women and women protecting themselves from the excessive exploitation they witnessed in Israel was a way of putting a boundary on capital's insatiable consumption. Customs that valued and celebrated uncommodified women's labor protected them against uncontrolled capitalist exploitation. This created barriers for women who *wanted* to work, most of whom were from the professional middle class, but working classes of semi-proletarianized peasants and refugees were saved from the extensive exploitation in the market. All but the poorest women have become cleaners and agricultural workers in Israeli production, because they are morally restricted to tasks of household reproduction and to one (nonprofessional) option for employment in the West Bank: sewing. The uncommodified tasks of household reproduction, women's customs, were also the resources that carried Palestinians through the curfews and closures of the Intifada and have subsidized the households of Palestinian men who work for "undocumented" wages in Israel. Simultaneously, customs created a compliant pool of workers for textile production.

Ted Swedenburg (1990, 1991) argues that settler-colonial activities, including "(1) the conquest of Palestinian land, (2) the preservation-dissolution of Palestinian villages, and (3) the denial of the legitimacy of Palestinian nationalism," were crucial determinants of Palestinian characteristic uses of the peasant as signifier (1990: 19):

the peasant's representative power was acquired through an erasure of internal differences and a forgetting of social antagonisms. As the *fellah* was fashioned into a signifier of national resistance, he/she ceased to evoke conflicts with landlords, moneylenders, and the state officials. (Swedenburg 1991: 169)

The image of the peasant was "generalized into a homogeneous composite" and "sanitized" in order to be widely acceptable (Swedenburg 1990: 25).[6] Consequently, peasant custom "unifies by cutting across differences based on class, sect, region and kinship" 24); "papers over or denies internal contradictions" (25); and "cover[s] over horizontal differences based on class and gender inequalities" (25). The *fallah*, or peasant, was "made the symbolic representative of the cultural and historical continuity of the Palestinian people. Their traditional lifestyle was seen to encapsulate the shared values deemed worthy of preservation" (1991: 168).

Customs worked as an expression of dignity. Customs prohibited "proper" women from becoming Western styled sex/advertising objects. One of the most powerful images generating communal identity for West Bankers was that of an immoral, promiscuous, and alienated society in the "West." Uncontrolled desire, immodesty of dress, pictures of naked women in films and magazines, all ubiquitous in the streets of cities in Israel, as in Europe or America, celebrated the consumption of the thin, vulnerable female body. The absence of proper custom indicated moral depravity and the breakdown of community. In a sense, the Palestinian community under occupation dignified "its identity by projecting beyond its own borders the sexual practices or gender behaviors it deems abhorrent" (Parker, Russo, Sommer, and Yaeger 1992: 10; see also Bowman 1989).

Customs in the West Bank, as in the refugee camps of Lebanon (Peteet 1993), usually depended upon Palestinian women as the bearers of "authentic" Palestinian culture. This was similar to other nationalisms that emerged as movements based on tradition and community embodied partly in gender in which images of women as part of home and hearth were valorized as representations of the nation (Chatterjee 1993: 69; Werbner and Yuval-Davis 1999).[7] Challenging "patriarchy and tradition" was not, however, part of the agenda because women did not want to open an internal front (Augustin 1993; Jad 1990; Jawwad 1990; Peteet 1991; Giacaman and Johnson 1994). Despite the powerful images and stories of peasant women struggling in the national cause, as in other settings (Kandiyoti 1991; Moghadam 1994; Badran 1995), women's daily life concerns were subordinated to the imperatives of a reconstructed patriarchal nationalist elite.[8] Men were allowed to become "modern," but the nationalist imperative to preserve customs and traditions became a restrictive burden for women.

Customs primarily distinguish the local from the larger, family from the onslaught of capitalism, Palestinians from the Zionist occupation. Like the porous geopolitical border that included Palestinians economically even as it excluded them politically, customs include and exclude in partial, incomplete ways. Customs can serve to cross the borders as well, to negotiate marriage, or, as described in the next chapter, to connect the homeland to the diaspora.

7. Diaspora and Homeland

Abu Thaki and Amman

In the late fall of 1994, Umm Samud's youngest son, twenty-one-year old Taysir, stayed up late running around packing and waiting for a 3:00 a.m. shared taxi to take him to the bridge to Jordan to visit his mother's older sister and brother, Hajji Latifa and Abu Thaki. Over and over, he excitedly sang the same lyric of an Arabic pop song. He looked at me with a tremendous smile and said, "Tomorrow I will sleep in Hajji's apartment!" Ahed, Taysir's older brother, teased Taysir that his excitement was because his aunt, Hajji Latifa, spoiled him with presents like clothes and pocket money.

Ahed and I sat at the kitchen table and watched while Taysir, his mother Umm Samud, and father Abu Samud packed nearly seventy kilos of food in boxes and bags to carry to Hajji Latifa and Abu Thaki. All the food was home processed by Umm Samud, and most was home grown: green peas, pole beans, okra, green barley (*friqi*), and *za'tar* were sewn into fabric bags; grape leaves and pickled olives stuffed into plastic bottles; white goat cheese sealed in gallon sized aluminum tins; oranges and lemons packed in cardboard boxes; and blocks of olive oil soap wrapped in plastic bags. The aunt living in Jordan had grown, working sons with greater incomes than Umm Samud's family, so I asked Ahed why they were sending all this food. Were these staples more dear in Jordan? Ahed said they were actually cheaper there, but outside Palestine food does not have the same good taste. Above all else, the bundles of food Taysir delivered to his aunt and uncle were a testament to Umm Samud's labor. She was sending her siblings her time and her commitment. She said it would be shameful for her son to arrive at his aunt's or uncle's home in Amman without gifts. Umm Samud sent her garden labors to her siblings in Amman as an act of devotion and a petition for support, and as a taste of Palestine crossed the river, Umm Samud reminded her siblings that she is still under the occupation.

At the departure station outside the town of Jericho, Taysir was not the only one weighed down with gifts of food to relatives in Jordan. Palestinian travelers arrived from across the West Bank to board special buses to the bridge crossing carrying 2-, 3-, and 4-gallon containers of olive oil, cartons of oranges, and other home produced edible goods. Those coming from Jordan before the mid-1990s were not allowed to pass with any food. Returning Palestinians usually brought manufactured goods, especially clothing and shoes, that were less expensive in Jordan. Of course, if they carried too many and they got caught, they paid the Israeli tariffs, which were often as high as 70 percent on clothing, or surrendered the items.

Despite the official state of war between Israel and the Arab world, the bridge to Jordan remained opened even after the Israeli occupation began in 1967. "No formal Israeli administrative body planned, initiated or discussed a policy allowing travel between the two sides of the river" (Gazit 1995: 184). Soon after the June 1967 War, a Palestinian produce truck tried to cross the river, but it was abandoned when Israeli soldiers opened fire. By mid-summer, Israeli officials realized that about 80,000 tons of produce would spoil, so "using General Security Service Intelligence Branch/Special Task channels, word was put out to the local population that the "Askar" (army) would allow the passage of agricultural produce to the East Bank" (185). Soon West Bankers began approaching the military liaisons requesting permission to travel to and from Jordan. About 2,000 exit permits a month were given at first, without limitations on departures from Gaza (189–90).

By July 1967, agricultural produce began to cross to the East Bank; on July 16 bus service began between Gaza, Hebron, and Ramallah; on August 27 the departure and return of students abroad was authorized; on September 6 the departure and return of workers abroad was authorized; by October and November the Allenby and Damiya Bridges were rebuilt over the Jordan River; on December 13 importation of goods from Jordan was allowed in accordance with Israeli customs and tariff regulations (see Gazit 1995). On April 26, 1968 local residents were allowed to submit requests on behalf of relatives abroad to visit the West Bank, and by the summer of 1968, 12,574 summer visitors crossed the bridge. These crossings were allowed by the Israeli military government because they made Palestinians more acquiescent to the occupation and subsidized the Israeli administrative budgets. Palestinians were allowed to export their vegetables and to import funds from their relatives in the Gulf.

Before the peace treaty between Israel and Jordan and the interim agreement with the Palestinian Authority, the civilian crossing was a crowded bureaucratic headache with long waits at the bridge, intimidating searches, confiscations, and detentions. Since the agreements procedures at the bridge became easier. Israelis, Jordanians, and foreigners crossed at new bridges in the north and south, while Palestinians continued to cross at the Allenby bridge near Jericho. However, after the arrival of the Palestinian Authority, Palestinians were dealt with on the West Bank side by Palestinian officials overseen by Israelis who were not to be seen, according to the Israeli-Jordanian peace treaty. Ultimately, the bridge was still controlled by Israel. Young men were still likely to face questions about their political sympathies and activities, only they faced Palestinian officials working with Israelis. The Palestinian Authority has detained and turned over "wanted" people to the Israelis. The trip did, however, become easier. By the summer of 1996, the hours of the Hussein-Allenby Bridge crossing were expanded from early morning until late at night and the lines were reduced significantly, except during holiday seasons.

By the mid-1990s, the crossing had become easy enough that Hajji Latifa, Umm Samud's older sister, was able to spend a few months of the year with her son and his family in Saudi Arabia, a few months in her apartment in Amman near her other son, and a few months in the West Bank village with her sister. Umm Samud had no daughters, so she usually worked alone in the house unless 'Alia or 'A'isha came by to help. But when Hajji Latifa came to visit, it filled Umm Samud's days with conversation and caring comfort. Umm Samud rarely traveled to Jordan, but her children made the trip with relative frequency.

Hajji Latifa left the village in the 1950s when she got married and moved to the larger West Bank town of Nablus. She and her husband taught school. Her husband died when the children were young, so in the 1970s, when the sons left home to pursue education and employment in Jordan, she soon followed. Hajji Latifa moved into her own apartment in Suwaylla, a mostly Palestinian part of Greater Amman. Just a few meters from her building was a mini-market called "Tulkarm Store," obviously owned (or at least named) by someone from her home region.

Her sons were both married with children. One lived and worked in Amman; the other became a successful engineer in Saudi Arabia. Hajji Latifa's son in Saudi Arabia was a generous man who never seemed to refuse any request made by his mother on behalf of Umm Samud or her children. He contributed significantly to their standard of living and even "loaned" the youngest several thousand Jordanian dinars to buy a car. Because of her sons, Hajji Latifa has been an important financial pillar to Umm Samud's household. Hajji Latifa's eldest son was also critical in funding the marriages of two of Umm Samud's sons in the late 1990s. He purchased their gas oven, refrigerator, microwave, dishwasher, clothes washer and dryer, television, VCR, and assorted other appliances.

Abu Thaki, Umm Samud's older brother, left the West Bank in 1956 when he was a young man. He was working near the village as a schoolteacher, but had aspirations beyond the agricultural hinterland in which he lived. Abu Thaki moved to the East Bank where he taught for a few years. Eventually, he applied to college in America; he was accepted, received a visa, and left in 1960. With his own savings and help from his father and family in the village, like his sister Umm Samud who sent him the money she earned as a seamstress, Abu Thaki moved to Washington state, where he attended a junior college for two years and then completed his B.S. in engineering at a state university. After nine years in America, he returned to Jordan with an engineering degree, fluency in English, a smart head on his shoulders, and the same disciplined character he left with. Abu Thaki established a construction business in Amman and married a woman from a family whose village of origin neighbored al-Qarya.

Abu Thaki and Hajji Latifa visited from Jordan in September 1994. Abu Thaki brought his daughter, Shakra, and her two children, a two-year-old girl and an infant boy. Shakra, like all Abu Thaki's children, was born and grew up in Amman. When she married she moved with her husband to the Gulf; she had not been to the West Bank in years, mainly because of the Intifada. Her baby boy had to be registered and physically present in the West Bank in order to obtain his "legal residence" papers from the Israeli authorities. If this was not done, Abu Thaki explained with disgust, he would only be allowed to enter as a foreign tourist and not as a returning Palestinian from the diaspora.

Abu Thaki and Shakra expressed polite skepticism about my research project soon after we met. Abu Thaki and I sat on the porch of Umm Samud's house eating breakfast together, scooping up olive oil, hummus, fried eggs, and homemade jam with pieces of Umm Samud's home baked bread. He said to me in his perfect English, "What are you going to write? That Palestinians eat with their hands and use different kinds of toilets?" Most adults in the village encouraged me to write about their customs and traditions ('adat wa taqalid), but Abu Thaki very critically and specifically asked if cultural anthropology of that sort did not reproduce the image of Palestinians as primitives, only to help the Zionists in the end. Shakra, too, asked if I thought I could ever get at what Palestinians really think, especially since there must have been suspicion about me being a Jew.

On the one hand, they expressed a fear that I might write in a derogatory manner about their poor relatives who continued to struggle so hard. On the other hand, they made it clear that their lives were not like their cousins'. On separate occasions they both mentioned that villagers were "simple" people, implying that their own outlook was more cosmopolitan. Abu Thaki and I spoke in English together, unfortunately making our conversation separate and private from almost everyone around us, certainly from his siblings. Shakra, too, not only spoke English, but managed to raise children in the Gulf who spoke English. Her two-year-old child kept asking for processed foods, "American" cheese, toasted cereal, and apple juice, which were familiar at their home in the Gulf but unavailable in the village.

Although firmly settled on the East Bank as a Jordanian citizen and successful businessman, Abu Thaki maintained close ties with his sister, brothers, and their children in the West Bank. In the early 1980s, Abu Thaki began to build a house in the village on a portion of the land he and his siblings inherited. He hired his brother-in-law Abu Samud, who with the help of his sons did the structural part of the building. Other workers were contracted by Abu Samud to finish the floor tiles, windows, electrical wiring, plumbing, and a very prestigious and expensive stone facade. The first phase of building, a ground floor with two bedrooms, kitchen, bath, and living room, was finished in 1984, and basic furnishings were bought. The house sat empty most of the year, except the week or two each summer when Abu Thaki visited.

Umm Samud's dedication to her brother was expressed not only in the homemade products she sent, but also in her care for his house. Before Abu Thaki visited from Jordan, Umm Samud cleaned the empty house in preparation, washed the dust off the kitchenware that had been hidden from robbers under the beds, laundered the linens and made the beds, and had her son and me carry the gas oven back from her kitchen to theirs. After Abu Thaki and his wife left, Umm Samud returned to pack the linens and kitchenware and cover the furniture and mattresses. Umm Samud took responsibility for caring for the house and regularly emphasized her dedication to her brother. She even named one of her sons after him. She told me repeatedly how she worked tirelessly as a seamstress to send him money in the United States when he was a student.

Abu Thaki's reasons for building the house were not completely transparent to me. He wanted a vacation home where his family could live while they visited the village for a few weeks each summer. He spoke of a day when his children would all be on their own and he would be able to retire, but he expressed doubt that he will ever move back. Perhaps he was claiming his inheritance vis-à-vis his siblings. The land his father left the five children was not yet divided by demarcation. However, there were already five houses built on the land and the number of claims grew as the grandchildren came of age. Perhaps by building the house Abu Thaki also invested in his own prestige in the village. The stone facade was an impressive testament to his success. It is as if the house legitimated his absence. Maybe building the home reconciled his relationship to the place of his birth, a place that has become so politicized. He was a pragmatic man, not a polemic one, but he did not want to abandon his claim to be and have part of Palestine. Building a home, even if he never lives in it, was a way of connecting himself financially and emotionally to the village and the land of Palestine. Of course, for Palestinians there is, unfortunately, always the possibility that they will be forced to return.

In the summer of 1995, Abu Thaki's eldest son, Thaki, visited the village for the first time in years. He visited his uncles, aunts, and cousins, but soon seemed bored with village life. He complained that there was nothing to do; his friends from home were not there. He was a teenager from the suburbs visiting his relatives on the farm. He wanted to take my car and go to the beach in Israel. I asked if he ever thought about moving back to the village, and he asked me if I were crazy; England or America maybe, but not the village.

Abu Harab and Kuwait

'Alia and 'A'isha, their younger siblings, and their parents, Abu and Umm Harab, suffered along with many Palestinians during the Gulf War and were forced into exile. I spent many evenings with their family, and Abu Harab was always eager to talk. One of his favorite topics was remembering his life back in Kuwait. In the West Bank Abu Harab's life was difficult in comparison with his memories of what he had struggled for in Kuwait

Unlike Jordan, in the early days after the creation of Israel, Kuwait was not an easy place to go and work. Umm Samud's eldest brother died in an attempt to reach Kuwait in 1951. The family says that he was taken into the desert by local Bedouin, robbed, and abandoned, and his body was never recovered.[1] But by 1958, agreements between Kuwait and Jordan made visas unnecessary for those carrying Jordanian passports. This opened the path for thousands of Palestinians, including those in the West Bank, who arrived alongside Egyptians, Sudanese, and Lebanese. In 1961, at twenty years of age, Abu Harab, Abu Samud's brother, joined the increasing flow of Palestinians and went to Kuwait. He had been in Syria for two years with his brother and uncle, but Kuwait offered a much better salary.

Abu Harab worked as a laborer building the undeveloped city-state. He worked in landscaping for two years and lived in conditions he described as primitive. The workers were mostly bachelors, living several in a room, without plumbing and usually without electricity; he called it a hut (*khuss*). He described the ordeal of having fresh water delivered daily by the barrel and stored it in clay jars. When I asked him to tell me about work he began by describing the tremendous heat and the dust. Dust storms would blow for a few days at a time, making it difficult to see farther than a meter. The dust was exacerbated by the whirlwind of construction building the city-state. He emphasized the difficulties, but showed a nostalgic smile for his youth and for the adventure he had lived. I imagined him telling these stories while still living in Kuwait to emphasize to his children that what they had was hard earned. By the mid-1990s, the stories resonated with a sense of betrayal and of loss.

During almost three decades, Abu Harab watched Kuwait grow from a land of pearl divers and dust to a land of air-conditioned shopping centers and paved roads. Living was cheap and wages were high. It was, from his point of view, a fortunate opportunity to save money and make a living. The work gradually got easier for Abu Harab. While he started as a landscaper and construction worker, he became an office worker. In 1963 he went to work for a Kuwaiti merchant company as a clerk in its Caterpillar equipment enterprise. He was later promoted and transferred to its local General Electric agency, where he remained employed until the Gulf War in 1990. Many Palestinians found employment in the quickly industrializing economy of Kuwait with companies like Ford, Mercedes, Fiat, and Pepsi-Cola, as well as in the Municipality and the Ministry of Public Works (Brand 1988: 127). By the 1970s, Jordan was exporting clerical and technical workers to the Gulf, while importing manual laborers from Egypt (Abdel-Jaber 1993: 148).

In the 1950s and '60s, men mostly came alone, but after the occupation of the West Bank they brought their families (Brand 1988; Lesch 1991). By 1971, after ten years in Kuwait, at thirty years of age, Abu Harab had saved a few thousand dinars and visited al-Qarya to engage a wife. He was set up with a third generation cousin, the daughter of Umm Samud's brother who died trying to cross into Kuwait. In 1972 he and his new wife moved into a family apartment in a largely Palestinian area called Abraq Khitan in Kuwait City.

Kuwait was expanding tremendously. Industrial and residential areas were being built. Kuwaitis and non-Kuwaitis moved into separate developments. Palestinians lived in areas such as Abraq Khitan, Salmiya, Fahalil, and Hawalli-Nuqra and Farwaniyyah, which were nicknamed the West Bank and Gaza Strip (Brand 1988: 117). Kuwaitis and other Gulf Arabs lived in their neighborhoods, and Iranians had their own areas.[2]

The Kuwaiti government sharply distinguished citizens and foreigners. "According to Article I of the citizenship law of 1959 (which was later amended in 1960, 1965, and 1966), Kuwaiti citizenship belonged to those (and their descendants) who resided in Kuwait before 1920 and maintained residence there through 1959" (Brand 1988: 113). Citizenship was reckoned by descent, not by place of birth. The rights of citizens and noncitizens differed greatly: noncitizens could not own immovable property, could not organize in the labor market, could not acquire licenses for importing, exporting, or opening most businesses, and 51 percent or more of every company had to be owned by a Kuwaiti. Consequently, most guest workers were sure to remain under Kuwaiti control.

When large numbers of Palestinians came after the 1967 war, new requirements were created for foreign workers: a visitor's card, a work card, or a no-objection certificate. These papers were issued by the Ministries of the Interior, of Social Affairs and of Labor, at the request of a Kuwaiti citizen. The Kuwaiti then became responsible in all legal and financial affairs for the non-Kuwaiti whose immigration he requested. This was the *kafil* or guarantor system, which became a basic part of employment in Kuwait (Brand 1988: 113). The *kafil* system put more pressure on Palestinians than on other guest workers because, unlike Egyptians or Pakistanis, they had no place to easily return if they lost their job or retired (Lesch 1991: 43).

I asked Abu Harab about these restrictions. He confirmed that such was the case and said that Kuwaitis were disdainful of Egyptians and suspicious of Palestinians, but despite these restrictions, Abu Harab said that life was very good in Kuwait. He and his wife had eight children there between 1973 and 1990. His eldest daughters fondly recounted to me how they lived in a tall apartment building and could visit friends without having to go outside. Their family took weekend drives to the beach or to shopping malls, or to visit friends in other parts of the city. In 1980, Abu Harab bought a brand new Buick, a huge eight-cylinder car, to drive the family around.

Despite being denied citizenship, Palestinians in Kuwait became an important and wealthy community. There was a political, educational,[3] and economic institutionalization of the community. The origins of Palestinian government-in-exile were born in Kuwait. Yasser Arafat, Khalid al-Hasan, Khalil al-Wazir, and Salim Za'nun were all living and working in Kuwait when they formed the Palestine National Liberation Movement (FATAH), which later took control of the PLO (Muslih 1988). By the late 1970s, organizations of Palestinian teachers, students, workers,[4] and women raised money for a fund, called the Sunduq al-Sumud (Steadfastness Fund), to support the Occupied Territories, held Palestinian cultural celebrations,[5] strengthened Palestinian-Kuwaiti and Syrian-Iraqi relations, and recommended that the PLO and the resistance organizations give popular organizations a clearer role in the Palestine National Council (Brand 1988: 123–24). The General Union of Palestinian Women sponsored "a wide range of cultural activities and social services. One focus was the preservation of Palestinian cultural heritage, particularly through a program of embroidery production" (Brand 1988: 134). They collected information on designs and styles, set up a museum, taught sewing and typing, provided financial subsidies to poor families, and, most important, developed the tuition subsidy program (Brand 1988: 134–35). Brand explains that

it was the Palestinians more than any other single expatriate group who helped shape the country's social, economic, and political development. The length of their residence, the size of the community, their dedication to work in both the public and private sectors, and their consequent entrenchment in the bureaucracy, economy, professions, and the media enabled the Palestinians in Kuwait to develop into one of the most cohesive and active communities in the diaspora. (Brand 1988: 108)

Migration from Jordan to the Gulf, which had increased during the 1950s and '60s with the Gulf's economic expansion and the tremendous boom in oil prices and revenues after 1974, began to decline with an economic slowdown in the 1980s. "Once most of the physical infrastructure had been constructed in 1974–82, the labor-receiving countries adopted new policies toward scrutinizing the inflow of foreign labor" (Abdel Jaber 1993: 154). Kuwaitis generally wanted to lower the number of foreign Arab workers in favor of less expensive and more compliant Pakistani, Sri Lankan, Indonesian, Filipino, and other non-Arab workers. Remittances to Jordan from the Gulf countries peaked in 1984 at about $1,237 million, dropping almost in half to $627 million by 1989 (Abdel-Jaber 1993: 152). The foreign labor force of Kuwait was still increasing, from 70 percent (217,000) to 86 percent (over 731,000) between 1975 and 1990 (Abdel-Jaber 1993: 149), but the composition of that labor force was shifting from Arab to Asian workers (Abdel-Jaber 1993: 155). There were growing fears that mass deportations might occur.[6] On the eve of the Iraqi invasion of Kuwait, there were about 400,000 Palestinians and about 600,000 Kuwaitis living in Kuwait (Lesch 1991: 42).

Abu Harab woke on Thursday morning, August 2, 1990 and left his home to go to work. He saw soldiers and tanks in the streets, but did not think for a minute that they were Iraqis. At 6:15 in the morning he turned on the radio to hear a Kuwaiti military broadcast calling on people to defend the country. Realizing what was happening, he left work and ran to the store to buy bread and food. At the store he found hundreds of other people doing the same. After two hours, with a few loaves of bread and cans of food, he drove home as the Iraqi army took over the streets, stopping vehicles, separating and detaining Kuwaitis by checking the identifications that had, until that moment, given them privilege. The border to Saudi Arabia was opened and about 460,000 Kuwaiti nationals immediately fled south (Humphrey 1993: 2).

For 40 days, Abu Harab got up at morning prayer and went to get rations of bread and food for his family. After 40 days the food ran out. In October he packed his family into the car and drove for three days, via Baghdad, to Amman. Half the Palestinian population fled in the fall of 1990, and by December there were about 150,000 left (Lesch 1991: 46). The Egyptians were the first to leave, along with the Sudanese and South and East Asians.[7] The Palestinians were the last because they had the most to lose. The major losses were suffered by those who had their own small businesses. They had to liquidate to the highest bidder (Abdel Jaber 1993: 157).[8] In December Abu Harab returned to Kuwait alone to see what was happening with his work, only to find a city ready for war.

In the wake of the Gulf War, life became precarious for the remaining 150,000 Palestinians in Kuwait, and few who left were allowed to return. Palestinians became the victims of Kuwaiti national restitution. They have been collectively punished by withholding government services and employment. Young Palestinian men have been the target of vigilante and police beatings and murder (Lesch 1991). Hypothetically, Lesch argues, 40 percent of the remaining 150,000 would leave if financial and travel restrictions were removed.

Arriving in Amman was not easy for Abu Harab and his family. When they went looking for apartments, rent was rising because of the increased demand and the inflated expectations of landlords. People thought the returning Palestinians were rich. Not only was the housing situation in Amman very bad, but the employment situation was even worse—terrible wages and no jobs. Jordan was suffering from absorbing war refugees and from their "neutrality" during the war which meant they were temporarily cut off from Saudi Arabian aid. After a few months, Abu Harab's cash savings were depleted.

After eight months in Amman, Abu Harab and his wife decided the family would return across the bridge to her home village al-Qarya, in the West Bank. In al-Qarya, where his father and brother had settled after the June War of 1967, he could find housing and an opportunity to work in Israel. The family of eight moved into Umm Harab's mother's home, where the elderly woman lived with her unmarried middle-aged daughter. I asked the old woman, Hajji Harab, about the new arrangements. She said, "Praise God my daughter returned to me from the desert and came rich with children." They added three more rooms to the house, along with a new kitchen and bath.

Abu Harab got a construction job in Israel. He was not particularly skilled as a builder and had to take more difficult, low skilled jobs. He had not done such work in years, and his back, shoulders, and especially his hands were no longer accustomed to such labor, but he was disciplined and eager to earn a living. However, he loved to talk about the electrical appliances that he once sold in Kuwait. He knew everything about their specifications and could not forget how useful that knowledge once was to him.

The younger children entered West Bank schools and adjusted well. But for the older three daughters moving to the village was more difficult. They went from a suburban environment in a wealthy country to a small village in the West Bank where they had no phone, no car, no friends, and absolutely nothing to do for entertainment. ʿAʾisha was sympathetic with her neighbors in the village, but she explained that they had suffered through several years of the Uprising and the atmosphere was very tense. People were afraid to go out, they did not always trust each other, and they did not visit very much. ʿAʾisha explained that it was very awkward for her to be told that she was coming home to her own country, when she had never been there and never wanted to leave Kuwait.

Borders and National Identity

The Green Line was central to the daily life of Palestinians in the West Bank, as discussed in Chapters 3–6, but because about half the people called Palestinians were actually outside historic Palestine, there was another border critical to West Bank Palestinian experience: the bridge to Jordan. The bridge to Jordan was the border that separated the Occupied homeland from the diaspora. It was often the single portal open to West Bankers who wanted to leave occupied Palestine either to seek their lives elsewhere or to enjoy themselves on vacation. Amman became a metropolitan city in the later part of the twentieth century, inhabited and built largely by Palestinians.[9] The United Arab Emirates and Saudi Arabia held even greater cities and opportunity, especially for those with professional aspirations. Such a life was nonexistent in the West Bank under the Occupation.[10] Amman provided a relief to the daily experience of Israelis having the "modern" metropolitan life and Arabs having only refugee camps, villages, or towns. In the diaspora, especially in Jordan, Palestinians became deeply incorporated at all levels of the national community and could make lives away from the fears of imminent violence experienced under Israel.

Although better fortune was found by some, living abroad had problems. The rights denied Palestinians in the West Bank were also denied under other governments. Kuwait was the most dramatic example. Few of the Palestinian children born in Kuwait came of age while living there. They were unable to return to their homes after the Gulf War because they were Palestinians, as the generation before was expelled from Palestine. For Abu Harab's family, leaving Kuwait was exile from a privileged exile. Jordan and to some extent Lebanon have been a middle ground, holding both opportunities and even greater poverty than in the Occupied Territories.[11] Leaving the West Bank, even voluntarily, was always difficult because for many it was a concession to Israel.

Instead of being absorbed into these countries, the trauma that began in 1948 "reinforced preexisting elements of identity, sustaining and strengthening a Palestinian self-definition that was already present" (Khalidi 1997: 22).

Transnational borders were a regular part of the lives of the West Bankers with whom I lived. Even those who lived in the towns or villages of their grand-parents were connected to people in the diaspora. Abu Harab and Abu Thaki were not extraordinary; there were greater tragedies and greater successes. Their different fortunes in the diaspora contained both sadness and hope. Their connection to the homeland emerged in different ways. Their stories show how borders create identity—in particular ways—out of territorial manipulations. The vulnerability at home and in the diaspora made these transnational rela-tionships more important. Complex inequalities and dependencies developed. Those in the Gulf and in Jordan knew that those in the West Bank maintained their land and customs in Palestine. They might need a place of refuge like those in Kuwait. For West Bankers, those in the Gulf provided remittances and connections to work in the diaspora. Affiliation or belonging to a community was a moral claim made especially clear in such moments of need or crisis. Building a house in the home village to which one is unlikely to return and sending garden vegetables or homemade products were practices that signify these transnational relationships built across the borders. These networks and relationships extend and elaborate the meanings of self and community.

Global flows of people have affected Palestine for centuries,[12] but the pro-cess of radical dispossession really began with the arrival of the British and Jewish settlers after World War I. In 1948–49, the "Catastrophe" (al-Nakba) and exile from parts of Palestine left about three quarters of a million people as refugees, many living in camps under Egyptian, Jordanian, and Lebanese rule. The 1950s and 1960s saw the growth of Palestinian migration from Lebanon and Jordan to the Gulf. In the 1960s, Palestinians moved from the West Bank to the East Bank and from Jordan to the Gulf. In 1967, a second wave of war refu-gees moved from the West Bank and Gaza to Jordan and Egypt. The oil boom drew many Palestinian families to the Gulf in the 1970s. But as the Palestinian community in Kuwait grew, the Jordanian army expelled the PLO and they fled to Lebanon. In 1982, the Israeli invasion forced their expulsion from Lebanon and flight to Tunisia. The Gulf War in 1990 and 1991 caused the flight and ex-pulsion from Kuwait. In 1994, Qaddafi called for the expulsion of Palestinians from Libya to mock the peace process. This long list of mass displacements and migrations would be dwarfed by a seemingly endless list of individual de-portations, expulsions, and flights to refuge or opportunity. The partition and occupation of their homeland have made Palestinians into a diaspora people. Many who lived inside historic Palestine were internally displaced from the homes of their parents or grandparents. About two out of three people of Palestinian descent were either refugees or in the diaspora.

Nowhere was identity clearer than at the border where people must present their documents. Palestinians were marked everywhere from no matter where they came. Most Palestinians had only travel documents, not passports, which were issued by Israel for West Bankers, by Egypt and Israel for those in Gaza, or by Lebanon for those in Lebanon. Palestinians in Jordan and Syria had passports from their respective countries, but they are marked as Palestinian (see Khalidi 1997: 2–3). Palestinians in 1948 Israel carried Israeli passports and were identified by religion. Since the mid-1990s, those in the autonomous Palestinian areas, the West Bank and Gaza, have been able to get Palestinian passports. "Even those few Palestinians who by the chance of birth, marriage, or emigration have managed to acquire United States, European, or other first world passports, find that barriers and borders remind them inexorably of who they are. This is especially true if they return to their homeland, which they have to do via points of entry controlled exclusively by Israel; or if they travel to virtually any Arab country" (Khalidi 1997: 3–4). Kearney (1991) suggests that Palestinians, like other transnational communities, "escape the power of the nation-state to define their sense of collective identity" (Kearney 1991: 59). While they might have escaped the power of any single nation-state to define their "collective identity," they did not escape the power of the system between nation-states to shape the meanings behind their territorial identities.

8. Borders and Apartheid

Borders have disrupted the lives of Palestinians since the drawing of the Mandate lines in 1917. The war in 1948 created a new border, and hundreds of thousands of refugees became stateless and dependent on host governments and the United Nations. The June War of 1967 altered the map again, expanding the Israeli borders into the remainder of historic Palestine, as well as into parts of Egypt and Syria. The Green Line that had separated the West Bank from Israel became an "open bridge" allowing Palestinians from the occupied territories to be incorporated as "foreign" labor. West Bankers entered the process of production, whether as men who migrated daily into Israel or as women who labored in workshops in the West Bank, without making the Israeli government or employers responsible for their welfare. Israelis who crossed the border found a pool of cheap labor in the West Bank to service their cars or to assemble the cut pieces of fabric that would be sold as clothes made in Israel. Palestinians provided labor to Israeli capital and consumers and then returned to their villages, where unpaid labor on farms and in the home subsidized their cheapness (Tamari 1981). The border also allowed Israeli merchants to dump goods, often inferior or outdated, on a captive population not protected by Israeli police. Workers and entrepreneurs who depended on border crossings experienced chronic limitations and potential for disaster. The maintenance of a porous border facilitated the subordinate economic integration of Palestinians into Israeli society while excluding them from the political community.

Oslo-based negotiations did not propose to significantly change the subordination of Palestinians to Israelis. By summer 2000, each side maintained its performances of borders and checkpoints, protecting against the infiltration of the other and simultaneously defining their own communities. Palestinians were urged to accept an autonomy in dozens of noncontiguous areas surrounded by ever increasing settlements, zones of Israeli control, and hundreds of kilometers of bypass roads.[1]

13. Bank advertisement in the Palestinian newspaper *Al-Quds*, October 1994. The words "closure, curfew, border, division of regions" are strewn through the barbs of razor wire. The bank proclaims itself to be the "sole solution." The bank's logo in the lower left-hand corner provides an alternate vision, as if it is a peephole into the future. In the logo, the domes of a mosque and a church stand protected behind a solid stone wall. Superimposed on the walled city is the outline of Palestine with its pre-1948 borders. These two images of the Palestinian border—dangerous barbed wire and a secure stone wall—evoke both pain and hope. Borders "illustrate the contradiction, paradox, difference, and conflict of power and domination in contemporary global capitalism and the nation-state, especially as manifested in local level practices" (Alvarez 1995: 447).

Negotiations only seemed to offer the reorganization of oppression. Even if Israel relinquished most of the West Bank to the Palestinian Authority, without a single soldier inside, as long as Israel controlled the borders it would control and subordinate the Palestinians. Redeploying Israeli troops away from Palestinian populations eliminated Israeli patrols in many neighborhoods and towns, but the number of checkpoints around these autonomous zones increased. Checkpoints became an even more important technique of control and coercion after redeployment. The new arrangements left Palestinians vulnerable to several forms of violence on a regular, systematic basis.

Seven years after the first Oslo agreement, the pathetic failure of Israeli and Palestinian leaders to achieve any resolution of the main issues (refugees, settlements, and Jerusalem) and the general failure of the Palestinian Authority to create a legitimate government made fertile ground for a renewed uprising in October 2000. Unlike the battles of the late 1980s and 1990s, these clashes included a number of armed Palestinians and Israeli helicopter gunships and tanks. Despite the overwhelming superiority of Israeli forces, Palestinians used rifles and stones to change their destiny for better or for worse.

Most Palestinians struggled within and against Israeli domination just by earning a living and maintaining a connection to Palestine. Although they could not control the geopolitical borders, their customs became one way of connecting and dividing people on their own terms. Palestinian customs shaped relationships within and across the borders. Umm Samud's customs of housework and cooking were a binding force with her family, those under her roof, and those in the diaspora. 'Adil's and Amal's different weddings displayed how Arab-Israelis and West Bank Palestinians distinguished themselves from each other, as moderns or preservers of tradition, even as they were intimately, but unequally, bound together by custom. Part of their dignity and dependency was defined against the other. Umm Samud's siblings in Amman, Abu Thaki and Hajji Latifa, despite leaving the village more than a generation ago, maintained their connection. Abu Thaki built a home in the village in which he would never live. Hajji Latifa had her son, who lived in Amman and Saudi Arabia, make large customary gifts so Umm Samud's sons could get married. Both visited often and Umm Samud sent both her siblings the products of her labors, things that tasted like home. Abu Harab had to flee Kuwait and return to the village. His story makes it quite clear that symbolic relationships between village and diaspora are sometimes critical because one needs to come home.

These different Palestinians confronted borders in different ways. No one is meant to be "typical." Customs are often described, by anthropologists and Palestinians, as reflections of a set of "core" values or collective culture shared by individual members. Someone else may see the deep semiotic patterns that link building a home, giving gold at a wedding, sending food to relatives, and similar acts, but none of these stories were retold here to reveal the underlying essence of Palestinian culture. I see Palestinian customs and traditions, ʿadat wa taqalid, as a folk category that included a mix of celebration, leisure, and household activities. These customs show how Palestinians shaped community within and against the borders imposed on them. This does not exhaust the many possible meanings of these customs, but it does shed additional light on the problems of the border and the informal solutions to overcome them.

The larger generalization (or theory) about the Palestinian-Israeli border situation is not about essential Palestinian culture, but about this powerful and modern technique of organizing space, identities and inequalities. Although significantly larger than the Green Line, the United States-Mexico border bears some resemblance to the Green Line: border permits allow workers to enter, large numbers of undocumented people also cross, large *maquiladoras* assemble parts for U.S. companies in Sonora and Chihuahua, Mexico, and Texans from El Paso take their cars to be serviced in Ciudad Juarez. On the one hand, the implementation of the North American Free Trade Agreement (NAFTA) made it easier for companies to move capital and commodities across the borders, largely by eliminating many taxes and tariffs and loosening or eliminating environmental, labor, and financial regulations. On the other hand, the United States doubled the number of border police and passed several pieces of legislation in 1996 to get tough on migrants (Heyman 1999). Combined with the "war on drugs," the militarization of the United States-Mexico border has not stopped the crossing of undocumented workers, it has only pushed them into an even more covert and therefore more vulnerable status. Capitalists largely liberated themselves from the shackles of their nationalisms to operate across borders. But those freedoms were not yet extended to workers. If this unequal treatment were justified by explicit racial, religious, or hereditary discrimination, as it once had been, it would have been widely condemned. But maintaining inequality according to spatial-territorial identities like nationality is rarely challenged. On the contrary, World Trade Organization agreements and International Monetary Fund and World Bank structural adjustment plans make such border policies global.

Citizenship affords certain rights and responsibilities to members in a territorially based state, but some states determine membership according to racialist concepts of a national community that overlap with concepts like shared customs, language, and religion, rather than on participation in the social process. National identity has become the "absolute geopolitical and social boundaries inscribed on territory and on persons, demarcating space and those who are members from those who are not" (Kearney 1991: 54; see also Anderson 1983). It is dangerous to organize states and the territories, budgets, and other state resources according to national classifications. Whether in Israel-Palestine, the United States, Yugoslavia, Germany, Japan, Saudi Arabia, or elsewhere, national citizenship has often become a modern version of racism that continues to organize, dominate, and exploit inequality and the conflicts it creates.

The new regime of autonomous zones and citizenship in the occupied territories resembled the homeland system of former apartheid South Africa. The legal basis of South African apartheid, created when the Afrikaner National Party came to power in 1948, implemented a program of separate development. All South Africans were registered at birth into separate racial categories: White, Indian, Colored, or African. Africans were denied citizenship by the descendants of white colonial settlers and assigned to live in one of ten Bantustans, or independent tribal homelands. Four homelands even had their own armies, passports, border posts, and embassies, while the other six remained "self-governing" areas inside South Africa. The difference in status between the homelands was not too significant because all were economically dependent on South Africa. Africans from the homelands were allowed into the South African labor market as migrant laborers who had to obtain travel passes and temporary residence permits (Human Rights Watch 1995: 59). The strength of the homeland system was partly in the ability of South African whites to impose their will militarily, but also in their propping up leaders in the name of tradition, like Chief Buthelezi in the KwaZulu territory, who opposed the African National Congress armed struggle and was an arm of the South African police. The South Africans had hierarchical distinctions based explicitly on whiteness that were administered largely by territorial arrangements.

This book should allow those interested in comparing the Israeli occupation to South African apartheid, or autonomous Palestinian territories to the Bantustans, a glimpse of how racialized categories administered according to territorially based citizenship work for some people living in the West Bank. My impression is that most in the United States rarely hear, read, or see this side of the conflict. Reporting in the United States regularly fails to see the chronic structural violence that existed before Palestinians began this third large uprising.[2] Instead of trying to understand the mechanisms of inequality, common journalists prefer old clichés about ethnic and religious fanaticism. Unfortunately, these clichés obscure the apartheid with portraits of abstract ethnic primordialism that distort mutual personhood.[3] Ironically, such work frames the problems caused by exclusive nationalism as if exclusive nation-states are the only possible solution.

Politicians in many countries have described the necessity of the border in populist rhetoric, saying it was for the protection of domestic labor markets. Never mind that workers who migrate across borders tend to take jobs that established groups refuse to take because of their low wages, low status, hard labor, or physical danger. Migrants usually do not compete with "domestic" workers, but tend to push more established workers up the occupational scale because they supply cheap labor and purchase goods in domestic markets driving overall economic growth (see Dowty 1987 or Ebeling and Hornberger 1996). This was clearly the case for Palestinians in the Israeli economy (Semyenov and Lewin-Epstein 1987).

Another argument for the necessity of borders has been to define the community eligible for distributive forms of justice like social welfare, health care, or education (see Walzer 1983). If a community is to supply any basic necessities to its members, there must be a limit to whom those services are provided. Borders serve to limit the distribution of "scarce" resources. But this inclusion or exclusion from social rights was something employers used to exploit workers by hiring undocumented foreign labor or moving production overseas. Just the threat of moving production can discipline a labor market. If employers were accountable to provide all workers with the same benefits regardless of territory or citizenship, workers could not be threatened and pitted against each other.

The people who clearly benefit from the maintenance of porous borders are the businesses big enough to be allowed to cross while their neighbors are pinned down and, therefore, rather compliant as workers. In capitalist democracies with relatively wealthy citizens and strong labor unions, it is increasingly difficult for employers to find domestic workers for heavy, manual jobs. Rather than try to break the unions or improve the jobs, firms have sought employees in the international labor market (Walzer 1983: 56). Maintaining borders that create undocumented workers provides a mechanism for employers to subvert domestic labor laws. These workers have no political rights and employers can pay below the legal wage and ignore illegal conditions of work.

Without the denial of political rights and civil liberties and the everpresent threat of deportation, the system would not work. Hence guest workers can't be described merely in terms of their mobility, as men and women free to come and go. While they are guests, they are also subjects. They are ruled, like the Athenian metics, by a band of citizen-tyrants. (Walzer 1983: 58)

Increasingly, the same effects are achieved by shipping the labor intensive parts of production out of the wealthy capitalist democracy to workers living under military dictatorships. In these cases, the tyrants seem one party removed from the point of oppression, but that is only an illusion created by the border. Much like their counterparts in other parts of the world, Israeli manufacturers and capitalists were actually subsidized by the protection of the state at the expense of workers and consumers. Borders, as they exist over much of the globe at the beginning of the twenty-first century, are a mechanism of tyranny: borders deny political rights or access to the distribution of social goods while they permit the integration of labor, material, and cultural resources.

However, the resulting "superexploitation" might not be the intention of border policy (Heyman 1998b). Economic and class interests do not sufficiently explain such politics. Exploitability that benefits employers "is not obviously sought by cohesive capitalist elites, but rather is the result of a complex political process" (Heyman 1998b: 173). The most obvious antecedent to border enforcement was fear of invasion. The Green Line was, in fact, an armistice line. The military had a need to defend the population from an invading army as Israel did in the wars of 1948 and 1973. By the beginning of the twenty-first century, however, several factors changed the old concept of militarily secure borders. Despite the smoke and flashes of Patriots, Iraq's use of SCUD missiles mocked the notion of secure borders. The militarily experienced and successful leaders of Israel, such as Yitzhak Rabin and Ehud Barak, understood that Israel's future military security could not depend on the army alone to defend borders as it did in the past. Furthermore, although missile attacks could and did occur, the military invasion of Israel was more remote after the Cold War because of Israel's overwhelming military power, including high-tech surveillance and espionage that have made it impossible to move troops and armor without detection, giving armies like Israel's a chance to mobilize if any army approached border areas.

The more pressing security fear for Israelis was categorized as "terrorism." This second aspect of security required policing against small groups or individuals who sought to attack Israelis. Tens of bombings in the mid-1990s, mainly on buses and markets in Tel Aviv and West (Jewish) Jerusalem, were the proximal cause of the increasing closures. But the closures never really kept Palestinians from entering. Tens of thousands of Palestinians entered Israel daily by going around the border checkpoints. By the late 1990s, workers went around the checkpoints in view of the soldiers, who turned a blind eye. Even if these crossing points were closed, as they were after every bomb that went off in Israel, the border could not really be sealed for those who make an effort.

Anyone who wanted to commit an act of violence could. The Islamic Resistance Movement (HAMAS) blew up two Israeli buses, one week apart, on the same day of the week, same route, same time of the morning, just to show they could strike at will.

The Palestinians believed that the border closures were intended as punishment to discourage them from sympathizing with the attacks, but the closures cannot be understood from an entirely strategic point of view. Terrorism was not a threat to the state, but because it was murderous and created mayhem, it was a threat to any elected government. For the government, border closures worked against the fear terrorism created among Israelis by assuring the public of their security. Fear of terrorism is a very real threat to any government that can be elected out of office, so it must have some highly visible response. The border closures have surely served at least this purpose, if no other.

More generally speaking, the border was necessary, not because of the threat of terrorism, but because the Palestinians were a *political* threat to Israel. The presence and existence of the Palestinians challenged the legitimacy of Israel as an exclusive state for Jews. In reference to migrant workers from more remote locations like Romania and Thailand, Rosenhek points out that the recognition of "social rights by the state might have undesirable implications for their legal and political status":

the granting of social rights to this population might signal their recognition as legitimate members of the polity. This situation, in turn, might encourage the articulation of claims-making by the migrant workers, legitimizing the eventual emergence of a rights-based politics around the issue of labor migration in Israel. (Rosenhek 2000: 59)

If the government acknowledged partial rights, the door would be open to challenge rights based on membership in the Jewish nation with rights based on participation and contribution to the society. From this perspective, the border is largely about regulating the nationality of the citizenry.

It is my hope that the regime of nation-states, in which there is corporate free trade and restricted migration of workers, will be challenged and that alternative forms of citizenship will be considered more deeply (see Joppke 1999). Postnational forms of membership could be based on international human rights standards (see Soysal 1994) or perhaps on multicultural forms of citizenship (Kymlicka 1995). Unfortunately, although the chronic failure to agree on partition has persisted for three-quarters of a century, alternative solutions, such as a single binational democratic state, seem extremely unlikely at the beginning of the twenty-first century.

Politically, such a state would dilute the power of both the PLO and the major parties of Israel. More significantly, most Israelis and Palestinians would not choose one binational state as a solution. Both favor their own state because of their respective transgenerational traumas. Having their own nation-state is important not only for security from the many forms of physical and structural violence, but also as a bulwark against symbolic violence due to non- or misrecognition.[4] Regardless of economic necessity, military parades and participation in the Olympics have become a prerequisite of dignity in the modern world, something critical for the healing of "mass traumas" (see Robben and Suárez-Orozco 2000), like the European genocide of Jews during World War II or the expulsion of Palestinians in 1948 and the occupation.

Peace cannot be achieved by further political partition. Peace will be achieved when popular opinion believes there is a just rule of law that favors complex forms of equality.[5] The collective legitimacy of such a system requires at least two overlapping principles: the elimination of tyranny based on national (or racial) affiliation and the enhancement of the recognition of mutual personhood. This strategic vision seems remote. The proper tactics to achieve it are not clear. The road is long and, like those in the West Bank, it probably has many military roadblocks. But, as the Rebbe Nachman of Brasolov said in his collection *Likutey Moharan* (2, 48), "The world is a very narrow bridge. The main thing is not be afraid."

Notes

1. A collection and analysis of these leaflets can be found in Mishal and Aharoni (1994).

2. During the first year of the uprising, Israeli authorities acknowledged the arrest of 18,000 Palestinians. In 1990, an estimated 30,000 Palestinians, approximately 13 percent of the adult male population, were detained (Palestinian Human Rights Information Center 1991). During the Intifada, there were usually about 14,000–15,000 Palestinians in custody, of whom about 40 percent were sentenced, the remainder either charged and awaiting trial, under investigation, or detained without charge (Palestinian Human Rights Information Center 1991: 23; see also B'Tselem 1992).

3. Similarly, the Human Rights Watch report on torture by Israeli forces, which includes interviews with forty-one former detainees, describes in intimate detail the beatings during arrest, being brought into interrogation, contortions of their body, exposure to extreme temperature, psychological abuse and sleep deprivation, beating and shaking, threatening, the complicity of Israeli doctors, and four cases of murder in custody (Human Rights Watch 1994).

4. Arguments affirming the illegality of these practices are based on the United Nations Universal Declaration of Human Rights (1948), the Geneva Convention for the Protection of Civilian Persons in Time of War IV (1949), the International Covenant on Civil and Political Rights (1966), the UN Declaration on Torture (1975), and the UN Convention Against Torture (1984). These tenets of international law challenge both the Israeli use of the British Defence (Emergency) Regulations of 1945 authorizing detention and the Landau Commission Report of 1987 authorizing the use of physical pressure against detainees.

5. Asad (1997) explains how violence can be either rational or irrational, depending on the observer more than on the act of violence itself.

6. For a discussion of the poetics of Israeli violence and the culture of the military see Ezrahi (1997), Ben Ari (1998), and Lomsky-Feder and Ben-Ari (2000)

7. As Cynthia Mahmood explains, the fact that so called "terrorist acts are often more expressive than instrumental in nature is oddly reciprocated by the industry of counterterrorism, which despite its rhetoric of brute realism is focused on strategies that appeal philosophically but are rarely pragmatic responses to the violence they purport to address" (Mahmood 1996: 81).

8. Border studies have been useful in examining the unequal intersections between international capital, state policy, and the local behavior of individuals (Asiwaju 1985; Chavez 1992; Donnan and Wilson 1994; Flynn 1997; Heyman 1995, 1998a,b, 1999; Sahlins 1989; Wilson and Donnan 1998). These studies, driven by a resurgence of scholarly and media interest in "globalization," have helped illustrate how com-

munities are based on changing networks of people that extend across different lands (Kearney 1986, 1995; Rouse 1991). Alvarez (1995: 449) distinguishes two trends in these border studies: the literal and the conceptual. The literalists study actual applied problems of the geopolitical border like policy, settlement, environment, labor, and health, whereas the a-literalists use the border as a metaphor for social and conceptual boundaries.

9. For many anthropologists, culture has been described as chains of analogies that penetrate different realms of knowledge.

10. This de-essentializing of culture became more profound as a critical gaze cast upon anthropology by authors like Asad (1973), Said (1978), Marcus and Fischer (1986) and Clifford (1988) influenced a generation of anthropologists uneasy with culture as a monolithic structure. Writers have set themselves to the deconstruction of racial/gender/cultural categories (Spivak 1988; Bhabha 1983, 1994) and celebrating hybridity, syncretism, and transculturalism (Rosaldo 1989; Hall 1990, 1991; Hall and Held 1993; hooks 1992), in an attempt to expose the modernist and colonialist claims to "whiteness" as "a myth sustained only by the Center's strangle hold on the global political economy" (Lavie and Swedenburg 1996: 163).

11. Studies in the borderlands of culture and gender, where people just do not fit neatly into categories like black or white, man or woman, challenge the notion that identities can be fixed, territorially or biologically, and focus instead on the processes and problems of constructing ideas about oneself and others, or us and them (Alvarez 1995: 447; Anzaldúa 1987; Flores 1994, 1995; Hicks 1991; Limon 1989, 1994; Rosaldo 1985, 1989).

12. In Arabic it is customary to address an adult as father (Abu) or mother (Umm) of his or her first-born male. For example, Abu Samud and Umm Samud are the parents of Samud. These personal names, like all others in this text, are pseudonyms, as is the name of the village. The main town of Tulkarm, however, is not a pseudonym.

13. For all the wealth of publications in English on the Palestinian-Israeli conflict, there are only a few ethnographies based on extended field research in the West Bank. Grenqvist (1931) describes customs of Palestinian marriage in the Bethlehem area, Moors (1995) interviewed women in about work and property, and Swedenburg (1995) interviewed veterans of the Great Revolt in 1936. Many journalists have written books about Palestinian daily life and personal histories, but few did much more than interviews using translators. One interesting exception to this is Binur (1989), an Israeli journalist who "disguised" himself as a Palestinian. His writing about being treated like a Palestinian further inspired the hands-on nature of my fieldwork, but unlike Binur, I did not, could not, and would not pass myself off as a Palestinian.

14. The point is not to privilege the epistemology of experience over other ways of knowing social history, but to include it alongside other ways of knowing, all of which are partial and incomplete.

15. I am inspired here mainly by the phenomenology of Frantz Fanon (1964, 1965, 1967) in which the study of a large number of instances is less important than the intuitive and deep understanding of a few individual cases (Fanon 1967: 169).

16. Robben (1995, 2000) explains how disappearance by the Argentine military

created a specific identity of resistance, the mothers of the disappeared, who are called the Madres de la Plaza de Mayo (see also Green 1994 and Afflitto 2000 on Guatemala).

17. Including both perspectives, Taussig's (1987) study of shamanism in Colombia and Nordstrom's (1997) work in war-torn Mozambique both artistically illustrate the interplay between and co-presence of the destruction of community, family, and identity and the creative resistance of magical healing. The grotesque, Nordstrom explains, "is a double-edged sword: it is used by the military and paramilitary forces to effect terror and thus control; and it is used by the citizenry as a way of defeating the holds of terror" (1997: 156).

Chapter 2

1. For a discussion of the uses of terms like "borders," "boundaries," and "frontiers" in describing history see Kratochwil (1986) and Lattimore (1968).

2. The "Children of Israel" are the main protagonists of the Hebrew Bible, and the name Philistine is mentioned in Genesis 9: 14. Other books of the Hebrew Bible describe the Philistines as a kingdom of people living on the Mediterranean coast.

3. Israel was the name given to Jacob, son of Isaac and grandson of Abraham, after he wrestled with God's angel one night in the desert (Genesis 32: 28). Genesis describes how Jacob had twelve sons who became the founding patriarchs of the twelve tribes—the Children of Israel (Genesis 35: 23–26). That is the charter myth behind the name "twelve tribes of Israel" that came to identify the Jewish people. By the ninth century B.C., Israel was the name of a small northern kingdom that was destroyed by Babylonians in the eighth century. The southern kingdom around Jerusalem was known as Judah (Judea) and that name lasted until the Roman period. Judea is the origin for the modern name Jew. The Romans crushed two Judean uprisings against their rule (A.D. 70 and 135) and destroyed the kingdom. The Romans renamed the region Palestinia. Palestine became the name of the region for the next 1800 years under a series of empires: Roman, Byzantine, Umayyad, 'Abbasid, Seljuk, Crusaders, Fatimid, Ayyubid, Mamluk, and Ottoman.

4. The classic, nonrelative definition of justice is that each person gets his or her due, as in the phrase just desert, and that can entail either reward or punishment. However, Harvey (1998) suggests that any understanding of justice must be situated within historically particular constructions of time and space. Consider the judicial ambiguity of the following act: a mother has two children with her and she gives ice cream to one and not the other. Obviously, this act could be just or unjust depending on the context, or how the event is defined in time and space. If our sympathy is with the child's perspective, this act indicates permanence, or something that "always" happens/exists, and the act is unjust. However, as any parent will probably agree, there are many possible reasons why not giving the second child ice cream, despite the child's crying protest of injustice (e.g., "you're not fair!"), is not unjust, but, on the contrary, a defining act of justice (a way of making and teaching a notion of justice). Making the judgement of a just or unjust act emerges from different perspectives of time and space, the child's or

the parent's. Obviously, in this example, the one with the power gets to choose which notion of justice will immediately prevail.

5. For those interested in further reading in Palestinian history I suggest Sayigh (1979), Khalidi (1997), or Kimmering and Migdal (1993).

6. In northern Palestine, the districts of Nablus and Acre were part of the *wilayat*, or province, of Beirut, along with the *sanjaqs* of Beirut, Latakia, and Tripoli. Southern Palestine was designated as the independent *mutasarriflik* of Jerusalem. These *sanjaqs* extended from the coastal plains in the west, past the central highlands running north to south, and down into the Jordan Valley. East of these hills, the interior lands were all part of the *wilayat* of Damascus divided into four *sanjaqs*: from north to south, Hama, Homs, Damascus, and Ajlun.

7. Through much of the seventeenth and eighteenth centuries Bedouin in the plains and feuding sheiks in the hills left thousands of villages deserted in Ottoman Syria, but the areas around Lebanon and Acre generally remained prosperous (Issawi 1988: 269).

8. In Palestine the Abu-Ghush ruled in the area of Jerusalem and Bethlehem, the al-ʿAmrs in the Hebron area, the ʿAbd al-Hadis in the Carmel region, the Tuqans in Nablus, and the Agha in the Galilee (Hourani 1966; Maʾoz 1975; Reilly 1981; Swedenburg 1991; Tabak 1991).

9. Sheik Zahir al-ʿUmar, who came from a local urban family in Nablus, established an autonomous state in northern Palestine for almost twenty-five years (Joudah 1987). After forming an alliance with Sheik Rashid al-Jabar of the Bedouin tribe the Banu Sakhr, Sheik Zahir annexed his neighbors' tax-farms, took Acre, Haifa, and Sidon, formed an alliance with ʿAli Bey in Egypt, and eventually occupied Damascus. The Ottoman navy and Zahir battled in the late 1760s until Zahir was defeated in 1775. He was succeeded by Ahmad al-Jazzar (r. 1775–1804), who, like his predecessor Zahir, pocketed grain taxes which had previously gone to provision the large cities of the interior, the Ottoman armed forces, and the pilgrimage to Mecca. Muhammad Agha Abu Nabat ruled in Palestine from the port of Jaffa in the early part of nineteenth century (Maʾoz 1975): "Though severe, his rule was just; he endeavoured to suppress robbery and brigandage, and thus made matters difficult for the bedawin, who rebelled against him" (Macalister and MacMahon 1906: 34).

10. "Although the Zionist challenge definitely helped shape the specific form Palestinian national identification took, it is a serious mistake to suggest that Palestinian identity emerged mainly as a response to Zionism" (Khalidi 1997: 20). Modern Palestinian nationalism "was rooted in long-standing attitudes of concern for the city of Jerusalem and for Palestine as a sacred entity which were a response to perceived external threats" (30). Consciousness of these threats stretched back at least to the time of the Crusades (c. eleventh century) and was continually stirred especially with the growing strength of Western Europe in the eighteenth century (29–30).

11. Stalin wrote the criteria for a nation in 1913: common language, territory, economic activity, and a particular psychological disposition from historical experiences that have produced a common culture. Lenin scorned the idea of national psychology or culture, but he, like Karl Kautsky, accepted that a nation needs both a language and a land (Harris 1990: 71). In 1928, Stalin changed the party's position on the Jews and

created a national homeland for them in Birobidzhan, near Manchuria, where approximately 40,000 Jews were relocated (Harris 1990: 232).

12. Said (1978) explains how British administrators such as Lord Cromer governed with the attitude that the "subject races did not have it in them to know what was good for them" (37).

13. Syria briefly had independence in 1920, then became a French Mandate until it was given independence in 1946.

14. Lebanon was a multi-religious community made up of Maronite Christians, Greek Orthodox, Greek Catholic, Druze, Shiʿa, and Sunni Muslims, where no group had a majority. The French engineered the construction of a constitution that established representational quotas for each group in a parliament based on a census of 1932. Key administrative positions, like president, prime minister, and president of parliament, always were to go to a Maronite, a Sunni, and a Shiʿa respectively. The delicate balance, which repeatedly collapsed (and eventually broke into civil war in the 1970s), was a mechanism through which the French could leverage the most influence. Any group would need their support to rule. After twenty-five years of French influence, Lebanon became independent in 1943.

15. The agreement advocated establishing an international administration of Palestine by Russia, France, Britain, and Sharif Hussein of Mecca in order to defer the issue and prevent squabbling between the wartime allies.

16. Farming, however, remained the primary livelihood of Palestinians, and the "family still remained the main unit of labour" (Graham-Brown 1990: 55).

17. According to the 1922 British census, there were fewer than 84,000 Jews in Palestine; slightly more than the Christian population of 71,000 people, and about 11 percent of the total population of 752,000, who were mostly Sunni Muslims. The 1945 British census recorded an increase to 1,743,000: 554,000 Jews, 1,101,000 Muslims, and 139,000 Christians.

18. In a letter dated October 24, 1915, Sir Henry McMahon of the British War Office excluded the lands west of Damascus, Hama and Aleppo because they were not "purely Arab" (Abboushi 1990: 1).

19. The revolt made many Jewish capitalist reluctant to rehire Palestinian workers, and Jewish labor was able "to achieve relative insulation from Arab competition through the device of near-total exclusion" (Shalev 1989: 102).

20. This commission also argued that economic viability would require a customs union.

21. Israeli society was ethnically divided into three classes of citizens. The first class of citizen were the "modern" Jewish Israelis of European decent. The second class were the Jews from Asian or African origins, particularly Moroccans and Yemenites. Israeli Arabs were the third class.

22. The number of refugees from the 1948 lands of Israel is greatly debated and ranges between 500,000 and 1 million (Morris 1987: 297–98).

23. Current statistics describe 42 percent (824,000) of the population of the West Bank and Gaza as refugees or descendants of refugees as designated by the United Nations. Refugees make up 62 percent (594,000) of the Gaza population and 26 percent (261,000) of the West Bank population. Fortunately for them, many are no longer

living in refugee camps. Of the total population of 1,962,000 (958,000 in Gaza and 1,004,000 in the West Bank), 18 percent (353,000) still live in camps; in Gaza the figure is 32 percent (306,000), but in the West Bank it is only 8 percent (80,000). To round out the statistical picture, in Gaza 31 percent (297,000) of the population live in Greater Gaza City and the remaining 37 percent (354,500) live in smaller towns and villages. In the West Bank 34 percent (341,000) live in twelve towns and 58 percent (582,000) live in approximately 430 villages. The West Bank is predominantly rural, but has a few pockets of crowded refugee camps, usually adjacent to towns or large villages (Heiberg and Ovensen 1993).

24. Figures on the relative size of different sectors of the economy vary. The World Bank and the United Nations calculated agricultural production in the West Bank and Gaza as 20 percent of the GDP in 1985, declining to 15 percent by 1995 (UNSCOT and World Bank 1999: 46). These figures seem to reflect market agriculture rather than home production for subsistence.

25. Wage employment in Israel drove up the cost of hiring farm workers in the West Bank. Water was severely restricted, remaining only 20 percent above the 1967 level in the mid-1980s, while the Israeli settler population, which made up only 2–3 percent of the West Bank population in the late 1980s, was permitted to use 20 percent of the water (Graham-Brown 1990: 58). "Military order 1039 of 1983 imposed quotas on production of grapes, plums, tomatoes and aubergines" (60).

26. Leaders of the movement came mainly from the Merkaz HaRav Yeshiva— the institute led by Rabbi Abraham Kook and then after his death by his son, Rabbi Tzvi Yehuda Kook—and many early settlers came from the Bnei Akiva youth movement and the Hapoel Hamizrachi political party, both organizations dedicated to the ideas of religious Zionism. Amanah, the main institution that sponsors settlement, was established in 1976. The Yesha Council politically represents the settlements to the government and carries out other administrative functions (Lustick 1988).

27. In the 1977 elections, Labor actually had more votes than Likud, 43 to 32 seats. However, in coalition with the National Religious Party's 12 seats, 15 seats from the Democratic Movement for Change, and a few smaller parties, Likud commanded a majority of the 120 seats. The Tehiyah party, which took three seats in the 1981 election, included Hanan Porat of Gush Emunim, but was created by secular ultranationalists who left Likud because of Begin's treaty with Egypt relinquishing the Sinai. They saw this as a dangerous precedent for further land-for-peace, which they viewed as only a tactic employed by the Arabs to fulfill their true goal to eliminate the Jewish state entirely. Tehiyah, in coalition with the National Religious Party, has been a significant threat to the Likud establishment. By the 1984 election, the National Religious Party and the Gush ended their cooperation inside the Knesset (Lustick 1988).

28. Following the Camp David Accords, the Begin government did two things: it increased the settlement of the occupied territories, and it granted "limited autonomy," which resulted in an increase in foreign money in the territories and development assistance. "This was the time of sumud in its first, more passive version, when the main aim of both the Palestinians and of their supporters outside seemed to be simply to provide the resources to allow them to remain in place—to survive, not to be forced out— in the teeth of the policies being pursued by an increasingly aggressive Israeli over-

lord." This was partly motivated in order to cope with Israel's terrible inflation during the 1970s (Owen 1989: 47).

29. Since 1976, the Israeli government has collected a value-added tax (VAT) on all goods and services, in violation of international law, which maintains that an occupier may not institute new taxes in the territory under its control. Most of the military budget was derived from the taxation of the local population. The Occupied Territories might even have been a source of revenue to the Israeli treasury (Al-Haq 1990: 242).

30. The current leadership emerged in the crucible of the Lebanese civil war. In the summer of 1982 the Israeli army invaded and forced the evacuation of between 11,000 and 14,000 PLO personnel. The PLO set up its new headquarters in Tunisia. PLO soldiers were relocated in several countries, mainly Tunisia, Sudan, Yemen, and South Yemen, where they received military training by their host governments. Syria played host for most of Fatah's leftist opposition.

31. The Wye River Memorandum, signed on October 23, 1998, focuses (four of seven pages) on the issue of security and the need for multilateral cooperation against terrorism. The primary human rights groups monitoring the situation, such as the Palestinian Centre for Human Rights, Human Rights Watch, and the Palestinian Human Rights Monitoring Group, have warned that this new agreement is a dangerous precedent. Few Palestinians "on the ground" trust the bilateral participation of Israeli security forces or trilateral participation of the CIA.

Chapter 3

1. No major restrictions were imposed on movement between Israel and the newly Occupied Territories; checkpoints were not established at the entrances to Jerusalem despite its annexation because of the "negative consequences of any such action" (Gazit 1995: 192). Thousands of summer visitors from the territories visited Tel Aviv and Israeli beaches making the bureaucratic burden of issuing visitor permits unmanageable (192).

2. The Israeli labor market was already divided by ethnicity and religion. Jews of European descent tended to have higher occupational statuses than Jews of Asian or African descent. Both groups of Jews generally had a higher status than Arab-Israelis. See Ben-Porat (1989) or Semyenov and Lewin-Epstein (1987) for a discussion of income and occupational gaps in Israeli society.

3. Five periods may be discerned regarding Palestinian employment in Israel: (1) 1967–73, rapid growth to 61,500; (2) 1974–80, small increase with a shift toward Gazan workers; (3) 1981–87, rapid increase; (4) 1988–92, unstable and decline of annual work hours; (5) 1993–98, significant decline (Farsakh 1998).

4. In 1990, 199,516 arrived, of whom 92.8 percent were from the USSR; in 1991, about 176,100 arrived, of whom about 84 percent were from the (former) USSR, and 11.3 percent (20,014) from Ethiopia. The flow continued through the mid-1990s at about 70,000–77,000 per year, of whom about 85 percent were from the former USSR (Ministry of Construction and Housing 2000).

5. Housing starts quadrupled between 1989 and 1991, from approximately 20,000 to well over 80,000, with almost 74 percent of the latter figure being funded my the government. Housing starts were cut in half in 1993–94, but rose again in 1995 with only 38.5 percent funded by the government. The later 1990s saw contraction again, but significantly more house construction continued compared to the 1980s (Ministry of Construction and Housing 2000).

6. The Druze are an Arabic speaking people living in Palestine, Lebanon, and Syria, who developed within and against the Islamic community in the eleventh century. They and the Bedouin are the only Arabic speaking people who can serve in the Israeli army, primarily because they are thought to have no loyalty to the Palestinian nation or to Arab states across the border. Israelis commonly told me that the Palestinians hate the Druze the most because they are the most brutal, and that Druze hate the Arabs because they had been persecuted by orthodox Islam. But it is more likely that the ethnicization of this army unit and its aggressive character are the consequences of Israeli policy, formal and informal, that has always sought a native pillar against the Palestinian national movement.

7. In the summer of 1996, I asked Palestinians who worked at 33 different sites in Israel, how many West Bankers at their work have permission and how many do not. Collectively we counted 46 workers with permission and 150 without. With this information I can guess that in the summer of 1996 there were about three illegal workers for every legal worker that came from the Tulkarm district. When I suggested this figure to Palestinians and Israeli labor contractors, they suggested that it was probably too low. Four Arab-Israeli contractors in construction and two Jewish-Israeli farm owners told me that they still rely significantly on West Bankers. "As much as before the closures?" I would ask. Most said yes, some said more.

8. The General Federation of Palestinian Trade Unions published higher figures than the Palestinian Bureau of Statistics. They reported that there were about 48,000 workers with permits in Israel, of whom about 600 were women.

9. Occasionally, illegal workers taken into custody end up dead, such as Ahmad ʿAsfur, who was arrested on a crossing in December 1997 and pronounced dead in an Israeli hospital in October 1998.

10. Burawoy (1985) explains that domination organized by state force plays a critical role in reproducing relations of production, but it is less critical in reproducing relations within production. For Burawoy, workers are usually compliant to exploitation when subject to surveillance and threats with very limited use of coercion. The Palestinian cases here illustrate that for migrant workers force can also directly shape the relations of work.

11. The Israeli state has always played an important role in shaping of economic relations in Israel and the Occupied Territories. The Israeli regime often attempted to "mobilize class power and class organizations toward nationalistic aims" (Ben-Porat 1989: xiii). State intervention in who got what employment opportunities and the state's corporatist relationship with the labor union were manipulated to control the direction of the economic growth for political purposes, particularly to control immigration and emigration of Jews (Shalev 1984: 384; see also Grinberg 1991).

12. In the wake of World War II, Western European countries sought "to procure

a limited supply of *cheap and disposable alien labor* to facilitate" the reconstruction of their economies (Zolberg 1991: 309, emphasis original). Each European country developed a "special relationship with a segment of the periphery" (Zolberg 1991: 316; see also Burawoy 1976; Sassen 1988). When the economy boomed in the 1950s and early 1960s, migrant laborers from across the planet made their way to the urban quarters of Europe and America. Among the people sending workers, exporting labor provided foreign exchange through remittances, which became important as international capitalist organizations like the International Monetary Fund and the World Bank made such funds a precondition for loans (Zolberg 1991: 316). But when the postwar reconstruction ended, Europeans began to close their doors to immigrants. By the mid-1990s, the presence of first, second, and third generation migrants became a contentious and often violent issue in countries like France, Germany, and Japan.

Chapter 4

1. Men working in the West Bank were concentrated in light manufacturing and in wholesale and retail sales and repairs. Most of them were working in small establishments with under ten workers. Most of these shops had a sole proprietor, who was usually present, often working in the shop (Palestinian Bureau of Statistics 1995). There is little doubt that these figures are too low. Most employers probably kept employees unregistered to avoid taxes. More recent figures estimate extensive growth in employment during the late 1990s. The total number of people employed in the West Bank and Gaza Strip was thought to be 386,874 in 1998 (United Nations Special Coordinator in the Occupied Territories 1999: 22).

2. Manufacturing clothes was the only job, besides a slight margin in education, in which there were actually more women than men (Palestinian Bureau of Statistics 1995). Other significant kinds of work for women (categories of over 2,000 workers) included education (2,817), health and social work (2,697), and retail trade in personal goods (2,173).

3. Of 925 garment workshops in the West Bank, about half (468) had 1–4 workers, another quarter (224) had 5–9 workers, only 11 had more than 50 workers, and only 3 had more than 100 (Palestinian Bureau of Statistics 1995).

4. Working as a seamstress, along with teaching, had been one of the few options for women to earn a living other than through the drudgery of agricultural labor or domestic/cleaning services. Only the poorest of women, who refused to be dependent on their male relatives or community charity, pursued these latter options (Moors 1995: 153–89).

5. Some of these artisan workshops still exist. The next oldest daughter of the family, twenty-one years of age, who studied at al-Najah University in Nablus, worked over the summer break for a dress shop where four women and the owner-tailor made fancy dresses, especially bridal wear.

6. Textiles and clothes accounted for 18 percent of total industrial production in the West Bank, but contributed only 5.3 percent to the total industrial revenue (Mansour and Destremau 1997: 41).

7. Women work as machinists and supervisors over other women, whereas men work as cutters, pressers, in maintenance, and as capitalists (see also Moors 1995: 203).

8. The wage rate is unclear for women; they are often told not to discuss their wages with other workers. Sometimes, "those who changed jobs were often too shy to ask beforehand what their wages would be, and many worked six days a week for years without ever asking for the vacation they were legally entitled to" (Moors 1995: 209). "On average, at the end of the month women receive about half of what men make" (207). The main logic of this wage differential is that men are expected to be the providers for their families.

9. "Young women may keep part of their wages to buy clothes and sometimes gold, but they mainly work to help the household until they marry," whereas for older women, either beyond the age of marriage or divorced, working provides their only income and keeps them from being completely reliant on male kin (Moors 1995: 212).

10. Moors (1995) reports the same thing among her many interviews during the 1980s in Nablus.

11. For a discussion of how the enforcement of gender propriety is bound up with worker segregation and inequality, see Beechey (1983), Chadorow (1979), Humphrey (1987), and Willis (1979).

12. Cairoli (1998) describes how female garment workers in large factories in Morocco "transform the public space of the factory into the private space of the home in an attempt to assuage the contradiction inherent in their presence inside the factory, outside the home, in a role ideologically reserved for men" (187). Her rich descriptions of the shop floor illustrate the local embodiment of relations within production, relations of work, and the importance of gender identity in shaping surplus extraction.

13. *Yedioth Aharanoth*, March 21, 1996 (my translation).

14. Another such plan was to put a factory in the Tulkarm District on land belonging to Khadurri College, a Palestinian agricultural training college. I spoke to administrators at the college in May 1995, who told me that they were upset that Palestinian Authority President Arafat and Israeli Prime Minister Rabin had agreed to such plans without consulting the people of Tulkarm or the trustees of the college. Local people objected to the confiscation of the college's land, especially because it was for an Israeli company. Eventually Israel dropped all plans to build there because of the objections of the local leadership (*Al-Quds*, July 16, 1995: 8).

Chapter 5

1. For a more extensive discussion of Palestinian women working in clothing assembly in the Occupied Territories, see Rockwell (1985) and Moors (1995).

2. "There are thousands of people (mainly women) working at home as subcontractors for Palestinian firms. In developing countries, the garments sector and the food processing sector rely the most heavily on informal employment" (Mansour and Destremau 1997: 41).

3. By comparison, in the East Asia and Eastern Europe minimum wage was

around $50 to $80, around $150 to $200 in Turkey, around $60 to $90 in Egypt, and $100 to $150 in Jordan (Mansour and Destremau 1997: 25).

4. By often reported custom (Grenqvist 1931; Moors 1995), women rarely claim their inheritance, allowing all property to pass to their brothers as a means of solidifying fraternal alliance. Married women are expected to depend on their husbands to provide food and shelter. This usually allows them to leave their property in the hands of their brothers. Brothers, in turn, are expected to help their sister should her husband abandon or neglect her.

5. The proposal that making a sacrifice will ward off the "evil eye" might be interpreted in several ways. On the one hand, I have witnessed people using the blood of a sacrificed sheep as a physical prophylactic against harm. They might touch the blood to their face, usually under the ear. In this practice the blood itself seems to have a property of healing or protection. On the other hand, the sacrifice is only a sacrifice, and not merely the slaughtering of an animal, if the meat is distributed among family members. In this sense, it seems that the circulation of the meat is what is crucial. This seems quite similar to theories of the gift explored by Mauss (1990) in which accumulation without reciprocity, without giving back, is not only dishonorable but can bring social, economic, and spiritual hardship.

6. In 1967–68, 2,500 tons of chemical fertilizer were bought in the West Bank; but by 1969–70, 15,000 tons of chemical fertilizers were purchased. The number of tractors went from 147 in 1967 to 1,534 in 1977 and 1,883 in 1979–80; in addition, most farmers have been compelled to buy Israeli seed (Graham-Brown 1990: 60).

7. Even this high figure probably is too low because goods going from Israel to the West Bank pass unregistered.

Chapter 6

1. Sometimes it was not so subtle. During the Uprising, Palestinians urged each other not to buy Israeli products, especially those that had substitute Palestinian products. The primary beneficiaries of this boycott were a soft-drink company, a dairy, many local bakers, and cigarette manufacturers. Some young men monitored the boycott by asking for a cigarette and giving you a lecture if you were smoking the wrong brand.

2. The Society for Family Restoration, Jam'iyat In'ash al-Usra, also housed a girls' orphanage, a nursery school and day-care center, several vocational schools for young women, a catering service, and a women's clothing cooperative.

3. In the 1970s, a number of grassroots organizations associated with the national movement devoted themselves to sponsoring "an array of projects designed to rescue the past: collecting testimony from refugees in order to document the histories of destroyed villages; gathering and publishing folklore and folktales; sponsoring folkloric dance and music troupes; and encouraging traditional crafts, particularly women's needlework" (Swedenburg 1991: 168).

4. Much of this work reiterates a few key points: (a) the women's movement

emerged as part of the national movement; (b) it was primarily elite women providing charity to the poor throughout most of the twentieth century; (c) in the 1970s popular women's committees arose as part of the nationalist struggle; and (d) women's issues have remained subordinate to the national issue. Even the populist-oriented women's organizations of the 1970s and '80s that supported the emancipation of women in terms of equal pay, social protection, and unionization hesitated mentioning women's status in society.

5. In the summer of 1996, for example, 'A'isha, the second eldest daughter of Abu Harab, got married to a man from Tayiba. Her mother and female relatives all said that the man, who now lives in Europe, came back to marry an Arab girl with good morals, and he particularly wanted a woman from the West Bank. They clearly said it with pride.

6. In cases where the forces of globalization are subjugating and exploiting populations based on their being different, choosing to maintain clear borders through custom is also a defense against subordination or annihilation. It "is a process of appropriating the concept of fixity of form and content from the Eurocenter for the margin's own recovery and healing" (Lavie and Swedenburg 1996: 165; see also S. Mahmood 1996; Shohat 1992).

7. Chatterjee (1993) describes how colonial rule in India was premised on notions of cultural difference that claimed the superiority of the British. Their liberal rhetoric eventually conflicted with the colonial reality, and resistance grew against their rule, arguing in favor of eradicating all forms of colonial difference (1993: 74). On the other hand, they increasingly emphasized the cultural particularity of the Hindu nation. This lived contradiction, between universalism and particularism, between needing to learn from and emulate Europe, but also to resist and maintain autonomy, became manifest in customs of gender. As the national movement developed, women were increasingly urged to protect and cultivate the Hindu tradition against the attack being made by Western practice. Female sensuality, like the lure of gold, was considered *maya* (1993: 62), part of the outer, material world and a threat from Europe.

8. The patriarchal attitude was evident in statements by the Ministry of Economy and Planning of the Palestinian Authority, specifically from a document called the General Program for National Economic Development, 1994–2000 (Giacaman, Jad, and Johnson 1996). The most persistent flaw of development thinking has been a two-track policy of social welfare. On the one hand, there is an attitude of entitlement for labor market participants, i.e., men; and on the other hand, there is an attitude of charity welfare for those not part of, or not expected to be part of the labor market, i.e., women.

Chapter 7

1. It was like Ghassan Kanafani's novella, *Men in the Sun*, which tells the tragic story of Palestinians attempting the clandestine journey with unscrupulous guides past international borders through uncompromising deserts.

2. In 1957 the Old City walls were torn down and careful urban planning, with separate residential districts, each with its own school, police station, clinic, market,

and the like, was instituted. The city's planning spatially laid the groundwork for later legal and political distinctions between Kuwaiti and non-Kuwaiti residents (Brand 1988: 112).

3. Several private schools were established in the mid-1960s to compensate for the Kuwaiti government's hesitancy to educate all Palestinian children. In 1967 the PLO was allowed to operate its own schools, where children saluted the Palestinian flag, celebrated and practiced Palestinian customs, and even formed scouting troops like the Zahrat and Ashbal, which, like American boy scouts, had paramilitary and political content (Brand 1988: 118–20). These schools were closed in 1976 and the children were reintegrated into Kuwaiti schools. But by the 1980s, the General Union of Palestinian Women in Kuwait had to organize a tuition fund, which by 1986 funded about 3,000 students, to care for large numbers of Palestinian children who were again denied matriculation (Brand 1988: 120–21).

4. Kuwait law forbade non-Kuwaiti unions; the General Union of Palestinian Workers was allowed to function as part of the PLO, but only in disputes among Palestinians (Brand 1988: 130).

5. The Palestinian cultural festivals featured embroidery, traditional handicrafts from the Occupied Territories, music, food, dance, and films (Brand 1988: 136).

6. Brand (1988) foreshadowed the tragedy that would befall the Palestinians two years later when she wrote:

Already suffering from increased visa and residency restrictions, problems with educating their children, and with the economic recession in the Gulf, evidence of Palestinian involvement in the explosions [at the U.S., British, and French embassies and the Kuwaiti international airport in December 1983], many believed, would trigger the imposition of even greater restrictions, and perhaps — the greatest fear of the community in Kuwait — mass expulsions. (Brand 1988: 124–25)

7. The exodus included 731,000 Yemenis from Saudi Arabia, 250,000 Jordanians from Kuwait, and 390,000 Egyptians from Iraq (Abdel-Jaber 1993: 156–57).

8. Former government employees were eventually paid their entitlement, but workers in the private sector, except those in large businesses, rarely received their due.

9. When Jordan took over the West Bank it acquired "a flourishing middle class involved in commercial activities and in the elaborate civil service that had developed under the mandate" as well as a trade union tradition (Brand 1988: 154).

10. Ramallah, Nablus, Bethlehem, and Gaza all have cultivated a metropolitan styled area — broad streets where pedestrians and cars cruise the arcades — but they are only large towns in comparison with Jerusalem, Amman, Tel Aviv, Beirut, Damascus, or especially massive Cairo with its population of around 20 million.

11. For a discussion of the Palestinian community in Lebanon, see Sayigh (1979) and Peteet (1991). An overall comparison of diaspora communities can be found in Aruri and Farsoun (1980).

12. For over a thousand years of Islamic rule, elites from across the Muslim world (including Christians and Jews) settled in Palestinian towns. Until the nineteenth century, the Palestinian peasantry suffered from cycles of attacks by Bedouin which forced them to take refuge in the hills. By the 1830s, Egyptian armies subdued the Bedouin, settled foreign populations to labor in commercial agriculture, and pulled Palestinians

into the constellation of international trade. By the later 1800s, however, those peasants became increasingly disenfranchised by Ottoman reformations. Some began to seek relief by immigrating to the Americas and Europe.

Chapter 8

1. According to Mustapha Barghouti, head of the Palestinian Medical Relief Services, by the spring 2001 the West Bank was divided into fifty separate sections divided by hundreds of military checkpoints, not including the many cement and dirt barricades and trenches that hinder travel (Wahdan 2001).

2. The first uprising was in 1936–39, the second was the Intifada of 1987–93.

3. When the renewed uprising began in the fall 2000, Deborah Sontag reported on the front page of the *New York Times* that

Many Israelis, especially the doves are staggered by this swift tumble from the brink of a resolution back down into the depths of the elemental ethnic hatred at the root of their blood soaked conflict. But the Palestinians are not. For an overwhelming majority of them, the peace felt only skin deep-not bone deep-and very fragile. (October 9, 2000)

Suggestions that Israelis and Palestinians were on the brink of peace, to which Israelis were committed, but about which Palestinians were hesitant because of "elemental ethnic hatred," were common stereotypes, masking daily experiences that fuel the fires of resistance.

4. "Where the politics of universal dignity fought for forms of nondiscrimination that were quite 'blind' to the ways in which citizens differ, the politics of difference often redefines nondiscrimination as requiring that we make these distinctions the basis of differential treatment" (Taylor 1994: 39).

5. Complex equality is a system in which "no citizen's standing in one sphere or with regard to one social good can be undercut by his standing in some other social sphere, with regard to some other social good" (Walzer 1983: 19).

References

Abboushi, W. F.
    1990   *The Unmaking of Palestine*. Brattleboro, Vt.: Amana Books.
Abdel-Jaber, Tayseer
    1993   "Inter-Arab Labor Movements: Problems and Prospects." In *Economic Development of the Arab Countries, Selected Issues*, ed. Said el-Naggar. Washington, D.C.: International Monetary Fund.
ʿAbd al-Jabbar, Naji
    1989   "Mathaf al-Turath al-Shaʿbi [Museum of Popular Heritage]." *Al-Turath wa al-Mujtamaʿ* 20: 111–20.
Abdulhadi, Rami
    1990   "Land Use Planning in the Occupied Territories." *Journal of Palestine Studies* 19, 4: 46–63.
Abu-Ghazaleh, Adnan
    1991   *Palestinian Arab Cultural Nationalism, 1919–1960*. Brattleboro, Vt.: Amana Books.
Abu-Habda, ʿAbd al-ʿAziz
    1981   "Al-Batal al-falastini fi al-hikaya al-shaʿbiya [The Palestinian Hero in Popular Stories]." *Al-Turath wa al-Mujtimaʿ* 15: 108–17.
    1993   "Dawr al-sahafa al-mahalia fi ʿamalia al-ihtimam bi-tarathna al-shaʿbi al-falastini [The Role of Local Journalists in Preserving Our Popular Palestinian Heritage]." *Al-Turath wa al-Mujtimaʿ* 22: 121–36.
Abu-Lughod, Lila
    1991   "Writing Against Culture." In *Recapturing Anthropology*, ed. Richard Fox. Santa Fe, N.M.: School of American Research Press.
    1993   *Writing Women's Worlds*. Berkeley: University of California Press.
Afflitto, Frank
    2000   "The Homogenizing Effects of State-Sponsored Terrorism: The Case of Guatemala." In *Death Squad: The Anthropology of State Terror*, ed. Jeffrey Sluka. Philadelphia: University of Pennsylvania Press.
ʿAllush, Musa
    1981   "Al-shaʿir al-shaʿbi Hanna Abu-Thiyab [Popular Poet Hana Abu-Theeab]." *Al-Turath wa al-Mujtimaʿ* 15: 85–102.
    1982   "ʿAzif al-rababa Saqur al-Basha [The Rababa Player Suqur el-Basha]." *Al-Turath wa al-Mujtimaʿ* 16: 80–90.
Alvarez, Robert, Jr.
    1995   "The Mexican-U.S. Border: The Making of an Anthropology of Borderlands." *Annual Review of Anthropology* 24: 447–70.
ʿAnani, Nabil
    1988   "Kayfa yataʿamal al-atfal ma turathna al-shaʿbiya [How to Deal With Children Regarding Our Popular Heritage]." *Al-Turath wa al-Mujtimaʿ* 19: 126–30.

Anderson, Benedict
  1983   *Imagined Communities: Reflections on the Origin and Spread of Nation-alism*. New York: Verso.
Anzaldúa, Gloria
  1987   *Borderlands/La Frontera: The New Mestiza*. San Francisco: Spinsters/ Aunt Lute.
Aretxaga, Begona
  2000   "A Fictional Reality: Paramilitary Death Squads and the Construction of State Terror in Spain." In *Death Squad: The Anthropology of State Terror*, ed. Jeffrey Sluka. Philadelphia: University of Pennsylvania Press.
Aruri, Naseer and Samih Farsoun
  1980   "Palestinians Communities and Arab Host Countries." In *The Sociology of the Palestinians*, ed. Khalil Nakhleh and Elia Zureik. New York: St. Martin's Press.
Asad, Talal
  1997   "On Torture, or Cruel, Inhuman, and Degrading Treatment." In *Social Suffering*, ed. Arthur Kleinman, Veena Das, and Margaret Lock. Berkeley: University of California Press.
  1972   "Anthropological Texts and Ideological Problems: an Analysis of Cohen on Arab Villages in Israel." *Review of Middle East Studies* 1: 1–39.
Asad, Talal, ed.
  1973   *Anthropology and the Colonial Encounter*. Atlantic Highlands, N.J.: Humanities Press.
Asiwaju, A. I., ed.
  1985   *Partitioned Africans: Ethnic Relations Across Africa's International Boundaries, 1884–1984*. Lagos: University of Lagos Press.
Augustin, Ebba, ed.
  1993   *Palestinian Women: Identity and Experience*. London: Zed Books.
Avineri, Shlomo
  1985   *Moses Hess: Prophet of Communism and Zionism*. New York: New York University Press.
Badran, Margot
  1995   *Feminists, Islam, and Nation: Gender and the Making of Modern Egypt*. Princeton, N.J.: Princeton University Press.
Baer, Gabriel
  1966   "Land Tenure in Egypt and the Fertile Crescent, 1800–1950." In *The Economic History of the Middle East*, ed. Charles Issawi. Chicago: University of Chicago Press.
Barth, Fredrik, ed.
  1969   *Ethnic Groups and Boundaries: The Social Organization of Cultural Difference*. Boston: Little Brown.
Beechey, Veronica
  1983   "What's So Special About Women's Employment? A Review of Some Recent Studies of Women's Paid Employment." *Feminist Review* 15: 23–45.

Ben-Ari, Eyal
   1998   *Mastering Soldiers: Conflict, Emotions, and the Enemy in an Israeli Military Unit*. New Directions in Anthropology 10. New York: Berghahn.
Ben-Arieh, Yehoshua
   1979   *The Rediscovery of the Holy Land in the Nineteenth Century*. Detroit: Wayne State University Press.
Ben-Porat, Amir
   1989   *Divided We Stand: Class Structure in Israel from 1948 to the 1980s*. New York: Greenwood Press.
Bernstein, Deborah
   2000   *Constructing Boundaries: Jewish and Arab Workers in Mandatory Palestine*. Albany: State University of New York Press.
Bhabha, Homi K.
   1983   "The Other Question . . . Homi K Bhabha Reconsiders the Stereotype and Colonial Discourse." *Screen* 24, 6: 18–36.
   1994   *The Location of Culture*. New York: Routledge.
Binur, Yoram
   1989   *My Enemy, My Self*. New York: Penguin.
Bowman, Glen
   1989   "Fucking Tourists: Sexual Relations and Tourism in Jerusalem's Old City." *Critique of Anthropology* 9, 2: 77–93.
Bourdieu, Pierre
   1984   *Distinction: A Social Critique of the Judgment of Taste*. Trans. Richard Nice. Cambridge, Mass.: Harvard University Press.
Brand, Laurie
   1988   *Palestinians in the Arab World: Institution Building and the Search for State*. New York: Columbia University Press.
B'Tselem
   1989   *The Military Judicial System in the West Bank*. Jerusalem: B'Tselem.
   1991a   *The Interrogation of Palestinians During the Intifada: Ill-treatment, "Moderate Physical Pressure" or Torture?* Jerusalem: B'Tselem.
   1991b   *Bi-Annual Report: Violations of Human Rights in the Occupied Territories 1990/1991*. Jerusalem: B'Tselem.
   1992   *The Interrogation of Palestinians During the Intifada: Follow-up to March 1991*. Jerusalem: B'Tselem.
Burawoy, Michael
   1976   "The Function and Reproduction of Migrant Labor." *American Journal of Sociology* 81 (March): 1050–87.
   1985   *The Politics of Production*. London: Verso.
Cairoli, M. Laetitia
   1998   "Factory as Home and Family: Female Workers in the Moroccan Garment Industry." *Human Organization* 57, 2: 181–89.
Chatterjee, Partha
   1993   *The Nation and Its Fragments: Colonial and Postcolonial Histories*. Princeton, N.J.: Princeton University Press.

Chavez, Leo
    1992   *Shadowed Lives: Undocumented Immigrants in American Society.* Ft.
            Worth, Tex.: Harcourt, Brace, Jovanovich.
Chodorow, Nancy
    1979   "Mothering, Male Dominance, and Capitalism." In *Capitalist Patriarchy
            and the Case for Socialist Feminism,* ed. Zillah R. Eisenstein. New York:
            Monthly Review Press.
Clifford, James
    1988   *The Predicament of Culture: Twentieth-Century Ethnography, Literature,
            and Art.* Cambridge, Mass.: Harvard University Press.
Cohen, Abner
    1969   *Arab Border Villages in Israel.* Manchester: Manchester University Press.
Donnan, Hastings and Thomas Wilson, eds.
    1994   *Border Approaches: Anthropological Perspectives of Frontiers.* New
            York: University Press of America.
Dowty, Alan
    1987   *Closed Borders: The Contemporary Assault on Freedom of Movement.*
            New Haven, Conn.: Yale University Press.
Ebeling, Richard and Jacob Hornberger, eds.
    1995   *The Case for Free Trade and Open Immigration.* Fairfax, Va.: Future of
            Freedom Foundation.
Ein-Gil, Ehud and Aryeh Finkelstein
    1978   "Changes in Palestinian Society." *Khamsin* 5: 16–23.
Ezrahi, Yaron
    1997   *Rubber Bullets: Power and Conscience in Modern Israel.* Berkeley: Uni-
            versity of California Press.
Fanon, Frantz
    1964   *Toward the African Revolution, Political Essays.* Trans. Haakon Cheva-
            lier. New York: Grove.
    1965   *A Dying Colonialism.* Trans. Haakon Chevalier. New York: Grove.
    1967   *Black Skin, White Masks.* Trans. Charles Lam Markmann. New York:
            Grove.
Farsakh, Laila
    1998   *Palestinian Workers in Israel: 1967–1997.* Ramallah: MAS.
Federation of Palestinian Chambers of Commerce
    1998   *Transaction Costs for Palestinian Business.* Ramallah: Federation of Pal-
            estinian Chambers of Commerce.
Flores, Richard
    1994   "Los Pastores and the Gifting of Performance." *American Ethnologist* 21,
            2: 270–85.
    1995   "Private Visions, Public Culture: The Making of the Alamo." *Cultural
            Anthropology* 10, 1: 99–115.
Flynn, Donna
    1997   " 'We are the Border': Identity, Exchange, and the State Along the Benin-
            Nigeria Border." *American Ethnologist* 24, 2: 311–30.

Gazit, Shlomo
    1995   *The Carrot and the Stick: Israel's Policy in Judea and Samaria, 1967–68.*
            Washington, D.C.: B'nai B'rith Books.
al-Ghul, Fayiz
    1992   "Al-fuklur [Folklore]." *Al-Turath wa al-Mujtima⸴* 21: 40–45.
Giacaman, Rita and Penny Johnson
    1994   "Searching for Strategies: The Palestinian Women's Movement in the
            New Era." *Middle East Report* 186, 24, 1: 22–25. Reprint in *Women and
            Power in the Middle East*, ed. Suad Joseph and Susan Slyomovics. Phila-
            delphia: University of Pennsylvania Press, 2001.
Giacaman, Rita, Islah Jad, and Penny Johnson
    1996   "For the Common Good? Gender and Social Citizenship in Palestine."
            Middle East Report 198, 26, 1: 11–17. Reprint in *Women and Power in
            the Middle East*, ed. Suad Joseph and Susan Slyomovics. Philadelphia:
            University of Pennsylvania Press, 2001.
Giacaman, Rita and Muna Odeh
    1988   "Palestinian Women's Movement in the Occupied West Bank and Gaza
            Strip." In *Women in the Arab World*, ed. Nahid Toubia. Atlantic High-
            lands, N.J.: Zed Books.
Ginbar, Yuval
    1993   *The "New Procedure" in GSS Interrogations: The Case of Abd Al-Nasser
            'Ubeid.* Jerusalem: B'Tselem.
    1998   *Routine Torture: Interrogation Methods of the General Security Service.*
            Jerusalem: B'Tselem.
Graham-Brown, Sarah
    1990   "Agriculture and Labour Transformation in Palestine." In *The Rural Mid-
            dle East*, ed. Pandeli Glavanis and Kathy Glavanis. London: Zed Books.
Green, Linda
    1994   "Fear as a Way of Life." *Cultural Anthropology* 9, 2: 227–56.
Grenqvist, Hilma
    1931   "Marriage Conditions in a Palestinian Village." *Humanarum Litterarum*
            3, 8: 1–195.
Grinberg, Lev Luis
    1991   *Split Corporatism in Israel.* Albany: State University of New York Press.
Hall, Stuart
    1990   "Cultural Identity and Diaspora." In *Identity, Community, Culture, Dif-
            ference*, ed. Jonathan Rutherford. London: Lawrence and Wishart.
    1991   "Ethnicity: Identity and Difference." *Radical America* 13, 4: 9–20.
Hall, Stuart and David Held
    1990   "Citizen and Citizenship." In *New Times: The Changing Face of Politics
            in the 1990s*, ed. Stuart Hall and Martin Jacques. London: Verso.
    1993   "Culture, Community and Nation." *Cultural Studies* 7, 3: 349–63.
Hammami, Rema
    1990   "Women, the Hijab, and the Intifada." *Middle East Report* 20, 3/4: 24–28.
Al-Haq
    1984   *Torture and Intimidation in the West Bank: The Case of al-Fara'a Prison.*
            Ramallah: Al-Haq.

1989   *Perpetual Emergency: A Legal Analysis of Israel's Use of the British Defence (Emergency) Regulations, 1945, in the Occupied Territories.* Ramallah: Al-Haq.

1990   *Punishing a Nation: Israeli Human Rights Violations During the Palestinian Uprising December 1987–December 1988.* Boston: South End Press.

Harris, Nigel

1990   *National Liberation.* Reno: University of Nevada Press.

Harvey, David

1998   *Justice, Nature, and the Geography of Difference.* Malden, Mass.: Blackwell.

Heiberg, Marianne and Geir Ovensen et al. eds.

1993   *Palestinian Society in Gaza, West Bank and Arab Jerusalem: A Survey of Living Conditions.* Oslo: FAFO.

Heyman, Josiah

1991   *Life and Labor on the Border: Working People of Northeastern Sonora, Mexico, 1886–1986.* Tucson: University of Arizona Press.

1995   "Putting Power into the Anthropology of Bureaucracy: The Immigration and Naturalization Service at the Mexico-United States Border." *Current Anthropology* 36, 2: 261–87.

1998a   *Finding a Moral Heart for U.S. Immigration Policy.* American Ethnologist Monograph Series 7. Arlington, Va.: American Anthropological Association.

1998b   "State Effects on Labor Exploitation: The INS and Undocumented Immigrants at the Mexico-United States Border." *Critique of Anthropology* 18, 2: 157–80.

1999   "United States Surveillance over Mexican Lives at the Border: Snapshots of an Emerging Regime." *Human Organization* 58, 4: 430–38.

Hicks, Emily

1991   *Border Writing: The Multidimensional Text.* Minneapolis: University of Minnesota Press.

Hiltermann, Joost

1992   *Behind the Intifada: Labor and Women's Committees in the Occupied Territories.* Princeton, N.J.: Princeton University Press.

1991   "The Women's Movement During the Uprising." *Journal of Palestinian Studies* 20, 3: 48–57.

1990   "Trade Unions and Women's Committees: Sustaining Movement, Creating Space." *Middle East Report* 20 (May/August): 32–36.

Hockstader, Lee

2000   "Trophy Photos Betray Israeli Police Abuse." *Washington Post*, September 19: A16.

hooks, bell

1992   *Black Looks: Race and Representation.* Boston: South End Press.

Hourani, Albert

1966   "The Political and Social Background of the Eighteenth Century." In *The Economic History of the Middle East 1800–1914*, ed. Charles Issawi. Chicago: University of Chicago Press.

1981   "The Ottoman Background of the Modern Middle East." In *The Emergence of the Modern Middle East*, ed. Albert Hourani. Berkeley: University of California Press.

1991   *A History of the Arab Peoples*. Cambridge, Mass.: Harvard University Press.

Human Rights Watch

1991   *Prison Conditions in Israel and the Occupied Territories*. New York: Human Rights Watch.

1994   *Torture and Ill-Treatment: Israel's Interrogation of Palestinians from the Occupied Territories*. New York: Human Rights Watch.

1995   *Slaughter Among Neighbors*. New Haven, Conn.: Human Rights Watch and Yale University Press.

1998   *Israel's Closure of the West Bank and Gaza Strip*. New York: Human Rights Watch.

Humphrey, Michael

1993   "The Political Economy of Population Movements in the Middle East." *Middle East Report* 181, 23 (March/April): 2–7.

Isaac, Jad

1989   "A Socio-Economic Study of Administrative Detainees at Ansar 3." *Journal of Palestine Studies* 28, 4: 102–9.

Israeli Central Bureau of Statistics

1999   *Statistical Abstract of Israel*. Jerusalem: State of Israel.

Israel Economist

1990   "Industrial R&D in Israel." *Israel Economist* (February): 4–7.

Issawi, Charles

1982   *An Economic History of the Middle East and North Africa*. New York: Columbia University Press.

1988   *The Fertile Crescent 1800–1914: A Documentary Economic History*. Oxford: Oxford University Press.

Jad, Islah

1990   "From Salons to Popular Committees: Palestinian Women, 1919–1989." In *Intifada: Palestine at the Crossroads*, ed. Jamal Nassar and Roger Heacock. New York: Praeger.

1995   "A Feminist Analysis of Tribalism and 'Municipal Elections.' " *Al-Quds*, September 12.

Jawwad, Islah Abdul

1990   "The Evolution of the Political Role of the Palestinian Women's Movement in the Uprising." In *The Palestinians: New Directions*, ed. Michael Hudson. Washington, D.C.: Center for Contemporary Arab Studies, Georgetown University.

Joppke, Christian

1999   "How Immigration Is Changing Citizenship: A Comparative View." *Ethnic and Racial Studies* 22, 4: 629–52.

Joudah, Ahmad Hasan

1987   *Revolt in Palestine in the Eighteenth Century: The Era of Shaykh Zahir al-ʿUmar*. Princeton, N.J.: Kingston Press.

Kana'ana, Sharif
    1986   "Al-fuklur ma huwa? [What Is Folklore?]" *Al-Turath wa al-Mujtima'* 18:
            7–24.
    1993   "Dawr al-Turath al-Sha'bi fi Ta'ziz al-Huwiya [The Role of Popular Heri-
            tage in the Preservation of Identity]." *Al-Turath wa al-Mujtima'* 22: 7–25.
Kandiyoti, Deniz, ed.
    1991   *Women, Islam, and the State.* London: Macmillan.
Kearney, Michael
    1986   "From the Invisible Hand to Visible Feet: Anthropological Studies of Mi-
            gration and Development." *Annual Review of Anthropology* 15: 331–61.
    1991   "Borders and Boundaries of State and Self at the End of Empire." *Journal
            of Historical Sociology* 4, 1: 52–74.
    1995   "The Local and the Global: The Anthropology of Globalization and
            Transnationalism." *Annual Review of Anthropology* 24: 547–65.
Khalidi, Rashid
    1997   *Palestinian Identity: The Construction of Modern National Conscious-
            ness.* New York: Columbia University Press.
Khoury, Philip
    1983   *Urban Notables and Arab Nationalism.* Cambridge: Cambridge Univer-
            sity Press.
Kimmerling, Baruch and Joel Migdal
    1993   *Palestinians: The Making of a People.* New York: Free Press.
Kleinman, Arthur and Joan Kleinman
    1997   "The Appeal of Experience; The Dismay of Images: Cultural Appropria-
            tions of Suffering in Our Times." In *Social Suffering*, ed. Arthur Klein-
            man, Veena Das, and Margaret Lock. Berkeley: University of California
            Press.
Kratochwil, Friedrich
    1986   "Of Systems, Boundaries, and Territoriality: An Inquiry into the Forma-
            tion of the State System." *World Politics* 39, 1: 27–52.
Kymlicka, Will
    1995   *Multicultural Citizenship.* Oxford: Oxford University Press.
Lattimore, Owen
    1968   "The Frontier in History." In *Theory in Anthropology: A Sourcebook*, ed.
            Robert Maners and David Kaplan. Chicago: Aldine.
Lavie, Smadar and Ted Swedenburg
    1996   "Between and Among the Boundaries of Culture: Bridging Text and
            Lived Experience in the Third Timespace." *Cultural Studies* 10, 1: 154–
            79.
Lein, Yehezkel
    1999   *Builders of Zion: Human Rights Violations of Palestinians from the Oc-
            cupied Territories Working in Israel and the Settlements.* Jerusalem:
            B'Tselem.
Lenin, Vladimir
    1939   *Imperialism, the Highest Stage of Capitalism.* New York: International
            Publishers.
    1974   *On the Jewish Question.* New York: International Publishers.

Lesch, Ann
    1991   "Palestinians in Kuwait." *Journal of Palestine Studies* 20, 4: 42–54.
Limón, José Eduardo
    1989   "Carne, Carnales, and the Carnivalesque: Bakhtinian Bathos, Disorder
            and Narrative Discourses." *American Ethnologist* 16, 3: 471–86.
    1994   *Dancing with the Devil: Society and Cultural Poetics in Mexican-Ameri-
            can South Texas*. Madison: University of Wisconsin Press.
Lomsky-Feder, Edna and Eyal Ben-Ari, eds.
    2000   *The Military and Militarism in Israeli Society*. Binghamton: State Univer-
            sity of New York Press.
Lowy, Michael
    1976   "Marxists and the National Question." *New Left Review* 96: 81–100.
Lustick, Ian
    1980   *Arabs in the Jewish State: Israel's Control of a National Minority*. Austin:
            University of Texas Press.
    1988   *For the Land and the Lord*. New York: Council on Foreign Relations.
Macalister, R. A. Stewart and E. W. G. Macmahon
    1906   "A History of the Doings of the Fellahin During the First Half of the Nine-
            teenth Century from Native Sources." *Palestine Exploration Fund Quar-
            terly*: 33–50.
Macfie, A. L.
    1996   *The Eastern Question, 1774–1923*. New York: Longman.
Mahmood, Cynthia Keppley
    1996   *Fighting for Faith and Nation: Dialogues with Sikh Militants*. Philadel-
            phia: University of Pennsylvania Press.
    2000   "Trials by Fire: Dynamics of Terror in Punjab and Kashmir." In *Death
            Squad: The Anthropology of State Terror*, ed. Jeffrey Sluka. Philadelphia:
            University of Pennsylvania Press.
Mahmood, Saba
    1996   "Cultural Studies and Ethnic Absolutism: Comments on Stuart Hall's
            'Culture, Community, Nation.' " *Cultural Studies* 10, 1: 1–11.
Mansour, Antoine and Blandine Destreman
    1997   *Palestine and Israel: Subcontracting in the Garment Industry*. Ramallah:
            MAS.
Ma'oz, Moshe, ed.
    1975   *Studies on Palestine During the Ottoman Period*. Jerusalem: Magnes
            Press.
Marcus, George and Michael Fischer
    1986   *Anthropology as Cultural Critique: An Experimental Moment in the Hu-
            man Sciences*. Chicago: University of Chicago Press.
Mauss, Marcel
    1990   *The Gift*. New York: Norton.
Ministry of Construction and Housing
    2000   *Monthly Bulletin* (April). Jerusalem: Department of Information and Eco-
            nomic Analysis.

Mishal, Shaul and Reuban Aharoni
    1994   *Speaking Stones: Communiqués from the Intifada Underground.* Syracuse, N.Y.: Syracuse University Press.
Moghadam, Valentine, ed.
    1994   *Gender and National Identity: Women and Politics in Muslim Societies.* Atlantic Highlands, N.J.: Zed Books.
Moors, Annelies
    1995   *Women, Property, and Islam: Palestinian Experiences, 1920–1990.* Cambridge: Cambridge University Press.
Morris, Benny
    1987   *The Birth of the Palestinian Refugee Problem, 1947–1949.* Cambridge: Cambridge University Press.
Morris, David
    1997   "About Suffering: Voice, Genre, and Moral Community." In *Social Suffering*, ed. Arthur Kleinman, Veena Das, and Margaret Lock. Berkeley: University of California Press.
Musharqa, Salih
    1996   "Ya ʿummal falastin intatharu [Oh Palestinian Workers Wait]." *Al-Milad* 3 (January/Kanun al-Thani): 56–58.
Muslih, Mohammed
    1988   *The Origins of Palestinian Nationalism.* New York: Columbia University Press.
Nasr, Mohamed
    1997   *The Impact of the Peace Process on the Textile and Garment Industry in Palestine.* Ramallah: MAS.
Nasser, Jamal and Roger Heacock, eds.
    1990   *Intifada: Palestine at the Crossroads.* New York: Praeger.
Nordstrom, Carolyn
    1997   *A Different Kind of War Story.* Philadelphia: University of Pennsylvania Press.
Owen, Roger
    1989   "The West Bank Now: Economic Development." In *Palestine Under Occupation: Prospects for the Future*, ed. Peter Krogh and Mary McDavid. Washington, D.C.: Georgetown University Press.
Palestine Exploration Fund
    1895   *Thirty Year Prospectus.* London: Palestine Exploration Fund.
Palestinian Bureau of Statistics
    1995   *Establishment Census Report.* Ramallah: Palestinian Bureau of Statistics.
Palestinian General Federation of Trade Unions
    1998   "Palestinian Labourers Face Undeclared War: Martyrs, Injured, High Fines." *Labourer's Voice* (October). Ramallah: Palestinian General Federation of Trade Unions.
Palestinian Human Rights Information Center
    1991   *The Cost of Freedom.* Chicago: Palestinian Human Rights Information Center.
Parker, Andrew, Mary Russo, Doris Summer, and Patricia Yaeger, eds.
    1992   *Nationalism and Sexualities.* New York: Routledge.

Perry, Nigel
    1995   *Making Education Illegal*. Birzeit: Human Rights Action Project /Birzeit University.
Peteet, Julie
    1989   "Women and National Politics in the Middle East." In *Power and Stability in the Middle East*, ed. Berch Berberoglu. Atlantic Highlands, N.J.: Zed Books.
    1991   *Gender in Crisis: Women and the Palestinian Resistance Movement*. New York: Columbia University Press.
    1993   "Authenticity and Gender: The Presentation of Culture." In *Arab Women: Old Boundaries, New Frontiers*, ed. Judith Tucker. Washington, D.C.: Center for Contemporary Arab Studies, Georgetown University.
    1994   "Male Gender and Rituals of Resistance in the Palestinian Intifada: A Cultural Politics of Violence." *American Ethnologist* 21, 3: 31–49.
Piven, Frances Fox and Richard Cloward
    1971   *Regulating the Poor*. New York: Vintage.
Reilly, James
    1981   "The Peasantry of Late Ottoman Palestine." *Journal of Palestine Studies* 10, 4: 82–97.
Rishmawi, Mona
    1988   "The Legal Status of Palestinian Women in the Occupied Territories." In *Women in the Arab World*, ed. Nahid Toubia. Atlantic Highlands, N.J.: Zed Books.
Robben, Antonius
    1995   "The Politics of Truth and Emotion Among Victims and Perpetrators of Violence." In *Fieldwork Under Fire*, ed. Carolyn Nordstrom and Antonius Robben. Berkeley: University of California Press.
    2000   "State Terror in the Netherworld: Disappearance and Reburial in Argentina." In *Death Squad: The Anthropology of State Terror*, ed. Jeffrey Sluka. Philadelphia: University of Pennsylvania Press.
Robben, Antonius and Marcelo Suárez-Orozco, eds.
    2000   *Cultures Under Siege: Collective Violence and Trauma*. New York: Cambridge University Press.
Rockwell, Susan
    1985   "Palestinian Women Workers in the Israeli-occupied Gaza Strip." *Journal of Palestine Studies* 14, 2: 114–36.
Rosaldo, Renato
    1985   "Chicano Studies, 1970–1984." *Annual Review of Anthropology* 14: 405–27.
    1989   "Border Crossings." In *Culture and Truth: The Remaking of Social Analysis*. Boston: Beacon Press.
Rosenfeld, Henry
    1972   "An Overview and Critique of the Literature on Rural Politics and Social Change." In *Rural Politics and Social Change in the Middle East*, ed. Richard Antoun and Iliya Harik. Bloomington: Indiana University Press.
    1978   "The Class Situation of the Arab National Minority in Israel." *Comparative Studies in Society and History* 20, 3: 374–407.

Rosenhek, Zeev
    2000   "Migration Regimes, Intra-State Conflicts and the Politics of Exclusion and Inclusion: Migrant Workers in the Israeli Welfare State." *Social Problems* 47, 1: 49–67.

Rouse, Roger
    1991   "Mexican Migration and the Social Space of Postmodernism." *Diaspora* 1, 1: 8–23.

Roy, Sara
    1991   "The Political Economy of Despair: Changing Political and Economic Realities in the Gaza Strip." *Journal of Palestine Studies* 20, 3: 58–69.

Sahlins, Peter
    1989   *Boundaries: The Making of France and Spain in the Pyrenees.* Berkeley: University of California Press.

Said, Edward
    1978   *Orientalism.* New York: Random House.
    1994   *Culture and Imperialism.* New York: Random House.

Samara, ʿAdel
    1989   "The Political Economy of the West Bank 1967–1987: From Peripheralization of Development." In *Palestine: Profile of an Occupation.* Atlantic Highlands, N.J.: Zed Press.
    1995   "Al-marʾa wa al-intaj wa-ras al-mal: tashghil wa-mawqaʿ al-maraʾ al-falastinia munthu al-intidab al-britani wa-hata al-hukum al-thati [Women, Production, and Capital: Employment and the Situation of Palestinian Women since the British Mandate until Self Rule]." Part One, *Kanaan* (January-February): 53–57; Part Two, *Kanaʿan* (March-April): 59–66.
    2000   "Globalization, the Palestinian Economy and the 'Peace Process.'" *Journal of Palestine Studies* 29, 2: 20–34.

Sassen, Saskia
    1988   *The Mobility of Labor and Capital: A Study in International Investment and Labor Flow.* Cambridge: Cambridge University Press.

Sayigh, Rosemary
    1979   *Palestinians: From Peasants to Revolutionaries, a People's History.* London: Zed Books.
    1983   "Encounters with Palestinian Women Under Occupation." In *Occupation: Israel over Palestine,* ed. Naseer Aruri. Belmont, Mass.: Association of Arab-American University Graduates.
    1989   "Palestinian Women: Triple Burden, Single Struggle." In *Palestine: Profile of an Occupation.* Atlantic Highlands, N.J.: Zed Press.

Scheper-Hughes, Nancy
    1992   *Death Without Weeping.* Berkeley: University of California,

Seifert, Ruth
    1996   "The Second Front: The Logic of Sexual Violence in Wars." *Women's Studies International Forum* 19, 1/2: 35–43.

Settlement Report
    1996   *Journal of Palestine Studies* 25, 4: 128–36.

Semyonov, Moshe and Noah Lewin-Epstein
    1987   *Hewers of Wood and Drawers of Water: Noncitizen Arabs in the Israeli*

Labor Market. Ithaca, N.Y.: International Labor Organization Press, Cornell University.

Shafir, Gershon
1989   *Land, Labor, and the Origins of the Israeli-Palestinian Conflict, 1882–1914.* New York: Cambridge University Press.

Shalev, Michael
1984   "Labor, Sate and Crisis: An Israeli Case Study." *Industrial Relations* 23, 3: 362–86.
1989   "Jewish Organized Labor and the Palestinians: A Study of State/Society Relations in Israel." In *The Israeli State and Society: Boundaries and Frontiers*, ed. Baruch Kimmerling. Albany: State University of New York Press.

Shehadeh, Raja
1989   *Occupier's Law: Israel and the West Bank.* Washington, D.C.: Institute for Palestine Studies.

Shohat, Ella
1992   "Notes on the 'Post-Colonial.' " *Social Text* 32/33: 99–113.

Sider, Gerald
1986   *Custom and Class in Anthropology and History.* Cambridge: Cambridge University Press.
1987   "When Parrots Learn to Talk, and Why They Can't: Domination, Deception, and Self-Deception in Indian-White Relations." *Comparative Studies in Society and History* 29, 1: 3–23.
1992   "The Contradictions of Transformational Migration: A Discussion." In *Towards a Transnational Perspective on Migration: Race, Class, Ethnicity and Nationalism Reconsidered*, ed. Nina Glick Schiller, Linda Basch, and Cristina Blanc-Szanton. Annals of the New York Academy of Sciences 645. New York: New York Academy of Science.
1993   *Lumbee Indian Histories: Race, Ethnicity, and Indian Identity in the Southern United States.* Cambridge: Cambridge University Press.

Sluka, Jeffrey, ed.
2000   *Death Squad: The Anthropology of State Terror.* Philadelphia: University of Pennsylvania Press.

Soysal, Yasemin
1994   *Limits of Citizenship.* Chicago: University of Chicago Press.

Spivak, Gayatri Chakravorty
1988   "Can the Subaltern Speak." In *Marxism and the Interpretation of Culture*, ed. Gary Nelson and Lawrence Grossberg. Urbana: University of Illinois Press.

Swedenburg, Ted
1988   "The Role of the Palestinian Peasantry in the Great Revolt, 1936–1939." In *Islam, Politics, and Society*, ed. Edmund Burke III and Ira Lapidus. Berkeley: University of California Press.
1990   "The Palestinian Peasant as National Signifier." *Anthropological Quarterly* 63, 1: 18–30.
1991   "Popular Memory and the Palestinian National Past." In *Golden Ages,*

Dark Ages: Imagining the Past in Anthropology and History, ed. Jay O'Brien and William Roseberry. Berkeley: University of California Press.

1995   *Memories of Revolt: The 1936–1939 Rebellion and the Palestinian National Past*. Minneapolis: University of Minnesota Press.

Tabak, Faruk

1991   "Agrarian Fluctuation and Modes of Labor Control in the Western Arc of the Fertile Crescent, c. 1700–1850." In *Landholding and Commercial Agriculture in the Middle East*, ed. Caglar Keyder and Faruk Tabak. Albany: State University of New York Press.

Tamari, Salim

1980   "The Palestinians in the West Bank and Gaza: the Sociology of Dependency." In *The Sociology of the Palestinians*, ed. Khalil Nakhleh and Elia Zureik. New York: St. Martin's Press.

1981   "Building Others People's Homes: the Palestinian Peasants' Household and Work in Israel." *Journal of Palestine Studies* 11, 1: 31–66.

1990a   "From the Fruits of Their Labour: the Persistence of Share Tenancy in the Palestinian Agrarian Economy." In *The Rural Middle East: Peasant Lives and Modes of Production*, ed. Kathy Glavanis and Pandeli Glavanis. Atlantic Highlands, N.J.: Zed Books.

1990b   "Revolt of the Petit Bourgeoisie." In *Intifada: Palestine at the Crossroads*, ed. Jamal Nassar and Roger Heacock. New York: Praeger.

Taussig, Michael

1987   *Shamanism, Colonialism, and the Wildman*. Chicago: University of Chicago Press.

1992   *The Nervous System*. New York: Routledge.

Taylor, Charles

1994   *Multiculturalism*. Princeton, N.J.: Princeton University Press.

United Nations Special Coordinator in the Occupied Territories

1999   *UNESCO Report on the Economic and Social Conditions in the West Bank and Gaza Strip*. Gaza: United Nations.

United Nations Special Coordinator in the Occupied Territories and the World Bank

1999   *Donor Investments in Palestinian Development*. Jerusalem: United Nations.

Wahdan, Hadeel

2001   "Israeli Closure." *Palestine Report* 7, 39: <www.jmcc.org/media/reportonline/report.html>.

Walzer, Michael

1983   *Spheres of Justice: A Defense of Pluralism and Equality*. New York: Basic Books.

Werber, Pnina and Nira Yuval-Davis

1999   "Introduction: Women and the New Discourse of Citizenship." In *Women, Citizenship and Difference*, ed. Nira Yuval-Davis and Pnina Werber. New York: Zed Books.

Wiesel, Elie

1982   *Night*. New York: Bantam Books.

Willis, Paul

1977   *Learning to Labour*. Westmead: Saxon House.

Wilson, Thomas and Hastings Donnan, eds.
    1998   *Border Identities: Nation and State at International Frontiers*. New York: Cambridge University Press.

Wood, Davida
    1993   "Politics of Identity in a Palestinian Village in Israel." In *The Violence Within: Cultural and Political Opposition in Divided Nations*, ed. Kay Warren. Boulder, Colo.: Westview.

Zolberg, Aristide
    1991   "Bounded States in a Global Market: The Uses of International Labor Migration." In *Social Theory for a Changing Society*, ed James Coleman. Boulder, Colo.: Russell Sage and Westview.

Zureik, Elia
    1976   "Transformation of Class Structure Among the Arabs in Israel: From Peasantry to Proletariat." *Journal of Palestine Studies* 6, 1: 39–66.
    1979   *Palestinians in Israel: A Study of Internal Colonialism*. New York: Routledge and Kegan Paul.

Index

Acknowledgments

Much of the research presented here was funded by the Social Science Research Council's Near and Middle East Program and the Fulbright-Hayes DDRA Program. Support was also received from the PSC-CUNY Faculty Development Grant and the Sheldon Scheps Memorial Summer Fund, Department of Anthropology, Columbia University.

Many scholars in New York shaped my thinking, including (in alphabetical order) Talal Asad, Toufiq Ben Amour, Ted Bestor, Richard Bulliet, Elaine Combs-Schilling, Libbet Crandon-Malamud, William Fisher, Amitav Ghosh, Morton Klass, Roger Lancaster, Barbara Price, William Roseberry, Abraham Rosman, Paula Rubel, Seymour Spilerman, Michael Taussig, and at Beloit College, Kathleen Adams and Lawrence Brietborde. Gerald Sider's theoretical guidance, practical advice, and personal inspiration have been central to my anthropology, as have many discussions with my friend and colleague Kirk Dombrowski. In Palestine, at Birzeit University in the Ramallah District, I had the opportunity to study with Salim Tamari and Ali Jarbawi. Both provided critical advice at very formative moments of this project and their writings and comments on the Palestinian struggle continue to inform my work. Cynthia Keppley Mahmood also provided many appreciated suggestions about the manuscript in her capacity as series editor, as did two anonymous reviewers. Jill Davis made many helpful comments on drafts of the text. Iris Gasser patiently executed the maps.

I am grateful and indebted to many people in Palestine who provided assistance along the way. I cannot list everyone, but acknowledge the kind support of many students and professors from Birzeit University (and elsewhere) including Albert Alghazarian, Ibrahim Khuraishi, Ahmed Sabawi, Ahed Hallis, Iyad al-Alool, Mohamed Zureiki, and Ahmed Rafiq Awad. Much thanks also to Jameel and Harra Qaquun, Dar Abu Shanab, Dar Sheik Ali, Dar al-Hajj, and Dar Melhem. My family deserves the most thanks, for making the larger project possible: Bob, Shirley, Ben, Hashem, Abed, Tha'er, Gert, Jonathan, Rachelle, Bassma, Masood, Joan, and Jacob.